T3-BSD-315

THE LATIN KINGDOM OF JERUSALEM

Europe in the Middle Ages
Selected Studies

Volume 11B

General Editor
RICHARD VAUGHAN
University of Hull

NORTH-HOLLAND PUBLISHING COMPANY – AMSTERDAM · NEW YORK · OXFORD

THE LATIN KINGDOM
OF JERUSALEM

By
JEAN RICHARD

Translated by
Janet Shirley

1979

NORTH-HOLLAND PUBLISHING COMPANY – AMSTERDAM · NEW YORK · OXFORD

Library
Jesuit School of Theology
in Chicago

© NORTH-HOLLAND PUBLISHING COMPANY – 1979
All rights reserved. No part of this publication may be reproduced, stored in a
retrieval system, or transmitted, in any form or by any means, electronic, mechanical,
photocopying, recording or otherwise, without the prior permission of the copyright
owner.

Library of Congress Catalog Card Number: 78-1747
North-Holland ISBN: 0-444-85262-X

Published by:
North-Holland Publishing Company – Amsterdam/New York/Oxford

Distributors for the U.S.A. and Canada:
Elsevier North-Holland, Inc.
52 Vanderbilt Avenue, New York, N.Y. 10017

D
182
.R513
vol. 2

Library of Congress Cataloging in Publication Data
Richard, Jean, 1921 (Feb. 7)–
    The Latin Kingdom of Jerusalem.

    (Europe in the Middle Ages; 11)
    Translation of Le royaume latin de Jerusalem.
    Bibliography: p. 471
    Includes index.
    ʰ. Jerusalem – History – Latin Kingdom, 1099–1244.
I. Title. II. Series.
D182.R513   956.9   78–1747
ISBN 0-444-85262-X

This book originally appeared in French in 1953 under the title *Royaume Latin de
Jérusalem*, Presses Universitaires de France, Paris

Printed in The Netherlands

PART 3

The kingdom of Acre

PART 3

The kingdom of Acre

Legally speaking, there never was a kingdom of Acre. The sovereigns who reigned over the Frankish possessions in the Levant after Frederick II, and those who had only theoretical or lapsed claims to them, always used the title of king of Jerusalem. The kings of Cyprus, the dukes of Savoy, King René and even the nineteenth-century kings of Naples and Austro-Hungarian emperors laid claim to this kingdom and adorned their list of titles with the name of the Holy City. But Jerusalem, reoccupied in 1229 in accordance with the treaty of Jaffa, in 1244 ceased for many hundred years to belong to Christians. None of the titular kings returned to the Holy Land to take up residence there, unless one counts the short periods spent by some of the Lusignans of Cyprus in Syrian cities. In any case, once Frederick II was crowned, none of them put in an appearance in Jerusalem itself, and this absence is symbolic: after the emperor's departure men ceased to care about the recovered capital, which stood for something essential only in the eyes of crusaders from the West and, more or less genuinely, of Frederick himself.

In fact the real capital of the kingdom was Acre, the great seaport where countless ships came bringing the products of the West and collecting those of the East, the great turbulent city where the Guelf revolt of 1232 began. The expressions used in contemporary texts, "the lordship of the kingdom of Jerusalem" and "the lordship of Acre", are strictly interchangeable. The 'kingdom' of Acre, or rather the confederation of lordships and towns of which Acre was the chief, the Frankish state that succeeded to the kingdom of Jerusalem, preserved a Latin presence in Syria until 1291, although with constantly diminishing territory. Yet in spite of this loss of land,

in spite of the Moslems' alarming victories, the history of the kingdom of Acre is not one of desperate Christian struggles against the
enemy, but one of intertribal warfare for the supremacy of one family
or another in Acre, for Genoese or Venetian hegemony in the eastern
Mediterranean, for the monopoly exercised by one Italian commercial
company or another over the market of Acre or Tyre. To these almost
constant civil wars were added insoluble dynastic complications, so
that no authority could make itself strong enough to put down the
different factions in Acre. The rivalry between the Lusignans of
Cyprus and the Angevins of Sicily contributed to the weakening of
the kingdom at the time of the Moslems' major offensive, which met
none but a divided resistance, the result of a divided country.[1]

In any event, by the time these rivalries appeared the monarchy of
Jerusalem had already suffered such a loss of power and prestige that
the dynastic conflicts were able to flourish unchecked. The various
claimants and the inhabitants of the kingdom all seem to have thought
of the Holy Land as a country without a master. We have already
seen the early stages· of the loss of nationhood suffered by the
kingdom of Jerusalem; from now on this loss was complete, and all
the instructions issued to the succession of regents who administered
the kingdom came from the West. Frankish possessions in Syria
survived until 1291, but the Latin kingdom perished long before that
date. The reason for the decline of the monarchy lies in the quarrels
between the Guelfs and the Ghibellines, and the very fact of these
quarrels' existence is enough by itself to prove that the Frankish Holy
Land was no longer a nation.[2]

CHAPTER 1

The Guelf revolt

The advancement of the Teutonic Knights

The event which finally undermined royal authority and split the kingdom of Jerusalem was the Guelf revolt of 1231–1233, or, as Philip of Novara expressed it, "the war between the emperor Frederick and Lord John of Ibelin". There were two reasons for this conflict, with its far-reaching effects: Frederick II's policy towards the nobles of Jerusalem, and the hostility of certain Cypriot barons towards the powerful Ibelin family. Frederick had long made clear his preference for an absolute rule very different from the feudal monarchy of Jerusalem; in his Sicilian kingdom, where the Norman kings had already established a centralized form of government, he wiped out the power of the feudal lords in the "war of the barons" of 1221. The Frankish nobles in Syria were bound to fear a similar fate; was not one of Frederick's principal lieutenants in the war of 1221 the same Thomas of Acerra, or of Aquino, who was sent to Acre as *bayle* in 1226? When the emperor arrived in the East, he made no secret of his intention of keeping a tight rein on the nobles of Jerusalem; he not only granted fiefs in the Holy Land to German barons such as Conrad of Hohenlohe, but above all he sought to increase the power of the Teutonic Knights and to make this order his chief instrument of government in his Eastern kingdom. We know what this German order was for Frederick:

No [community] ever depended more closely on the pope than this did on the emperor. He recruited huge numbers of young nobles to it, entrusted shipbuilding to it, and the postal services. A Teutonic Knight ruled Alsace. When the grand master attended court, he belonged to the *familia*. Hermann of Salza, from Thuringia [died 1239], was

Frederick's most admirable assistant.... By the bull of Rimini in 1226 Frederick established the order's programme and its privileges. It enabled him to set up an autonomous state, with the order itself as sovereign, within the 'monarchy of the empire'.[1]

Frederick began to shower benefits on the order before even reaching Syria; it was he who completed the donation of Count Otto of Henneberg, obtaining for the order the cession of the entire domain in which the castle of Montfort was later built; he had to pay large sums to James of La Mandelée, Count Joscelin's heir, to get him to renounce his claims to this domain. In 1226 the Teutonic Knights were exempted from taxation, in particular from the market tolls known as the *plateaticum*; in 1229 they were given the former royal palace in Jerusalem, in the Street of the Armenians.[2]

But in his policy of generosity to the Teutonic Knights, Frederick inevitably injured the rights of some of the barons of Jerusalem, who must already have been looking askance at this religious order which seemed bent on taking over all the castles in the kingdom. Thus, after the struggle between James of La Mandelée and Hermann of Salza's knights, another problem arose: by the treaty of 1229 the Christians had recovered Toron, the castle in the hinterland of Tyre of which the Humphrey family had been lords until the reign of Baldwin IV, and which Humphrey IV gave to the king when he married Isabelle of Jerusalem. It passed to Count Joscelin and then to William of Valence, and became part of Joscelin's inheritance again, at least in theory, when William disappeared in 1187. Frederick therefore thought himself entitled to give Toron to the Teutonic Knights, as having belonged to Joscelin, like the domain of Montfort, in virtue of the donation made by the count of Henneberg.[3]

The emperor had already embarked for the West, after appointing two Frankish lords as joint regents of the kingdom; they were Balian of Sidon and Garnier L'Aleman. The latter "became a brother of the Temple" almost immediately and was soon replaced by the constable of the kingdom, Odo of Montbéliard, lord *in partibus* of Tiberias.[4] Balian of Sidon tried to give effect to the imperial donation, but met an obstacle in the objections raised by an heiress of the Toron house: Alice of Armenia, mother of Raymond Roupen and daughter of Humphrey IV's sister Isabelle of Toron (wife of Roupen III of Lesser Armenia), put forward her claim. The marriage of Humphrey and Isabelle of Jerusalem was dissolved in 1190 and at that date Queen Isabelle solemnly restored the lordship of Toron to her ex-husband.

He died without direct heirs, so that his right to Toron passed to his sister, and his niece Alice claimed the right to call herself "lady of Toron, of Kerak, of Montreal and of Saint-Abraham". The matter was laid before the high court, which acknowledged the justice of the princess' claim. Balian of Sidon refused to accept this decision, and, to justify his refusal, produced the explicit order he had received from Frederick. The Syrian barons were not accustomed to obeying orders of this kind, and at the request of Alice, who showed that it deprived her of her fief without valid motive or *égard de cour*, consideration by the court, all the barons of the realm withdrew their service from the emperor's regent. Faced with this strike of military service, the most dangerous threat against royal authority, Balian had to give way.[5]

Frederick II versus the Ibelins

More serious still was the quarrel between Frederick and the Ibelins. Wishing to break the dangerous power of this proud line that enjoyed almost royal status in the East, Frederick II no sooner reached Cyprus than he drew John of Ibelin into an ambush and ordered him to give up the regency of Cyprus and to return to him the fief of Beirut, which, he said, John possessed 'unreasonably'. In a scene of great violence John of Ibelin held his own against the emperor. He surrendered the regency of Cyprus but refused to accept disseisin of Beirut, lawfully enfeoffed to him in 1197 by King Aimery and Queen Isabelle, and declared that he would submit only to the judgement of the barons' court. He took care to remain within the law, refusing to try to force concessions by violence out of the emperor, who had only a small number of troops with him.[6]

Frederick II still fully intended to recover Beirut, and John of Ibelin, well aware of this, began in 1228 to put his lordship into a state of defence. The emperor, now back in the West, decided to punish the Syrian party which had never stopped thwarting him during his campaign of 1228–1229; on his orders Balian of Sidon attempted to disseise the barons of the Ibelin party, that is, to confiscate their fiefs. John of Ibelin, lord of Beirut, his son John, lord of Arsuf, the latter's father-in-law, Rohard II of Cayphas, Philip L'Asne and John Moriau were all to be deprived of their honours. John now reaped the reward of his correct behaviour; he called upon his peers to stand by him, in virtue of Amalric's *Assise sur la Ligèce* which laid down such a punishment for a lord guilty of seizing his vassals' fiefs without judgement given, and all the barons of Syria once more withdrew their service from Balian.[7]

Loyal though he was to the emperor, whose negotiations with the Moslems he had supported while the barons of the country held aloof, Balian of Sidon could not govern in these conditions. Frederick therefore replaced him by one of his most devoted adherents, Riccardo Filangieri, marshal of the Empire. With the alleged objective of strengthening the defence of the Holy Land, where a sudden attack by local Moslem peasants had put Jerusalem in danger, a force that although small was very large by Syrian standards was embarked at Brindisi in 1231; 600 knights, 100 "young men with covered horses", that is, squires, 700 infantrymen and 3,000 armed sailors arrived off Cyprus under the command of Filangieri[8] and landed in Syria. Filangieri, who ordered the castellan Aymar II of Layron to hand Tyre over to him, and Balian of Sidon to deliver Acre into his charge, which they did, was well known to the Syrians; he had arrived in the Holy Land somewhat before Frederick II and had enforced the observance of the truce with a brutality that shocked the Franks, little accustomed to such energetic behaviour. He was alleged, among other things, to have attacked a Frankish raiding party returning from a foray into Moslem lands; Ernoul describes it thus:

They [the crusaders at Sidon] one day sent their foragers into Pagandom to seek food. The foragers went there and brought back great plenty of livestock and of booty, such as bread, corn, meat, men, women and children. The emperor's marshal, who was at Acre, heard that the Christians had gone into Pagandom and were bringing out great booty; he mounted, and ordered his knights and his people to mount, and went to meet them. When the foragers saw the marshal and recognized his insignia they were very pleased, for they thought he was coming to their assistance, in case they needed help. But they had no such purpose, and instead charged them, killed, wounded and beat them, and took away what they had won and sent it back into Pagandom.

It was also held against Filangieri that he had systematically prevented the Syrian barons from taking any part in negotiations with the Moslems; the barons wrote at the time to complain to the pope about this.[9]

Civil war in Cyprus

To all these causes of conflict were added others peculiar to the
kingdom of Cyprus, where the war began. Some of the Cypriot
barons took offence at the omnipotence of the Ibelins at the time
when Philip of Ibelin and then his brother John exercised the regency
on behalf of King Henry I. One of the most important among them,
Aimery Barlais, related through his mother Isabelle to the royal house
of Jerusalem, and son of one of the companions of Guy of Lusignan,
had long been a friend of John of Ibelin; but when Queen Alice
(daughter of Henry of Champagne and widow of King Hugh I)
married Bohemond, son of the prince of Antioch, in about 1223,
despite opposition from the Ibelins and the Barlais,[10] she found she
could not appoint her husband as *bayle*, and gave the regency to
Aimery Barlais. Philip of Ibelin and Anselm of Brie, leaders of the
Cypriot barons, fought against him. Aimery was deposed, John of
Ibelin became regent, and Aimery Barlais, together with his cousin
Amalric of Beisan, began to gather the opponents of the Ibelins
around themselves. Two other malcontents were quick to join them;
these were Gawain of Cheneché, who had been accused of murder
before the Ibelin regent and compelled to make peace with his
adversary in humiliating circumstances, and his kinsman William of
Rivet. Lastly a relative of the Ibelins, Hugh of Gibelet, joined this
party, and its members all appealed to Frederick II.[11] When the
emperor reached Syria he stripped John of Ibelin of the regency and
gave, or rather, in accordance with medieval custom, sold it to the
five associates. These took their revenge on the Ibelins and their party
by overwhelming them with taxes, so as to procure the money with
which to pay the emperor.

An act of marked hostility provoked the final break: the regents
arrested Philip of Novara, a close friend of John of Ibelin, and by his
own account, tried to kill him. With the help of the Hospitallers,
Philip gathered supporters and began the fight against the five regents.
John of Ibelin hastened to his aid with his own forces, and defeated
the enemy troops near Nicosia on 14 July 1229, suffering heavy
losses. The siege of the great castles of Cyprus, in which the regents
and the young king in their charge took refuge, lasted until the middle
of 1230, without Frederick being able to offer his supporters any help
other than a decree of confiscation of the Ibelin fiefs. The victorious

John of Ibelin was reconciled with Aimery Barlais, outwardly at least, and regained control of the kingdom of Cyprus.[12]

Siege of Beirut and rebellion of Acre

When he heard what was happening in Cyprus, the emperor sent Filangieri to the East, but John of Ibelin was warned by informants in sufficient time to go and put Cyprus into a state of defence. Filangieri commanded King Henry, as Frederick's vassal, to expel the Ibelins from his lands, as they were under the ban of the kingdom of Syria. Henry refused, and when the imperial fleet appeared off the coast of Cyprus, Filangieri saw the royal army ready for battle. Being unable to land in Cyprus, he came ashore instead under the walls of Beirut, took the town unopposed and laid immediate siege to the castle. Its small garrison put up a strong resistance in 1231 and in 1232, thus giving John of Ibelin time. He declared that he was the liege man of the king of Cyprus and that he had been wrongfully deprived of his fief in Syria, and he obtained a promise of help from Henry I of Lusignan in the winter of 1231. An army from Cyprus disembarked the following February in the county of Tripoli; the Tyre anchorage was in the hands of the imperialists, who were also blockading Beirut. No sooner were they ashore than the barons who supported Frederick – Aimery Barlais, Amalric of Beisan and Hugh of Gibelet, but not William of Rivet and Gawain of Cheneché, who were dead – rejoined the imperial army, together with their following of eighty knights.[13]

While John of Ibelin, thanks to his command of Cyprus, was preparing to raise the siege of Beirut, the situation in Syria was very confused. Riccardo Filangieri had no difficulty in obtaining possession of the castle of Tyre, as his authority was valid; then he went to Acre to show his letter of appointment, which correctly bore the golden imperial *bulla*, and to be recognized as the *bayle* of the kingdom. At this point his predecessor Balian of Sidon, at last free to express his thoughts, spoke in the name of the barons and knights of Acre; he requested that in accordance with the promise made by Frederick to respect the customs and *assises* of the kingdom, the Ibelins should receive justice. Above all he asked that the siege of Beirut should be raised. Filangieri put off making any reply and went to Beirut, hoping that the castle would fall and present these troublesome Syrians with a *fait accompli*. But the leaders of the Frankish nobility, Balian of Sidon, Odo of Montbéliard, John of Caesarea and Garnier L'Aleman, were not to be fooled by delays which they well understood, and they sent two envoys to bring back the marshal's answer; he at last declared that he was only carrying out the emperor's commands.

The nobles of Acre now decided to take action. They found a means of organizing themselves in the confraternity of St Andrew, a devotional brotherhood dating from the time of the first kingdom of Jerusalem, which no doubt resembled that of the Holy Spirit whose statutes we possess.[14] The confraternity of St Andrew of Acre received every Guelf sympathiser in the town into its ranks, barons, knights, burgesses and commoners. Without yet proceeding to actual warfare, this league of self-defence got in touch with Filangieri's opponents, particularly John of Ibelin. As soon as he landed and came within reach of Beirut, John of Ibelin asked the men of Acre for help, and forty-three knights joined him, as did John of Caesarea and Rohard of Cayphas. Soon afterwards the patriarch and the grand masters of the orders (Frederick having ceased to be excommunicate in July 1230, and now receiving aid from Gregory IX), as well as Balian of Sidon and Odo of Montbéliard, offered to mediate, along with representatives of the Italians in Syria. This attempt at reconciliation failed, and recourse was had to arms. John of Ibelin organized a blockade of the town of Beirut, within which Filangieri was besieging the castle, and succeeded in getting reinforcements into the castle, enabling it to hold out much longer against the imperial troops. The Cypriot forces then reached Sidon, and John of Ibelin tried to unite all Franks about himself. Balian, his eldest son, went to Tripoli to negotiate with Bohemond IV the marriage of Isabelle, sister of the king of Cyprus, to Henry 'du Prince', son of the prince of Antioch-Tripoli, from whom were to descend the kings who sat after 1267 on the throne of Cyprus. But Bohemond did not wish to fall out with Filangieri, the military orders wanted to preserve their neutrality (on 17 June 1232 Gregory IX wrote to the patriarch Gerold blaming him for assisting the rebels and withdrawing the legation from him),[15] and a significant number of the barons of Tripoli, chief among them Bertrand Porcelet, father-in-law of Aimery Barlais, were opposed to the Ibelins. Balian was threatened with death, and Bohemond IV ordered him out of his lands. Meanwhile John himself, leaving his son John of Arsuf in command of the garrison of Beirut, went to Acre. He there transformed the confraternity of St Andrew into a real commune, gathering together the "barons and knights of the kingdom of Jerusalem" and the "burgesses of Acre". The sworn commune chose John of Ibelin himself as its mayor, and appointed other officials to carry out various municipal duties.[16] The result of the transformation thus achieved was to detach Acre from the royal domain, and henceforth Filangieri counted the powerful fraternity amongst his enemies.

It may have been now, in April 1232 rather than a month later, that John of Ibelin with the support of the patriarch Gerold of Lausanne and of the people of Acre surprised and captured a fleet of thirteen or seventeen imperial *chalandres*, flat-bottomed transport vessels, at anchor off the town.[17] At any rate, the Cypriot army moved from Sidon to Acre and it was decided to make for Tyre, and to attack Filangieri and expel him from Tyre. But Frederick's marshal received warning of this plan, and his brother Lotario, commanding in Beirut, raised the siege of the castle there and brought up his men to reinforce the imperial army. Riccardo Filangieri then ordered the patriarch of Antioch to offer his services as mediator to John of Ibelin. John, who had got as far as Casal Humbert on the way to Tyre, returned to Acre to discuss these proposals. Thereupon Filangieri in a swift march surprised the Cypriot forces before dawn; their commander Anselm of Brie had omitted to post guards; and a contingent from the imperial galleys completed the rout of the Cypriots, who lost all their equipment, but not many men, in the defeat of Casal Humbert on 3 May 1232. In any case, the arrival of troops from Acre, stirred to action at last by this treachery, prevented Filangieri from following up his victory and destroying the Cypriot army.

But the marshal wasted no time; he despatched Aimery Barlais and his men to Cyprus and soon afterwards landed himself in the island, which John of Ibelin had left undefended. The easy conquest, in which only the castles of Dieu d'Amour and Buffavento offered any resistance, stripped Frederick's enemies of their chief possession, and Filangieri pursued without pity those Cypriot nobles who had chosen the Ibelin side. Meanwhile John of Ibelin was busy re-equipping his forces, with money raised from the sale of two *casals* by his nephews John of Caesarea and John of Ibelin. He also made efforts to obtain a fleet, and in order to avoid the danger threatened by the Pisans' devotion to the imperial cause, he concluded an alliance with the

Genoese. It was rumoured that Frederick II had ordered his marshal to imprison all the Genoese in Acre; on 10 August 1232 the commune of Genoa sent off a fleet of ten galleys and two ships under the command of Ansaldo Bolleto and Bonifacio Panzano.[18] Twenty-seven days after Casal Humbert, the army, thanks to the Genoese, was able to set sail for Famagusta, where it arrived on 6 June 1232. They disembarked by night, taking Filangieri by surprise and capturing first Famagusta and then the great fort of Kantara. Soon afterwards they marched on Nicosia, exasperated by the devastation of the island at the hands of the Longobards, as the Syrian Franks called Frederick's Calabrian troops. They took Nicosia, doing so with the less difficulty because Filangieri fell back upon the mountains in the centre of the island. Hastening to relieve Dieu d'Amour, where food was short, the Cypriots encountered the imperial army and fought the battle of Agridi on 15 June 1232. Owing to an unwise charge by the imperialists, this was a total defeat for Filangieri, who lacked infantry, although he was much stronger in cavalry than his opponent. The defeat at Casal Humbert was cancelled out, a large number of 'Longobards' killed or captured, and almost the whole of Cyprus recovered. Only the fort of Kyrenia held out, which it was able to do for nine and a half months thanks to its position in the northern mountains by the sea, looking across to Cilicia where Filangieri found refuge, and thanks also to the imperialists' command of the sea.

Kyrenia fell at last, through the efforts of the Genoese: the fleet under Bolleto and Panzano had agreed to take part in the siege, which ended on 3 April 1233.[19] The Guelf revolt had freed Cyprus from imperialist occupation, but the situation in Syria still had to be cleared up. Filangieri was occupying Tyre, and the Guelfs Beirut, Acre, Caesarea and Arsuf. Jerusalem was a dependency of the emperor, and the lords of Sidon and of Jaffa, Balian and Walter of Brienne respectively, hesitated, as did Odo of Montbéliard the constable, between Ghibelline loyalism and Guelf defence of Frankish liberties. The Pisans supported the emperor; the Genoese had just come to the aid of the Ibelins but were soon to be reconciled with Frederick II,[20] who could also count on the support of Bohemond V, prince of Antioch-Tripoli (Bohemond IV died in March 1233). The Temple and the Hospital, although Frederick had seized their domains in Sicily, were reluctant to declare against the emperor, who had the support of the Teutonic Knights.

In this anarchy the rights of Frederick II were not disputed. John of Ibelin made his stand clear in 1228: the emperor, husband of Queen Isabelle, was the lawful master of the kingdom. Isabelle died, leaving an infant son, the future Conrad IV, Conrad II of Jerusalem. Immediately Alice, elder daughter of Henry of Champagne, at that time wife of the future Bohemond V although their marriage was later broken on the grounds of kinship, came to Acre to lay claim to the throne of Jerusalem. This was in 1230, and the barons agreed without hesitation that the crown belonged to none but young Conrad. Alice, a perpetual claimant who again and again in later years tried to make good her claims to the throne of Jerusalem and to the county of Champagne, saw her claim dismissed, and two knights, Geoffrey Le Tort and John of Bailleul, were sent to Frederick II to request that the lawful king should come and reside in the Holy Land, according to custom. Frederick answered that within the year "he would do what he ought".[21]

After the revolt of 1231–1233 the Guelfs did not dare reverse the decision made in 1230, and negotiations were begun. The papacy had not waited till then to try to put an end to dissensions so harmful to the Holy Land; in July 1232 Gregory IX persuaded Frederick to refrain from sending another force against the rebels, and Frederick did no more than maintain a strong garrison in Tyre.[22] The patriarch Gerold was sharply reprimanded in June 1232 for favouring the Ibelins, but at once went to Rome to tell the pope the facts of the situation, including Filangieri's harsh behaviour. He came back free from blame and confirmed – an unarguable mark of confidence – in the legation, which was henceforth always held jointly with the patriarchate. Frederick II then, with Gregory IX's approval, tried to arrive at a peace settlement by making concessions but without surrendering his rights as king. He ordered the bishop of Sidon to offer the Syrian barons a general amnesty in return for their submission, and as they detested Filangieri, the emperor offered to put the government of the Holy Land into the hands of one of their own number, Philip of Maugastel. The Guelf party could find no objection to Philip except to call him a typically effeminate *poulain*. But Frederick could not allow a royal city to set itself up as an independent republic – the very cause of the Guelf-Ghibelline struggles in Italy – and he refused to accept that the confraternity of St Andrew should rule Acre, and insisted on its dissolution. Early in 1233 the bishop of Sidon took these proposals to the unchallenged leaders of Frankish Syria, the ex-regent Balian of Sidon and the constable Odo of Montbéliard. They summoned the *parlement* of the realm to meet in the church of the Holy Cross at Acre. Violent discussions arose, and the loyalist party was getting the best of it – Balian and Odo were about to cause an oath to be taken to Frederick – when John of Caesarea had the tocsin rung, the Guelf confraternity gathered, and the rioters, reinforced by the Genoese of Acre, tried to kill the two barons and the bishop in the church. John of Ibelin, warned by the bishop of Sidon who was asking him for a purely formal submission ("that you should go to a place where it seems that he has power and you should simply say, 'I put myself in the mercy of the emperor as my lord'"), replied with the fable of the stag enticed into the lion's den and refused to be drawn to a place where the emperor exercised real power. He remembered too clearly the trap into which he had been led in 1228 and as a result of which his eldest son Balian, left in Frederick's hands as a hostage, had endured a harsh captivity.

In spite of the disturbance in the church of the Holy Cross and John of Ibelin's refusal, negotiations continued between Odo of Montbéliard and the emperor. The patriarch of Antioch and the grand master of the Teutonic Knights reached a preliminary agreement. The pope wrote expressing pleasure at this on 22 March 1234, and on 7 August 1234 he asked John of Ibelin simply to offer his submission to the emperor by messengers, as he was reluctant to trust himself among imperial troops.[23] He also sent a legate to Acre, Theodoric, archbishop of Ravenna, authorized to obtain the Guelfs' submission to the lawful sovereign and to dissolve the commune. If they would not confirm the proposed treaty, the pope ordered a return to the status quo. The Guelfs did refuse to submit, and then the legate proclaimed the dissolution of the confraternity, and banned the communal bell, emblems of the town's liberties, and at the end of 1234 placed Acre under an interdict. A delegation from Acre consisting of Philip of Troyes and Henry of Nazareth brought back the same proposals, dissolution of the commune and recognition of Filangieri. Tension again became acute, so much so that in letters written on 28 July 1235 Gregory IX sought to guard against an imminent threat of war. He asked the three grand masters to assist the imperial regent and to prevent John of Ibelin and the men of Acre attacking Tyre or some other imperial city.[24]

Another ambassador, Geoffrey Le Tort, then went to Rome, and succeeded in getting Gregory IX to reverse the decisions made by the archbishop of Ravenna. The pope now wrote to Frederick II telling him to raise the interdict on Acre and to make peace with the "burgesses and syndics of Acre". As for Filangieri, the pope advised Frederick to suspend him for the time being, "because there are mortal enmities between the marshal and the opposing party" (22 September 1235). Finally, on 19 February 1236, Gregory IX suggested that Bohemond V of Antioch be appointed regent of the kingdom; "having taken the oath according to the custom of the kingdom and received the oaths of the men of the kingdom", he would enjoy all regalian rights and occupy the city of Tyre, the castle of which would be entrusted to the Teutonic Knights. (It was Hermann of Salza who negotiated this treaty with Philip of Troyes and Henry of Nazareth.) The commune of Acre would be disbanded and a *bayle* appointed in Acre by Filangieri, by arrangement with the constable Odo of Montbéliard. The Syrians would obey the *bayles*, the *bayles* would respect the customs and *assises*. Lastly, Frederick's grievances against the Ibelins would be examined through due process of law.[25]

This attempt at reconciliation failed like the rest. In any case, Frederick was preparing to break with the pope[26] (he was excommunicated again in 1239), and the pope now realized how great a gulf had been created by the Ghibellines' violence. Gregory IX had recommended a close alliance between Cyprus and Acre to Geoffrey Le Tort, as the best guarantee for peace in the Holy Land. However, Frederick was now reaching a definite settlement with the Hospitallers, and he confirmed their privileges in June 1239. The Templars, in contrast, adopted a more emphatically Guelf policy. The death in 1236 of John of Ibelin, the Old Lord of Beirut, removed one of the main Guelf leaders (Balian of Sidon died in 1239 and Odo of Montbéliard in 1244), and the Old Lord's heirs, his sons Balian of Beirut and John of Arsuf, and his nephew John, future count of Jaffa, inherited his grievances but not his authority. Grousset could write: "Under the humble title of regent or of mayor of the commune of Acre, the Old Lord of Beirut had in fact been a real sovereign.... But these were exceptional cases, after which anarchy resumed its sway."[27]

The state of the kingdom

During the troubled years between the departure of Frederick II and the crusade of 1239 the Holy Land continued to live an almost normal life. Ruled first by Balian of Sidon, then by Odo of Montbéliard, and by Filangieri in the part that obeyed the emperor, it experienced brief moments of civil war. In Acre, the Pisan and Genoese inhabitants manifested lively antipathy towards each other, but there was nothing new about that. Central government might be divided, but local government continued in the name of Conrad II, who was everywhere acknowledged. The viscounts of Acre, Stephen Boutier in April 1232 and Philip of Troyes in September 1232, presided over the court of the burgesses at Acre, while the constable Odo of Montbéliard presided over the high court. In the newly recovered Jerusalem, although the roads were not yet safe, Filangieri appointed castellans: Baldwin of Picquigny in 1235, successor of Renaud of Cayphas, castellan from 1229 to 1230 and then chamberlain of the kingdom, and after him Peter or Walter of Pennedepie, a knight from Picardy who ruled the Holy City from 1241 to 1244. Under the presidency of the viscount, who in 1235 was Girard of Saiges, the burgess court of Jerusalem dealt with the sale of lands and houses, and the revenues of the kingdom's former capital were such as to enable Filangieri to charge an annual payment of 400 bezants upon them for the castellan's salary.[28] Work was done on the city's fortifications, but political difficulties paralysed every attempt at the complete restoration of the enceinte. The money that arrived in Syria supplied the Guelf-Ghibelline quarrels, not the defence of the kingdom. Therein lay the great danger: intact in appearance, and indeed on the point of reaching a degree of territorial expansion unknown since 1187, the Latin kingdom was irreparably divided, and once the few years' respite afforded by the death of the sultan al-Kamil in 1238 were over, its foreign policy revealed a fatal lack of cohesion. Disputed by different powers, each of which shuffled off its responsibilities onto the others, it was not long before the kingdom suffered a disaster almost as grave as that of Hattin, one which reminded men that so dangerously exposed a territory was no place for the partisan games which the Franks of Syria were beginning to enjoy.

CHAPTER 2

The fall of Jerusalem

The crusade of 1239

The treaty made at Jaffa in 1229 was designed to last ten years, and seemed likely to be broken almost immediately, both because the Templars disliked it, as an enforced peace, and because it created an awkward corridor between Jerusalem and the coast. None the less it lasted some ten years before warfare between Franks and Moslems broke out again.

In 1235 Pope Gregory IX, looking ahead to the expiry of the truce, and hoping perhaps to draw Syrian Christians together in a holy war, preached a new crusade. The hostilities then flourishing between the different Moslem states, where Ayubid-Seljuqid enmities were at their height, gave good grounds for hope. But the pope set the date for the expedition's departure as late as 1239, and his appeal roused little enthusiasm except among the barons of France, who had taken no part in the crusades since 1204. Once again, it was Burgundy and Champagne that sent the largest contingents to the new campaign. Duke Hugh IV of Burgundy, the count of Mâcon, who now sold his county to the king of France, and the counts of Chalon, Nevers, Forez, Bar, Sancerre and Joigny took the cross at the same time as Theobald IV, count of Champagne and king of Navarre. But serious problems arose in the mustering of the crusading army.

In 1237 Gregory learned of the death of the aged John of Brienne, regent of the Latin Empire of Constantinople, which left that Empire in a critical situation. The pope had already written to the king of Navarre, in December 1236, suggesting to him that he should direct the crusade towards Constantinople, pointing out how greatly the

Latin Empire needed help. It was there, he said, that the Greek
schism could be ended; the vows made by the pilgrims to free the
Holy Land could be fulfilled in this way, since the destruction of the
Latin Empire would be a disaster for Syria. And Gregory IX began to
apply money collected for the crusade to the support of Baldwin II, the
young emperor.

The barons were not pleased and refused to change their destination, although in 1239 some 700 knights did leave for Constantinople.
They now chose as their leader none other than Frederick II, an
obvious choice because of his title of king of Jerusalem; but it was a
choice which displeased the pope, who in March 1239 had just
excommunicated Frederick, and who feared a renewal of the 'crusade' of 1228–1229. He even tried to cancel the crusade, but without
success. Fortunately for the pope, Frederick, who in 1238 had promised to take part in the expedition in person, or to send his son
Conrad, declared that his war with the Lombards would prevent him
keeping his promise. He was reluctant, too, to embark on a struggle
against the sultan of Egypt just as he was beginning the long contest
with the papacy that was to last until he died. Instead the barons
chose the king of Navarre, who took over command of the expedition.[1]

The crusade was warmly welcomed in the Holy Land. On 7
October 1238 the assembled prelates of Syria, with Walter of Brienne,
count of Jaffa, the constable Odo of Montbéliard, Balian of Sidon and
John of Caesarea, wrote from Acre to the leaders of the crusade to
give them information and advice. It was useless, they said, to wait
until the truce expired, for the Saracens were not observing it (many
pilgrims had been killed or taken captive on the way to Jerusalem).[2]
They advised the crusaders all to embark at the same port, Genoa or
Marseilles (in fact most travelled via Marseilles, some by way of
Aigues-Mortes, and some, at Frederick's invitation, sailed from
Brindisi). The army should assemble in Cyprus, near Limassol; the
island could furnish all the provisions necessary to feed the 1,000 to
1,500 knights, and a council of war could be held and the decision
made whether to open hostilities in the Holy Land or in Egypt;
Limassol was equidistant from Acre, Damietta and Alexandria.
Lastly, "all those who govern in the country" – a formula eloquent of
the lack of central government in the kingdom of Acre – had forbidden the export of foodstuffs, and the crusaders could be sure of
supplies.[3]

The suggestion of landing in Cyprus was a good one. It showed that the barons of Syria disagreed about the purpose of the crusade, but it would have allowed all parties to reach an agreement, and would have enabled the crusaders to learn how matters stood in the East. The situation was that the sultan al-Kamil was dead; Damascus and Egypt, both ruled to begin with by his son al-Adil II, soon split up. First al-Salih Ayub and then al-Salih Ismail ruled in Damascus, and in June 1240 Ayub succeeded in taking Egypt from al-Adil, with the help of Dawud, king of Transjordania. What was needed was to play these princes off one against another, so as to extract all possible concessions from them, as Frederick II had done in 1229. The crusaders, however, went directly to Acre in September 1239, with never a thought in their heads but the slaughter of Saracens.

The campaign opened with the Moslem recapture of Jerusalem. Its castellan had cleverly enough taken advantage of the quarrels between the Ayubid princes to rebuild part of the city walls, in spite of the treaty of Jaffa. Naturally after the town fell the Guelfs accused "the emperor's *baillis*" of having neglected to provide "men, food, arms and engines", but we must remember the bias of Frankish sources. The Tower of David, which was the only fortification in existence in 1229, had been made the keep of a new citadel, and work was begun on completing the whole enceinte. Hearing of this, the king of Transjordania moved against the Holy City, took the town without difficulty and laid siege to the citadel, which held out for three weeks, while the Tower of David resisted for another six days after that. The defenders surrendered, and were escorted to the coast, while Dawud razed all the defences, including this time the Tower of David. This was in August and September 1239.[4]

In Acre, the council of war held there demonstrated yet again the disharmony that divided the Syrian barons, who wanted to go and attack Egypt on her own ground, from the newly arrived crusaders. Various plans were put forward: an attack on Damascus, on the fortress of Safed, nerve point of Galilee, or the rebuilding of the walls of Jerusalem. The decision eventually taken united all possible disadvantages:

The crusaders decided to go first of all and occupy Ascalon and refortify it, and after that to go and take Damascus. This twofold plan was no sooner known than it alienated both the sultan of Egypt, overlord of the Ascalon district, and the new *malik* of Damascus, al-Salih Ismail. The French crusade achieved the unlikely result of reconciling the Ayubid princes with each other.[5]

The crusaders marched against Ascalon at the beginning of November, even though the Egyptian army was concentrated at Gaza. Peter Mauclerc, count of Brittany, captured a caravan after a hard fight and won considerable booty. Henry, count of Bar (le-Duc), tried to do the same, falling upon the Egyptian vanguard which was now at Gaza. Together with the duke of Burgundy, Amalric of Montfort, Walter of Brienne, John of Ibelin, lord of Arsuf, Odo of Montbéliard and Balian of Sidon, the count of Bar set off, against the advice both of their commander, Theobald IV, who learned too late of the proposed expedition, and of the grand masters of the three military orders. All Theobald could do was to move his army up towards Ascalon to support his foolhardy subordinates. The expedition was most unwisely led, and was caught having dinner at midday on the sand dunes near Gaza. This was 13 November 1239. It was a disaster: 1,200 killed and 600 taken prisoner, while the Syrian barons, whose advice had been ignored, and the duke of Burgundy, managed to get away. The disheartened and divided army retreated next day upon Jaffa and Acre.[6]

Theobald of Champagne now considered intervening, at the request of a missionary who was friendly with the prince of Hama, in the quarrel between this prince and his neighbour of Homs; then he went and encamped in Galilee. Meanwhile al-Adil II was deposed and Ayub, the new sultan of Egypt, went to war against the king of Damascus. This ruler, fighting to hold his capital city against Dawud, king of Transjordania, appealed to the crusaders; he made a treaty with Theobald according to which both Franks and Damascenes would go to Jaffa or Ascalon to block the Egyptians' way into Syria. In return he ceded to the Latins the whole hinterland of Sidon, as far as the Litani, including Beaufort, all Galilee, including Tiberias and Safed, and he promised to cede the whole of the former kingdom of Jerusalem, except for the parts east of Jordan. Force was necessary to make the occupants of Beaufort obey their sovereign and deliver their castle to Ismail, who gave it to the Franks.[7]

The Moslems' dissatisfaction had a further consequence: the Damascene troops in the allied army went over to the Egyptians, and the Franks had to fall back on Ascalon. None the less Ismail suggested a joint expedition into Egypt. But a reversal of these alliances was already preparing, in circumstances that greatly endangered the unity of Frankish Syria. Had the Hospitallers, we may ask, received orders from Frederick II to conclude an immediate peace with Egypt? Did they act solely out of jealousy of the Templars? In any case, the grand master of the Hospitallers persuaded Theobald IV to make peace with Sultan Ayub so as to set free the prisoners taken at Gaza. In breach of their oath to Ismail, the Hospitallers, the Teutonic Knights, their grand masters acting in the name of Frederick,[8] and the crusaders made a treaty in these terms with the sultan of Egypt. The Syrian barons and the Templars refused to ratify it, and while Theobald and the greater part of the crusaders took ship for home in September 1240, the Syrian Franks, the Templars' forces and two leading crusaders, Hugh IV of Burgundy and Guigues of Nevers-Forez, remained stationed between Jaffa and Ascalon in order to keep faith with the Damascenes. Hugh IV took the opportunity to rebuild the walls of Ascalon.

At this point another crusader arrived: Richard, earl of Cornwall, brother of the king of England and brother-in-law of Frederick, his sister's husband. Richard's first intention was to reconcile the opposing parties, but this proved impossible. He then joined Hugh IV at Ascalon, where together they completed the rebuilding in March 1241. But it was necessary to put the fortress into the hands of a man who could defend it. Walter of Brienne, count of Jaffa, might have put forward his claims to the second city of the former "county of Jaffa and Ascalon", but he does not seem to have done so. Richard, although urged by the Templars to entrust the fortress to them, refused to consign it to an order whose arrogance had so much exasperated him. He chose to place Ascalon, and the large sums of money he gave for the completion of the works in hand, in the care of the emperor's representative, in this case Walter or Peter of Penne-depie, who as imperial castellan was governor of Jerusalem.

Relations between Richard, the Templars and the Syrian barons were good at first, but soon deteriorated. The Templars' arrogance proved intolerable; the earl of Cornwall, brother-in-law of the emperor and a great man in the West in his own right, found himself treated like a child by the grand master. He himself was unable to reconcile the two orders, and was therefore glad to take account of the opinions of the moderates, Walter of Brienne, Hugh of Burgundy and the grand master of the Hospital; the peace settlement of 23 April 1241 completed that of 1240. Richard succeeded in obtaining from Egypt extensions of the Damascenes' territorial concessions; the hinterland, the 'mountain' of Beirut, the entire lordship of Sidon, the land of Acre, with Bouquiau and Saint-Georges, the lordship of Toron

and Châteauneuf, Tiberias and the whole of Galilee, including Beauvoir, Safed, Nazareth, Mount Tabor and Lyon, the country round
Jaffa and Ascalon, including Mirabel, Ramleh and Ascalon itself, as
well as Gibelin, were now returned to the Hospital. In short the whole
region of Jerusalem and Bethlehem, not, as in 1229, the towns without
their surrounding countryside, was restored to the reconstituted
kingdom of Jerusalem. West of Jordan, only the regions of Nablus
and Hebron and that between Beisan and Jericho remained in Moslem
hands.[9]

This was no merely formal cession; the barons of Jerusalem
immediately put their ancestral rights into effect. Odo of Montbéliard
claimed his principality of Galilee and at once rebuilt the castle of
Tiberias. On the eastern bank of the Lake of Tiberias Philip of
Maugastel, the man whom Frederick had wanted to appoint as regent
in 1232–1233, recovered the *casal* of Corsy, which he granted to the
Teutonic Knights in 1241.[10] Giles of Sidon, whose father Balian seems
to have died in 1239, recovered possession of Beaufort and
established one of his vassals in the "land of the Schouf and of
Gezin". The lord of Sidon, who took the title of "lord of Saete and
Beaufort", also reoccupied the long disputed fortress of the Cave of
Tyron. The Templars, perhaps at the instigation of Benedict of
Alignan, bishop of Marseilles, who laid the first stone on 11 December
1240, rebuilt their castle of Safed.[11] We do not know whether the
Hospitallers undertook similar work at Beauvoir and Gibelin. Nor did
they merely fortify reoccupied strongholds; John of Ibelin, younger
brother and vassal of Balian, lord of Beirut (who was the eldest son
of John of Ibelin, the Old Lord of Beirut), in 1241 rebuilt his town of
Arsuf. As for Jerusalem, the work of fortification there had to start
again from the beginning; it was probably done by Riccardo Filangieri
and his local castellan, Walter of Pennedepie, who had gone to live in
Jerusalem when the first agreement with the sultan of Egypt was
made.[12]

Such were the results of the earl of Cornwall's crusade. But
although the earl succeeded by his diplomatic ability in achieving a
significant reconstitution of the kingdom, he was not able to effect a
union between its subjects. Even in matters of foreign policy the
Templars were recalcitrant, still refusing to abide by the treaties made
with Egypt: in 1242 they raided the Hebron district and provoked a
counter-raid by the king of Transjordania, who controlled Hebron. At
that the Templars on 30 October 1242 sacked Nablus and devastated

the country round the town. The sultan of Egypt then sent a force to blockade Jaffa, but the conflict went no further. Somewhat later the king of Damascus resumed hostilities against the sultan of Egypt; he had made an alliance with the king of Transjordania and the king, in order to obtain an alliance with the Franks, restored to them the Temple, hitherto reserved for Moslem worship. The sultan of Egypt, wishing to obviate the results of this concession, hastened to do the same himself, so that in 1243 the Templars at once began to build a new fortress on the site of their former home.

Simon of Montfort suggested as regent

Richard of Cornwall had attempted to reconcile the conflicting parties, but the hostility of the Guelfs, supported by the Templars, towards the emperor's authority had reached such a pitch that any understanding was out of the question. Before taking ship for the West on 3 May 1241 the English prince wrote of his sorrow at the decline of the kingdom "because it is divided, and ruled by usurpers".[13] He seems, however, to have made one last effort to re-establish peacefully the authority of his brother-in-law Frederick, the only man whom everyone in the Holy Land could accept. One month after his departure a decision was taken by the "barons and knights and citizens of the realm of Jerusalem", including the Guelf leaders, Balian of Ibelin and his brothers, their cousin John of Ibelin, Philip of Montfort, lord of Toron, and Geoffrey of Estraing, lord of Cayphas.[14] They asked that the emperor should restore them to "his grace, and forgive us all the wrongful disputes arising from the discord which has been in the land until the present day". They asked Frederick to give them Simon of Montfort, earl of Leicester, as regent, until Conrad should attain his majority or visit the kingdom, and to promise that he would maintain "every man according to his justice and in his right" – *à sa reisum et en sun dreit* – and rule "by the uses and customs and by the assizes of the realm of Jerusalem". For their part, they promised to obey this regent, to abolish the bell and the consuls and the captains of the commune of Acre (7 June 1241).[15] It seems likely that this letter, the original of which is in London, was to be given to Earl Richard so that he might discuss the matter with the emperor.

The choice of Simon of Montfort as a prospective *bayle* is an interesting one. His father was the leader of the Albigensian crusade, that minor baron from the Ile-de-France who conquered Toulouse, defeated Aragon and acquired almost all the domains of the powerful house of Saint-Gilles: Languedoc, Rouergue, and part of Gascony and of the Massif Central. Simon was quite another man than his brother Amalric who had shown himself incapable of preserving the "duchy of Narbonne". In Simon the heirs of the counts of Montfort-l'Amaury were to continue to pursue the destiny which for a hundred years sent them battling over all the Latin world, to come close to more than one crown. Simon, earl of Leicester, was to bring Henry III king of England to his knees before the battle of Evesham ended at once Simon's life and the near-royal destiny of the Montforts. We may wonder whether it was not the earl of Cornwall, worried by the ambition of his new brother-in-law (Simon married Richard's sister in 1238),[16] who sought to rid England of the man who later became leader of the baronial party, and at the same time to provide Syria with an energetic ruler who could unite all parties about him. Simon did subsequently become the head of a baronial party with theories very like those of the Ibelins. The failure of the earl of Leicester's candidacy may well mark the disappearance of one of Frankish Syria's last chances. We do not know why Frederick II did not accept the idea; in any case, Filangieri continued to govern Tyre and Jerusalem. The same cause brought Riccardo Filangieri a powerful enemy: from 1239 a cousin of Simon's had played an important part in Syrian affairs. He was Philip of Montfort, son of Guy of Montfort, lord of La Ferté-Alais, brother of the first duke of Narbonne, and of Helvis of Ibelin.[17] On his arrival in the Holy Land, where he had accompanied his cousin Amalric (who was captured at Gaza and died on his return to Italy), Philip in 1240 married the daughter of Raymond Roupen, heiress of Toron and Châteauneuf. Despite his comparatively obscure origins, Philip was not a man to be satisfied with a lordship of eighteen knights' fees. His marriage gave him a claim to the throne of Armenia, which he was by no means backward in pursuing.[18] He must have been an eager supporter of the accession of his cousin Simon to the throne of Jerusalem, vacant as it was in effect. Once this solution was out of the question, he conceived the idea of annexing the wealthy city of Tyre, the only surviving valuable part of the royal domain of Jerusalem. Having done this, the need to hold it made him one of the most determined enemies of the Frankish monarchy; he refused to support the monarchy until King Hugh of Lusignan recognized the Montforts' right to Tyre.

The Ghibelline conspiracy

After this interlude, during which the question of the alliance with Egypt or Damascus embittered existing discords, the war between Guelfs and Ghibellines began again owing to a step taken by Filangieri. He had observed the Franks' dissensions with interest, and he did not bear patiently the insults heaped upon their adversaries by the triumphant Guelfs. The Templars, especially, not content with conducting their own war against the Moslems of Egypt and the Transjordan, in defiance of the king-emperor launched an attack on their rivals, the Hospitallers and the Teutonic Knights.[19]

The Hospital had been Ghibelline since 1239, and its grand master, Peter of Vieille-Bride, instantly laid complaint before the emperor of this act of violence, as did the grand commander of the Teutonic Knights, whose order's headquarters at Acre had been devastated. Filangieri now had a pretext to intervene in the affairs of Acre, and he was able to do so the more easily because the Templars soon afterwards sent all their forces to join the army of Jerusalem then encamped at Caesarea under the constable Odo of Montbéliard.[20] None of the Ibelins were present in Acre. Balian was at Beirut, John of Arsuf was in his lordship of Arsuf, Guy and Baldwin in Cyprus; John of Caesarea had recently died, not long after his uncle Balian of Sidon. A Ghibelline party was beginning to take shape in the great town where Pisan support could be counted on. Two of the notables, John Vaalin and William of Conches, were in touch with the imperial marshal.

Filangieri went to Acre, too early, perhaps, unless he went only to get first hand knowledge of the situation. The grand master of the Hospital and his forces had left for the principality of Antioch, where the governor of Margat was at war with the sultan of Aleppo. Filangieri entered the Hospitallers' headquarters secretly, but Philip of Montfort, the only Guelf baron then in Acre, learned that the two above-mentioned citizens were in the process of persuading the inhabitants to acknowledge the authority of the *bayle* of Tyre rather than that of Odo of Montbéliard. They were already collecting the oaths of their supporters. Philip hastily assembled the Guelf party, got help from the Genoese and the Venetians, and arrested John Vaalin and William of Conches. Warned of the movement's collapse, Filangieri left the town unobtrusively by a side gate, the Porte du Maupas, narrowly escaping capture by the troops of Balian of Ibelin-Beirut, Latin and native infantry, Maronite and Moslem, from Mount Lebanon, on their way down to Acre. They besieged the Hospitallers' headquarters for several months, thinking Filangieri was inside. The siege was not raised until 1242 when Peter of Vieille-Bride and the Hospitallers returned from Margat and took up positions in the commandery of Vigne-Neuve, from which they could threaten Acre. The grand master had to swear that he had never been in collusion with Filangieri.

The Guelf reply: occupation of Tyre

When Frederick II learned of Filangieri's latest reverse he decided to replace him by Thomas of Aquino, count of Acerra, whose previous missions gave reason to hope that he would succeed better with the Syrian barons than Filangieri had done. But it was too late; the antagonism between Guelf and Ghibelline was now out in the open. Acre was thrown into the Ibelin camp, and the Hospitallers resolved on discretion. As for Balian of Ibelin and Philip of Montfort, they decided it was time to do away with the "evil nest" of Longobards at Tyre. They had intelligence in the town, Venetians perhaps, whom they managed to keep undiscovered; from them they now learned that Filangieri had left for the West after his recall, even though his replacement had not arrived.

It was not easy, however, to justify such an enterprise. Frederick II was still the lawful sovereign, in the name of his son King Conrad II, and Filangieri was Frederick's "*bayle* of Cyprus and Jerusalem, legate in Armenia, at Antioch and at Tripoli". A solution was found by the poet and jurist Philip of Novara. In the *assises de Jérusalem* it was laid down, no doubt with reference to the difficulties of Baldwin II's accession in 1118, that when the inheritor of the kingdom attained his majority he must come and take possession of his realm. Conrad II was born on 25 April 1228 and would soon be fifteen.[21] In Philip's opinion they could do nothing before April 1244, allowing Conrad sufficient time to make an appearance. After that, they could give the crown to the next heir after Conrad.

But the two Guelf leaders did not mean to wait so long. If they could not oust Conrad completely, they would provisionally appoint a regent who in due course would succeed Conrad if he continued absent. At that time Conrad had just required his Syrian vassals to pay him homage; the whole baronage of Syria assembled at a *parlement* in Acre held in the patriarch's palace.[22] Queen Alice of Cyprus, Count Henry's daughter, who had laid claim to the crown in 1230, came forward to do so once again.[23] All had been carefully prepared by the Ibelins; Philip of Novara, instigator of this coup d'état, aided by the jurist and burgess Philip Béduin, carefully noted down in advance all the arguments he put forward on behalf of Queen Alice, whose advocate he had made himself. She paid his services with the grant of a money-fief of 1,000 bezants a year, as well as paying his debts, which came to more than 1,000 marks of silver. Alice had just married Ralph of Coeuvres, brother of the count of Soissons. She obtained from the assembled barons the recognition of her right to the crown as the daughter of Isabelle of Jerusalem and half-sister of Mary of Montferrat, from whom Conrad derived his claim. The aged constable, Odo of Montbéliard, tried to get a year's postponement, but without success. The most he could obtain was a ruling that the queen and her husband must restore the kingdom to Conrad as soon as he should require it, if he ever came. Thereupon Ralph and Alice received possession of the kingdom; led by Balian of Ibelin and Philip of Montfort, the barons did homage to their new rulers, and Alice, as duly appointed regent, summoned the Longobards to restore Tyre. This they refused.

The royal army, with Philip of Novara as its paymaster, was quickly strengthened; galleys were armed, and the fleet augmented by Genoese and Venetian flotillas. At Tyre, the *bayle* had been replaced by his brother Lotario Filangieri, who as marshal of the kingdom of Jerusalem (Riccardo was marshal of the Empire) was carrying on an interim government. Lotario was a "valiant knight, wise and courageous",[24] but the Guelfs' sources of information inside Tyre rendered all defence vain. The knights passed along the shore outside the walls, their horses troubled by the rough sea, and entered the town through the postern gate of the Butchers, which was opened for them, while their galleys, despite volleys of arrows shot down at them from the Chain Tower, made their way in past the chain which their allies in the town had put out of action. The secret had been well kept, and Lotario, caught unawares by the rising and by the Guelf entry, only just had time to take refuge in the castle. At this point a vessel entered the roadstead and made fast to Philip of Novara's ship; it was the *barque de cantier*[25] of Filangieri's vessel, which had gone down off Cyrenaica. The wrecked survivors, the imperial marshal among them, had been driven back by the storm towards Syria, in spite of the efforts of their competent captain, the knight John of Gril, and came into Tyre not knowing what had happened there on 12 June 1243. At the suggestion of John of Ibelin, cousin of Balian and future count of Jaffa, Riccardo Filangieri was used as a hostage, and rather than see his brother hanged Lotario surrendered the castle to the Ibelins.[26] This was 10 July 1243.

Frederick II still possessed some domains in Syria. Bohemond V of Antioch–Tripoli remained faithful to the king-emperor, and so possibly did Walter of Brienne, count of Jaffa, whose possessions linked together the imperial towns of Jerusalem and Ascalon. But the emperor realized how precarious was the situation of these two towns while Ralph and Alice were subduing imperial territories in the north of the kingdom, and he ordered his new *bayle*, Thomas of Acerra, to entrust Ascalon to the Hospitallers until further notice.[27]

No sooner was Tyre taken than the victors began to quarrel over it. The Venetians, like the Genoese, had played an important part in the capture of the city, and in former times they had possessed one third of it. Their *bayle*, Marsilio Giorgio, lost no time in recovering former Venetian properties and drew up an inventory of them which he sent to Venice in October 1243. As for the town itself, in law it belonged to the crown. Ralph of Coeuvres therefore thought himself entitled to claim it as a dependency of the royal domain, but when Philip of Novara received the surrender of the imperialists, he had put Balian of Ibelin and Philip of Montfort in command of the castle. These now replied to Ralph that they were unable to do as he asked; Ralph and Alice only held the regency during the absence of King Conrad II, to whom, when he came, the two cousins would deliver the castle, unless Ralph could show an indisputable right. In fact, Philip of Montfort with all due speed linked Tyre to his domain of Toron, called himself "lord of Tyre and Toron", and even – ultimate usurpation of royal prerogative – struck coins there.[28] Realizing with fury that the two associates had given him nothing but the shadow of authority and meant to keep him in the background, Ralph took ship for France. The kingdom of Jerusalem now had no other head than Queen Alice (who died in 1246); she exercised only a theoretical power, without full royal prerogative, and was known as "the lady of the kingdom".[29] Odo of Montbéliard had resigned the regency. There was now no effective government in Syria, and it was on this defenceless and leaderless land that the storm was about to break.

Renewal of the war; disaster of Forbie

Yet circumstances were favourable. As we have seen, the dispute between the sultans of Cairo and Damascus had enabled the Christians to reoccupy the Temple at Jerusalem. Pope Innocent IV hoped to make immediate use of this war between Moslems, as had been done before 1239, and he wrote to the patriarch of Jerusalem, the successor of Gerold of Lausanne (Gerold died on 7 September 1239, and was the only thirteenth-century patriarch buried in the Holy Sepulchre), authorizing him to raise a levy among the Franks of Syria in order to rebuild the walls of the Holy City.[30] No authority, however, undertook the work – to whom, after all, did Jerusalem belong? The Templars had their headquarters there, and were setting about fortifying it, but was the rest of the city not under imperial rule? But Frederick's *bayle*, Thomas of Acerra, could not undertake the defence of Jerusalem; with Tyre in the hands of Philip of Montfort, Thomas had had to go and take up his residence in the county of Tripoli.[31]

While nothing more was done than the erection of some hurried defences under the direction of the imperial castellan, the Templars and their Guelf allies now ended their policy of playing off one adversary against another and drawing advantages from both;[32] they decided for an alliance with the sultan of Damascus and the kings of Transjordania and Homs against Egypt. For their part, the Damascenes promised to cede part of Egypt after it was conquered. Alarmed by this coalition, the sultan of Cairo called in those "great companies" which were then spreading in the East the same terror that France was to know from similar bands in the Hundred Years War. These were the Khwarismians, the battle-comrades of Jelal al-Din against Genghis Khan, then roaming in upper Mesopotamia. They came pouring south to Sultan Ayub's aid, on the way attacking

Tiberias, where they took the town but not the castle, and Jerusalem. The defenders of Jerusalem appealed for help to all the Frankish princes, and to the allies gathered near Gaza, but in vain. They managed none the less to hold out against the first assaults, but the castellan and the preceptor of the Hospital were killed making a sortie. The defenders then asked their neighbour, the Moslem king of Transjordania, for help in securing a safe retreat to the coast, but their convoy was attacked by the 'Corasmins' (Khwarismians) and by Moslem peasants. Of 7,000 Franks, some 300 reached Jaffa, whilst the besiegers, who remained before the town from 11 to 23 August, sacked Jerusalem, destroying the Holy Places and the tombs of the kings. The Latin kingdom had lost the Holy City for ever. The disaster was made irretrievable by the wiping out of the Frankish army at Forbie near Gaza on 17 October 1244; unable to take the wiser course of waiting for their precariously placed adversaries' position to weaken, the coalition of Franks and Moslems attacked the Egyptian and Khwarismian forces. The Franks fought like heroes, but were totally destroyed. The grand master of the Temple was killed and the grand master of the Hospital captured, as was Walter of Brienne, count of Jaffa. Philip of Montfort escaped and saved Ascalon from capture, bravely defended by the Hospitallers. The grand master of the Teutonic Knights, Gerhard of Mahlberg, may have been one of the three knights of that order who fled; he was dismissed from his post not long afterwards.[33]

Thus the Latin kingdom was punished for the internal divisions which made its external policy so erratic and incoherent. Frederick II had forbidden the breaking of the Egyptian alliance;[34] out of party spirit and the desire to profit by Damascene concessions, the Syrian barons and the military orders, instead of being content to build up the patiently reconstructed kingdom, pitchforked it into a most dangerous venture. Not long was to pass before the lands regained by Frederick II and by Richard of Cornwall melted away, and the kingdom of Acre was once more reduced to a thin strip along the coast.

CHAPTER 3

St Louis' crusade, 1245–1254

The consequences of Forbie

News of the second fall of Jerusalem and of the defeat at Forbie re-echoed sadly around Christendom. A Nestorian prelate then in Iran wrote in 1246 to tell the pope of his distress.[1] The bishop of Beirut went immediately to carry an appeal for help to the monarchs of the West, and in July 1245 the council of Lyons proclaimed a general crusade. St Louis, the king of France, had already taken the cross in December 1244. Unfortunately, the council of Lyons had also, for the third time, excommunicated Frederick II;[2] besides the French, only a few crusaders from England, Frisia and Brabant left for the East in 1248. The situation in the Holy Land deteriorated further during this delay. When Jerusalem fell, the 'Corasmins' had already occupied the country east of a line between Toron des Chevaliers and Gaza, that is, practically the whole of Judaea. After the battle of Forbie, the sultan of Egypt refused to let his dangerous allies into the Nile valley, and they spread over the almost defenceless Latin kingdom. Very soon the southern part of the Frankish possessions as far as Nazareth and Safed was overwhelmed; the Khwarismians even set up their tents two miles from Acre and it was feared that they meant to besiege the city. A disturbing aspect of the Moslem campaign was that it began to look like a permanent reoccupation: Ayubid officials took up residence in the recaptured *casals* and collected the taxes.[3] Late in 1244 the sultan of Cairo sent his forces to occupy Jerusalem, and also Judaea and Samaria, lost to him by the king of Transjordania. The capture of Damascus in October 1245 reunited Damascus and Egypt, and so destroyed any chance of the Christians profiting by Moslem dissensions. Meanwhile the pope was doing what he could to limit the scope of the disaster. Attempts were made first of all to purchase the prisoners taken at Forbie, for whom prayers were ordered throughout Christendom in 1245.[4] Matthew Paris, the English historian who is well informed about events in the Holy Land at this period, tells us that the Templars and the Hospitallers endeavoured to redeem their prisoners, and Sultan Ayub replied that he would not grant their request unless it was supported by Frederick II. If it were, he would release the captives without payment. To the Syrian Franks and to many Christians, Frederick seemed none other than Antichrist, and the two orders did not feel able to do as the sultan recommended. Ayub had, moreover, commented sarcastically on their dissensions – five years of fighting which Earl Richard had been unable to bring to an end – and on the flight of the Templars' standard-bearer, the "bearer of the Bauceant".[5]

Innocent IV had earlier written to the sultan to ask for a truce. Ayub's reply of 3 June 1245, in accordance with diplomatic protocol, commended the pope's desire for peace, but maintained that by the treaty of 1229 the sultan of Egypt could only negotiate with the Christians through Frederick II; the pope's letter had been sent on to the Egyptian ambassador at the emperor's court. This obstructive reply incensed the pope against Frederick, whose attitude seemed a betrayal of Christendom, and at first Innocent thought that Frederick had forged the letter. Further examination, however, showed it to be authentic. It was also learned that Frederick, the sovereign of the Holy Land, was preventing the transport to Syria of victuals and troops, on the pretext that "succour for the Holy Land", *subsidium Terre Sancte*, was the papacy's "very effective argument by which it extorts money from the faithful, money on which it grows proud and fat, by means of hypocritical preaching of the liberation of the Holy Land".[6]

The now relentless war between pope and emperor halted the relief intended for Frankish Syria, and the collaboration between Frederick and the sultan did much to render this war one of the bitterest of the Middle Ages.[7] In the Holy Land, in spite of the Moslem invasion, in spite of the urgency of the crisis, a fresh outbreak of the Guelf-Ghibelline quarrel almost occurred. The pope in due course accepted the fact that the Syrian Franks had rejected Frederick; in 1247 King Henry of Cyprus was released from the oath of loyalty taken to the emperor by his predecessors since 1197 and by himself, and on 17

April he was acknowledged as "lord of the kingdom of Jerusalem". Henceforth Cyprus depended only on the Holy See. The pope thus ratified the coup d'état of 1243 and, passing over the question of Queen Alice's illegitimate birth, he recognized Henry, Alice's son, as regent of the kingdom by hereditary right. His purpose was to try to ensure a measure of effective protection for the unhappy Latin kingdom; on 17 July 1247 he begged Henry "if it can be done, to bring into a better condition the land in which Jesus Christ was pleased to be born, to live and to die". Another letter of the same date commanded the subjects of the kingdom to cease obedience to Frederick II.[8] The imperial *bayle*, Thomas of Acerra, was still in residence at Tripoli; on 25 May 1248 Innocent IV was exclaiming in alarm and demanding his expulsion. Perhaps he had just learned of the continued existence of a Ghibelline party, resuscitated by the able count of Acerra and preparing a new coup d'état to restore Conrad II to his throne. The movement was said to be supported by members of the military orders, Hospitallers, perhaps, or Teutonic Knights. The pope ordered all possible steps to be taken to prevent such a restoration. Among others, he forbade Pisan ships to enter the port of Acre under the imperial flag, and he confirmed King Henry's lordship of the kingdom.[9] In any case, Balian of Ibelin-Beirut, appointed *bayle* at Acre by Queen Alice, had just died, on 4 September 1247. In Balian's place, Henry appointed his brother, John of Ibelin-Arsuf, who resigned the post in September 1248.[10]

Clearly, the kingdom's internal troubles could not fail to benefit the Moslems. Sultan Ayub had by no means halted his forward march; on 17 June 1247 the siege of Tiberias was brought to a victorious conclusion, and the Ayubid forces then moved against Ascalon and laid siege to it by land and sea. Ascalon was a strong fortress, and at the Hospitallers' request the king of Cyprus had reinforced it with 100 Cypriot knights under Baldwin of Ibelin and a fleet of seven galleys and two galleons, further strengthened by a Syrian squadron under John of Ibelin-Arsuf. The Egyptian fleet was flung back upon the coast, and the Franks withdrew to Acre to avoid bad weather. There they learned that on 14 October 1247 the Egyptians had managed to dig a tunnel, shoring it up with timbers from their ships, and through it had entered unexpectedly into the citadel of Ascalon. The news of the fall of Ascalon was disheartening for Christendom indeed; a stronghold on which Hugh of Burgundy and Richard of Cornwall had spent so much effort, and it held out so short a time![11]

Matthew Paris draws a sad picture of the state of things in the Holy Land: "The inhabitants of Acre themselves, fearful for their city and neither daring nor able to leave it, expected nothing but a siege or a pitiable surrender. They lacked food, were sustained by no hope of assistance and were consumed with fear." Mighty fortresses like Krak des Chevaliers and Châtel Pèlerin "seemed to their inhabitants prisons, not protection, a reason for fear, not for security". Many Christians lost every shred of courage at the sight of their enemies going unhindered about the country, and even went to the length of apostasy.[12]

The news that the crusade was about to set off restored some hope to the Syrian Franks; perhaps at least the Moslem reconquest would be halted. News of the coming of the king of France reached the Moslems from Frederick himself, the man who had offered to take the cross in 1245. He sent dispatch after dispatch to Sultan Ayub to keep him informed of the progress of the French expedition.[13] Alarm reigned in Egypt, said the western merchants who traded at Alexandria, and they profited by it nicely: it was rumoured in Europe that early in 1247 the sultan's agents had poisoned all the supplies of pepper for Christian ports in order to prevent the crusade setting out. Naturally purchasers at once bought up all the previous years' pepper they could lay hold of, and as soon as the old stocks were used up, the Italian merchants issued a denial of the rumours they had spread.[14]

The sultan of Egypt happened then to be at war with the king of Aleppo, who took Homs in 1248. The news of the preparations for the Frankish invasion compelled him to make peace. Perhaps the crusaders might have tried to negotiate with Ayub's enemies and in this way to obtain the cession of territories without bloodshed, but the king of France refused to use these means. Perhaps he feared to be blamed as Frederick had been for the treaty of Jaffa. St Louis landed in Cyprus on 17 September 1248 and wintered at Limassol, where Joinville says that literally 'mountains' of victuals had been collected. The length of time spent in winter quarters was harmful to the army, and could not be used for negotiation, although on 20 December St Louis received two envoys from a Mongol general who said that their master was anxious to enter into relations with the Franks in order to act jointly with them against the Moslems. The king was greatly interested in this suggestion, and sent an embassy to Mongolia in January 1249 under Andrew of Longjumeau. It did not return until 1251 and had no result.[15]

The Seventh Crusade

The fleet was at last assembled,[16] and on 30 May 1249 Louis IX's army, including 400 knights from the principality of the Morea and contingents from the kingdom of Cyprus and of Acre, 2,800 knights in all, embarked aboard it. The king's campaign is well known. He arrived on 4 June in sight of the coast of Egypt, near Damietta, taking the same route as the previous crusade in spite of the existence of the fortress of Mansurah, blocking the way to Cairo, and in spite of the warning pronounced in 1223 by the patriarch of Alexandria, who recommended an attack upon the less strongly defended Rosetta branch of the Nile. St Louis disembarked straight away on 5 June and put to flight the Egyptian army drawn up on the shore. Even the troops garrisoning Damietta fled, and they forgot to break down the bridge joining the town to the western bank of the Nile where the Franks were. On 6 June 1249 the Franks entered the empty city without striking a blow, and Damietta instantly became a Latin city, its mosques transformed into churches, and the religious orders installed in monasteries, while an archbishop took over the new cathedral of Our Lady and men worked on repairing the ramparts. Time was lost again, waiting first for reinforcements and then for the Nile flood to be past its peak. Meanwhile the Egyptians mustered their army afresh, and repaired the long neglected fortress of Mansurah.[17]

Next came the famous march on Cairo, undertaken only after long discussion. The count of Brittany was insistent that they should make rather for Alexandria, so as to choke Egypt by capturing both its major ports, thus compelling the sultan to make peace on the king's terms. But the count of Artois swayed the decision, even though the majority disagreed with him, and it was decided to follow the route of the Fifth Crusade, and Matthew Paris asserts that it was even decided to reject Sultan Ayub's offer to return all his conquests made in the Holy Land if the Franks would return Damietta to him. Ayub died not long after this, on 23 November 1249, but his successor Turanshah had time to reach the battleground. Meanwhile the Frankish army could not get off the island formed by the Damietta and Tanis branches of the Nile. St Louis advanced with care, avoiding the ambushes set for him by his opponent. Having reached a position opposite Mansurah, but on the further bank, late in December 1249, he beat off several Egyptian attacks and had trenches dug around his camp. The Franks tried to build a causeway across the Tanis branch of the Nile so as to cross by it to the eastern bank, but as fast as they built on the one side, the Egyptians dug out a channel for the river on the other. It was at this point that a local inhabitant, whether Bedouin, Copt or Moslem we do not know, informed the king of the existence of a ford. The crusading army would at last be able to cross the Nile.

An act of folly and of disobedience to the king's orders now wrecked the whole campaign. The king had commanded his troops to cross the ford in good order and to re-form on the far shore. No sooner had Robert of Artois, St Louis' brother, reached the eastern bank in command of the vanguard than he flung his men into an attack on the Moslem camp; this was 8 February 1250. The camp was taken by surprise, the Egyptian generalissimo killed and his army put to flight. Robert, not content with this incontestable victory, sought to complete it by pursuing the fugitives, wiping out the enemy and taking Mansurah. Brother Giles, grand commander of the Templars, tried to restrain him but was called a coward for his pains and could do nothing but join the count of Artois' mad ride. The king himself sent ten knights at a gallop to order the count to wait, but with no effect. Robert of Artois had entered Mansurah and was at the very foot of the citadel when Baibars, a Turkish commander, regrouped the Mamluks of the Egyptian army and flung them against the crusaders, whose wearied mounts could not sustain the shock of the encounter. Trapped inside the town, driven to and fro in a dreadful street battle by an enemy more numerous than themselves, the Templars and the count of Artois' men were almost all killed with their commander.

The royal army had not finished crossing the ford. The rearguard under Hugh IV of Burgundy was still on the western shore with the infantry when Baibars and his Turks and Arabs fell upon the corps commanded by St Louis. Divided as it was into three separate parts, it seemed as if the army must be destroyed. The vanguard had already perished; the centre, consisting of knights without infantry – and it was the foot who since 1189 had won the Franks' most splendid victories – was about to perish too, and the rearguard could do nothing. The personal heroism and prudence of St Louis enabled his knights to stand firm during an entire day in which they were showered with arrows to which their crossbowmen could not reply, and bombarded with projectiles containing Greek fire, while exhaustion prevented them returning the enemy's charges. The king even tried to send the count of Brittany and Humbert of Beaujeu to help the vanguard, but the overwhelming numbers of the Egyptians prevented this. In addition to all else, thirst and heat made it seem impossible to hold out. They held out, none the less, until the duke of Burgundy and Humbert of Beaujeu with the infantry were able to intervene late in the evening. The Egyptian army at last withdrew, and the dreadful day of Mansurah ended in victory. But St Louis' army could not now think of taking Mansurah; it had held its position on the road to Cairo, but it had been decimated and was not capable of taking the offensive.

Harassed by Egyptian attacks, which ended in another victory on 11 February, after which the enemy left them alone, the Franks were too slow in withdrawing towards Damietta. Sickness attacked their camp, and, as in 1221, the Egyptians built a fleet which regained control of the Nile, cutting off the Frankish army's supply of food and further damaging its health. Once the retreat was decided on, it was found difficult to accomplish, both because of fresh enemy attacks and because typhus was sapping the army's strength. St Louis attempted to negotiate with the new sultan Turanshah, but the sultan did not reply. The Egyptians were able to cross the Nile on the bridge which had still not been destroyed, and again began to harry the pathetic convoy of sick men, who continued to defend themselves. On 6 April 1250, one stage from Damietta, catastrophe occurred: the king fell ill, and at the very moment when Philip of Montfort had obtained hurried terms of surrender by which the army would be saved in return for the surrender of Damietta, a treacherous sergeant tricked the crusaders into laying down their arms. The sick men captured both ashore and aboard the Frankish ships were slaughtered, and all the rest, St Louis included, were imprisoned in Cairo.[18]

The French king was then required to surrender Damietta and to evacuate the whole of Frankish Syria. This he refused, as he had no authority over the Holy Land, at which he was threatened with torture. An agreement was reached in due course: Damietta should form the king's ransom, but 500,000 *livres* must be paid for the release of the army. The Holy Land would be restored to its condition previous to St Louis' arrival in the East, that is, the Moslems would evacuate the Cave of Tyron which they had taken at the same time that Damietta fell. All prisoners on both sides would be released, including those taken in the 1249–1250 campaign and in previous battles. This included the Forbie prisoners, held at Cairo for the past six years.

The ransom was enormous, but it would save what remained of the king's army and of the knighthood of the Morea, Cyprus and Syria. Now, however, the story took another turn, with the intervention of the Mamluks. These soldier-slaves, in some ways comparable to the janissaries of the Ottomans, formed the main fighting strength of the Ayubid army, and it was they who had halted the Frankish invasion at Mansurah. They turned against the new sultan, Turanshah, and on 2 May 1250 he was murdered by his own guards at the order of the future sultan, Baibars. Now arose that strange phenomenon which was to endure till the Ottoman conquest and indeed until the eighteenth century, the government of Egypt by sultans sprung from the ranks of a slave militia, Turkish at first and later Circassian: a vigorous and centralized government in which there was no trace of the past feudalism and where almost the only rule of inheritance was assassination.[19] The new Mamluk sultan, Aibek the Turcoman, soon confirmed the treaty made with the Franks by his former master.

Damietta, defended by Marguerite, queen of France, in spite of threats of desertion made by Italian troops, was handed over to the Mamluks on 6 May. They killed all the sick in the hospitals and considered killing the king and his barons as well. But, after a month's captivity, St Louis was at last set free, though Joinville had to threaten to break open the Templars' strong boxes before they would agree to lend the money for the ransom. The military orders, as we know, held no funds other than those deposited with them by crusaders, or such at least was their excuse for refusing the loan.

St Louis in Syria

St Louis could well have now considered his crusade accomplished, as many other crusading princes had done. In France the strange revolt of the Pastoureaux, that mass rising of peasants who on the pretext of going to free the king pillaged churches on their way, was posing a serious problem to the regent, Blanche of Castille. She feared, too, an attack from the king of England. At a council meeting in Acre on 26 June the crusading barons made plain their wish to return to France. None the less the king, following Joinville's advice, decided to remain. The charming scene[20] is well known in which the future historian of the Seventh Crusade, afraid he had annoyed the king, withdrew to a window where he stood thinking sadly, till he felt a pair of hands placed on his head. Thinking it was one of the men he had been arguing with, Joinville said, "Leave me alone, messire Philip", but it was the king, come to comfort the only one of his knights whose opinion agreed with his own; he also asked him not to speak of it yet. At a meeting on 3 July 1250 St Louis pointed out that they still had to obtain the release of the rest of the prisoners (which was done not without difficulty in 1252) and that he could not go away and leave the Holy Land undefended after the terrible loss of its manpower at Mansurah. Leaving his brothers and his barons free to consider their vows accomplished, Louis IX remained in Syria.

Syria was in great need of help, but since the arrival of the crusaders the Franks of the Holy Land had taken heart, as a number of small points show: on 7 August 1248 the monastery of St Mary of the Latins, a refugee at Acre, granted to the Hospital, with its priory of Caco, the *casals* of Montdidier and La Tour Rouge on a long lease. These areas near Caesarea must have been devastated by Moslem raids, and the very fact that their recovery was contemplated shows a returning optimism.[21] During the campaign of 1248–1249 the Egyptians followed up their earlier successes by capturing the Cave of Tyron in 1248, but a counter-offensive was begun by the army of Jerusalem, which was very probably reinforced by St Louis, although some of the barons, such as John of Ibelin-Jaffa and Philip of Montfort, constable of the kingdom since the death of Odo of Montbéliard in 1244, who had been with him in Egypt, had gone. Led by John of Ibelin-Arsuf, *bayle* of the kingdom, the knights of Acre pillaged the small Moslem town of Beisan on 28 January 1250, and surprised a large Turcoman horde, capturing some 16,000 beasts, their owners and the emir who was conducting them.[22]

In his treaty with the Egyptians St Louis had been careful to ensure that the Holy Land should be restored to the condition it was in in 1248. Jaffa, Arsuf, Caesarea, Châtel Pèlerin, Cayphas, Caymont, Nazareth, Safed and Beaufort marked the Frankish frontier, of which they were the principal fortresses. But the king of France was worried by the poor state of these towns' defences, and his presence in Syria was reflected in an immense programme of building works.[23] The king's masons and engineers went first to Acre, where they rebuilt a whole stretch of the walls, from the St Anthony Gate to that of St Lazarus by the sea, thus putting into a state of defence the suburb of Montmusart, hitherto left without adequate ramparts. The refortified quarter gained a new lease of prosperity: in 1254 a hospital was built in the *rue des Anglais* (street of the English) for poor pilgrims from Brittany. It was founded by Giles, archbishop of Tyre, who endowed it himself and dedicated it to St Martin, patron saint of Tours, the archiepiscopal see on which the Breton bishoprics then depended.[24]

The king went next to Cayphas and Caesarea, where the ramparts were rebuilt in 1251,[25] and then to Jaffa, which he set to work to make into a major fortress. Here too, greatly to the advantage of John of Ibelin, count of Jaffa, the town was fortified, between 1252 and 1253. Next came Sidon, where the Castle of the Sea was balanced by a second citadel, the Castle of the Land, and walls were built about the whole town. By means of these protracted and expensive building works, St Louis very much increased Frankish Syria's ability to defend itself. His efforts were continued in succeeding years: the Hospitallers obtained from the pope the grant of the property of two destroyed monasteries, Mount Tabor and St Lazarus of Bethany, on condition that they built at Tabor a castle to be defended by forty knights.[26] An act of 1255 established the future castle as the complement of the fortresses of Safed and Beaufort, enabling the Franks to defend western Galilee, which had lain open to every raid since the fall of Tiberias. The archbishop of Nazareth tried to play his part in this rebuilding of Frankish Galilee; in 1255, after ceding four *casals* near Cana[27] to the Hospitallers to round off their domain of Tabor, he tried to revive the little town of Sephoria, planting settlers there. But the archbishop was unable to make a success of this; enemy attacks still threatened, revolt was still latent among the Moslem peasants, and he could not hold his property. He obtained from the pope permission to withdraw with his chapter to Acre – one more prelate *in partibus* – and ceded the whole lordship of Nazareth with its nineteen *casals* and its wastelands to the Hospitallers in exchange for an annual rent of 14,000 bezants.[28]

Although this attempt to restore the former Frankish domain of Galilee did not succeed, it is worth mentioning because it shows that, thanks to St Louis, the kingdom of Acre had ceased to be merely on the defensive. Resettlement was beginning on lands that had scarcely been freed from the incursions of Turcoman foragers, and it was being attempted too in Samaria.[29] The king of France had made use of his release from captivity to embark, somewhat late perhaps, upon a skilled game of diplomacy; the Ayubid princes had not meekly accepted the Mamluk revolt that destroyed the head of their family and was threatening them. Damascus recovered its independence and offered its allegiance to al-Nasir Yusuf, the king of Aleppo, a direct descendant of Saladin, and the Ayubids mounted a campaign for the recovery of Egypt. They were crushed at the bloody battle of Abbasa on 2 February 1251 and the Mamluk regime could feel secure. St Louis took advantage of Sultan Aibek's worries to hasten the release of the captives, and from fear of endangering them he had to refuse the alliance suggested by Yusuf, who offered to return the kingdom of Jerusalem to him.

In March 1252 St Louis even considered an alliance with the Egyptians, who were now planning to go over to the offensive and recapture Damascus. A truce was signed for fifteen years, agreeing to the release of all prisoners taken since the accession of Frederick II to the throne of Syria in 1226, and the surrender to the Christians of the whole country west of the Jordan, including Jerusalem, Hebron and Nablus. Only the four strongholds of Gaza, Daron, Gibelin and, in Galilee, Grand Gerin, were to remain in the hands of the sultan, who undertook not to fortify them.[30] But, unfortunately, while the Frankish army was waiting at Jaffa for its allies to arrive, the caliph of Baghdad in April 1253 succeeded in bringing about a reconciliation between the Ayubids and the Mamluks. The Damascenes sought vengeance on the Latin kingdom, in whose fate, naturally, Aibek was no longer interested. On 6 May 1253 the Damascenes threatened Jaffa but were driven off by crossbow fire. They destroyed two *casals* near Acre, but John of Arsuf, *bayle* of the kingdom and constable since at least 1251, managed to prevent them laying waste the orchards and gardens. Sidon, though, was not able to defend itself; in June 1253 all who could do so took refuge in the Castle of the Sea, but the encircling walls were not finished and the town was taken and 1,200 Christians captured or killed.

St Louis hit back; until then he had forbidden his men to take part in isolated skirmishes, such as the raid on Ramleh led by the master of the order of St Lazarus whom Joinville had had to rescue.[31] Leaving the walls of Jaffa more or less finished – work continued on them for several years – the king went to Sidon and sent a detachment of his army into the interior. Commanded by Philip of Montfort, by the grand masters of the Temple and the Hospital, by John of Eu and Giles Le Brun, marshal of France, this force surprised Banyas and nearly succeeded in taking Subeibah, the all but impregnable

fortress dominating Banyas. Having failed in this attempt they withdrew and returned to Sidon. When he had completed the ramparts of
Sidon, St Louis returned to Acre on 7 March 1254, where on 12 April,
Easter day, he knighted Balian, the son of John of Arsuf, as he had
done Bohemond VI, the new prince of Antioch, in 1252. On 25 April
he took ship for France.

It may seem strange that where Frederick reaped nothing but
insults, the king of France could exercise an undisputed authority in
the Holy Land, subduing even the proud order of the Templars, and
compelling the grand master to break a private peace treaty
concluded between that order and the Damascenes by the marshal of
the Temple himself.[32] Yet St Louis had to work in a particularly
delicate situation, since Frederick, or rather his son Conrad, was still
the lawful king of Jerusalem. Conrad acted as king several times, in
1252, 1253 and 1254 confirming the Hospital's possession of property
in the country, Ascalon in particular, and appointing a chancellor of
the kingdom, one William of Ocre.[33] Frederick II died on 13 December 1250, bequeathing 100,000 ounces of gold to his Syrian kingdom
by way of conscience money; when Conrad II died, the pope recognized his son Conrad III, or Conradin, in September 1254 as the true
heir of the throne of Jerusalem. The king of France was well placed
to act; he had tried for a number of years to reconcile the pope and
the emperor, and his own relations with Frederick were still good.
Relying on this, Frederick asked Louis IX to re-establish his officials
at Acre and throughout the kingdom. St Louis refrained from doing
any such thing, but he was careful not to infringe the rights of Conrad
II in any way.[34]

That the king of France, without any legal title, could exercise an
authority which Richard of Cornwall had been unable to assert, was
undoubtedly due to his personal renown, to the sanctity which made
him the arbiter of Europe, to his fairmindedness and to his heroism.
Besides this, we must not forget that all these Syrian barons belonged
to French families. Scarcely one of them was without either fiefs in
France, such as Philip of Montfort had,[35] or at least near relatives
who were bound to the king by the closest feudal ties. It was not
solely a shared language and culture that made St Louis into the
untitled king of Frankish Syria, but also the personal tie of homage
which made him the natural head of the Syrian barons. Was not the
lord of the kingdom himself, the king of Cyprus, a cousin of that
count of La Marche whom the king had taught so severe a lesson?

Lastly, the generous material aid which Louis IX contributed to the Latin colony of the East was bound to rally all possible opponents to his side. With him, for the last time, unanimity reigned in the land of Syria.

The effects of his crusade were to be seen in the putting of what was left of the kingdom into a state of defence, and in the respect inspired in his enemies. John of Ibelin, count of Jaffa, *bayle* of the kingdom from the year 1254, completed the work of Louis' diplomacy abroad by negotiating a ten-year truce with the Damascenes in the year 1255. It excluded the county of Jaffa, and we can only wonder whether John was here sacrificing his domain to the common good, or, as Grandclaude thinks, contriving to channel all subsidies from the West to his own county.[36] In any event, the operations carried on from 1255 under the count of Jaffa and under Geoffrey of Sergines, the commander of the troops left in the Holy Land by St Louis, worked out well for the Franks. The Moslem emir of Jerusalem himself was defeated and killed in an encounter on 17 March 1256, and in the same year John obtained a ten-year truce for the whole kingdom, Jaffa included, operating both on the Egyptian and the Damascene frontiers.[37]

Peace had returned at last, after ten arduous years which had brought the kingdom to the edge of disaster. But now, just when every effort was needed to re-establish the Holy Land, the Frankish and Syrian barons devoted themselves instead to futile party man-oeuvring which very soon led to a terrible civil war. This paralysed the kingdom at a time when Islam was staggering under the blows of new actors on the scene, the Mongols.

CHAPTER 4

The kingdom of the merchants

Syrian commerce

In the middle of the thirteenth century the Latin kingdom was at the height of its commercial prosperity. The years of peace before 1244 had allowed East–West trade to develop, and Syrian commerce of this period seems to have been highly organized. Documents dating from about 1250 throw some light on the nature of its organization. It seems appropriate, then, to choose this period at which to examine the activities of merchants in the kingdom of Acre, and the more so because it was at this time that their role became a leading one. Crusading fervour gave way to economic realism; the Mamluk campaigns against Frankish Syria and Christian Armenia might be part of Islam's holy war, but they were also conscious attempts to put down Acre and Lajazzo, rivals of the port of Alexandria through which all eastern Mediterranean trade was to flow for several centuries.

Syria did not attract many merchants before the time of the crusades, except those from Amalfi, who organized pilgrimages to Jerusalem. Such Eastern products as were then known in the West passed through Byzantium into the hands of Italian merchants, mainly Venetians and Sicilians, some of whom also traded at Alexandria or Damietta. Some Moslem and a good number of Jewish merchants also carried goods to Western ports. The crusades opened up fresh markets for Pisa, Genoa and Venice.[1]

As we saw earlier, the coastal cities of Italy and Provence, Languedoc and Catalonia gradually created trading networks owning concessions in certain ports which naturally led them to trade through these ports to the exclusion of others. Thus the trade of Iran, Mesopotamia, Aleppo and Damascus flowed increasingly through the ports of Syria instead of through those of the Nile Delta, although the Delta kept an almost total monopoly of trade with India, Arabia and Egypt. Certain products, though, such as the alum of upper Egypt, travelled to the Frankish kingdom by way of the isthmus of Suez. Even Moslem trade was attracted to the great markets of Jerusalem, Acre and Tyre;[2] at the end of the twelfth century, according to Ibn Jobaïr, Damascus traders had their subsidiaries in the coastal towns, and even in time of war Moslem shipowners of Tyre could obtain permission from the Latin kings to take their ships to Egypt.[3] This transit of goods is recalled in a passage in the *Assises de la Cour aux Bourgeois*, dated by Prawer to about 1244: linen carried from Cairo to Damascus paid in the king's *fonde* one bezant and two *caroubles* (a *carouble* was a twenty-fourth part of a bezant) on every camel-load.[4]

This tariff and other documents tell us what goods passed through the customs at the Frankish ports. The list of these Eastern products was one that seemed to the people of the Middle Ages a catalogue of marvellous wealth; one has only to read the amazed description of the Holy Land and its produce given by James of Vitry to realize how his contemporaries were enthralled by anything that came from the East. From the ports of Tyre and Acre came many of the medicaments stocked in apothecaries' shops; the medieval pharmacopeia, based on the teaching of the school of Salerno, was wholly Eastern in origin. Senna, aloes and manna of Sinai came from Persia and Arabia, camphor and myrobolan plums from India and Afghanistan, rhubarb, myrrh and scammony from Syria, cassia and the bitter zedoary root from India and Java, and customs dues were payable on them all in the *fonde* at Acre. Spices were heavily taxed, eleven per cent on pepper, eight per cent on nutmeg, nine per cent on cloves, and we know how much spices were liked in the Middle Ages, in both food and drink; if we did not, the story of the poisoned pepper in 1247 would prove it. Most spices were brought overland from India; they were supposed to retain their aroma better than those brought by sea to Alexandria. At the end of their long journey, cinnamon, ginger and cardamom were put up for sale in the markets of the Latin cities of Syria. There, too, were products destined for Western industries, basic materials such as hanks of raw silk, bales of cotton, linen from Egypt, Damascus silk thread, zinc ore, and above all the components of dyes, so important to Western cloth manufacturers. These were alum, from Egypt or Aleppo, lac, used also as a medicine, from India and Indochina, cochineal or *graine d'écarlate*, sandalwood, the much sought after red brazil-wood from India and Sumatra, and indigo from Baghdad.

Churches imported incense from Arabia through these ports, heavily taxed at eleven per cent. Balm, though, had disappeared from Engedi and Jericho and came almost solely from Egypt, although Arabia sent *opobalsamum*, another product of the balsam tree which was less valued, but in demand for pharmacy and perfumery. Ivory, taxed at eight per cent, came from Ethiopia and Zanzibar. Perfumes were to be bought, too, in the Acre market: *mousqueliet*, that is musk from Tibet, paying eight and a half per cent, amber and benzoin. Luxury products were endless: pearls, precious stones, including among others balas rubies from Bactria, emeralds, sapphires, diamonds and cornelians from India, porcelain ("pottery from heathendom"), and above all the richly ornamented fabrics from all over the East: the gold brocaded *baudequins* from Baghdad, silken *camocans*, damasks from Damascus, *mousselines*, muslins, from Mosul, and carpets.[5] Lastly there were the kingdom's own products to add to the riches crammed into the warehouses of Acre:[6] sugar, product of Frankish Syria's principal industry, so much so indeed that Frederick II wrote to Filangieri telling him to send workmen from the works at Tyre to those at Palermo, without worrying about Syria's interests;[7] glass, mainly produced by Jewish craftsmen, leatherwork, wine from Nazareth and Sephoria, and fabrics which were the pride of the kingdom's weavers. The *Assises* regulated the production of *bouquerans*, fine linen or cotton fabrics, and of the silk *cendal* of Tyre and Tripoli; these silks had to be presented for inspection before being dyed in order to check their quality. Camel and goat hair *camelots* were also manufactured in the workshops of the Latin kingdom.

These goods did not all go to the West. Egypt imported much of its soap from the kingdom, also cotton, melons, citrons, oranges, dates, lemons and oil, especially sesame oil. The fisheries of Tyre and the coast gave rise to a sizeable fish-preserving industry; salt fish exported to 'heathendom' paid a tax of a quarter *carouble* per bezant.[8] A large part of the trade between Moslem countries was carried in Christian boats; thus in 1248 Marseilles was re-exporting cinnamon and cloves to Bougie.[9] Slaves are the last item on the list of goods exported to the West from Frankish ports.[10]

Less well known and just as interesting are the goods sent from Europe to the East. This was the first time that the balance of trade between Europe and Asia was not uneven, as it had been, according to Pliny the Elder, throughout classical antiquity. Gold had disappeared from Western currency at the time of the barbarian invasions and during Carolingian times. In the second half of the twelfth century it made its appearance once more in the West, and the Byzantine or Moslem gold bezant was at a premium on the French market. Charters of donations to abbeys mention the gold bezant along with the silver *deniers* that had been the only currency in use during the previous centuries, since the disappearance of the gold *solidus*.[11] Better still, the minting of gold coins began again in the West. St Louis, whose predecessors had minted only silver, issued golden 'royals', imitations of the bezant, and Genoese gold pieces and gold florins from Florence were already current: Italy, too, had begun to issue gold currency. We must conclude that the Moslem countries, with access to the gold mined in the Sudan, had to export it to Europe to pay for their purchases.

For centuries Europe had exported cloths to the East. Charlemagne, looking for a precious gift to send to the caliph Harun al-Rashid, chose Frisian cloth, which he knew to be highly esteemed beyond the sea. Contracts made by merchants of Genoa and Marseilles in the thirteenth century show that these cloths were still liked in the East. Ships carried bales of woollen and linen fabrics; when the *Sicarde-du-Saint-Esprit* left Marseilles for Acre she was carrying 450 quintals of cargo, 400 of which were woollen and linen textiles. The registers of a notary of Marseilles, for example, the *Notules d'Amalric* of 1248, read like a catalogue of the weaving industry: there were dark brown woollens from Douai, grey from Provins, green and blue from Châlons, red from Ypres, woollen stuffs from Louviers, Rouen and Cambrai, linens from Champagne, Rheims, Germany, Lille and Basel, furred mantles from Poitiers, dark Stamford cloths from England, striped stuffs from Paris, light woollens from Arras, canvas, barracans, woollen blankets, felt hats, gold thread from Genoa, capes from Bayonne, and furs and skins, all on their way to Acre. Hemp was in great demand, and so were metals not common in the East, such as copper – one ship carried copper pans – tin, mercury and lead. Almonds were carried, and salt pork, for the Westerners in Syria had to send home for the bacon that they could not do without and could not buy from Moslem lands where the pig was forbidden. Saffron, a much favoured seasoning, also came from the West, and even alum came from Castile to compete in the market of Acre with alum from Aleppo, which was also exported. Large quantities of coral were sent to Acre from the fishing grounds of Sardinia. To this undoubtedly incomplete list we may add iron, timber, which probably came mainly from Armenia, and saddles.[12]

The kingdom of Jerusalem consumed a considerable part of all this, but the bulk of the goods that came into its ports only stayed in the Acre warehouses until they were bought by Moslem merchants. Merchants of Damascus and above all of Mosul had agents at Acre who sent merchandise from Western lands on to the bazaars of the interior. It even seems probable that Egypt herself bought provisions in the Frankish towns along the Syrian coast. Marino Sanudo, writing not long after the fall of Acre, was surprised to find how dependent Egypt was on other lands; hardly anything reached her from the Moslem countries of the West – we saw that modern Tunisia and Algeria sometimes communicated with Egypt through Italian and Provençal merchants – nothing from Arabia, not much from Syria, and only spices from the Indian Ocean. It was from the Christian lands of the West that she received silver, lead, copper, tin, mercury, fine lawns and silks, linen, coral, saffron, oil, walnuts and almonds, mastic from the island of Chios, and even the slaves, timber, iron and pitch upon which the Mamluk sultans' military power depended.[13]

Trade with Egypt in these items was strictly forbidden, but it could not be entirely prevented. The *Assises* made such trading a hanging offence,[14] but when Prince Edward of England tried to enforce its prohibition, he was confronted with the privileges granted to Italian merchants to enable them to carry it on. In any case, the kingdom had no power over Western merchants beyond its own frontiers; it would have needed a fleet doing nothing but put down the contraband trade. In fact this went briskly on, its merchants risking nothing but a sentence of excommunication, which did not much trouble their elastic consciences.

The crown and the merchants

Even inside the kingdom, the king was often powerless against Italian, Provençal or Catalan traders; we saw earlier what a huge number of concessions the merchants obtained from the crown. The kings or their officials did sometimes recover an alienated royal right, but they were not able to rescind the vital privilege, exemption from taxation. The sum paid on bringing merchandise into Acre was often purely nominal, as for instance the one bezant per hundred paid by the Marseillais in virtue of a treaty of 1190. The communes would allow no attempts to do away with these privileges; when in February 1231 Frederick II ordered Filangieri to reimpose a *droit de chaîne*, custom dues, on the Genoese, the Genoese objected so strongly that the imperial *bayle* did not dare insist.[15] These privileges were constantly being augmented; Conrad II, for instance, granted franchises to the people of Messina, which were confirmed by the pope in 1255. For his part, on 28 July 1245 the pope authorized merchants from Ancona to trade in Acre and the whole of the Latin kingdom "without paying any customs charges". The "lordship of the kingdom of Jerusalem" could do nothing but ratify these fresh exemptions, and even at times was forced to add to them. Thus in 1257 the barons of the kingdom granted the men of Ancona a quarter in Acre, with church, palace and inn, near the sea, in order to induce them to promise to supply fifty armed men for the defence of the kingdom.[16] With so many exemptions, the revenue from the *chaîne* decreased more and more; it was no longer the inexhaustible supply of annual payments that the kings of the previous century had had at their command. Although the income from the *fonde*, the market, remained relatively high, though even that had lessened slightly, the revenue from the customs at Tyre in 1243 was only 1,240 bezants a year. John of Brienne exempted the Syrians themselves from paying the *chaîne*.

Thus the Latin kingdom gradually lost the profits it had reaped from international trade in the twelfth century. The power to exact large payments from caravans had gone, together with the fortresses of Transjordania and the Sinai peninsula. And the merchants, Italian and others too, tended more and more to behave like masters in the Frankish colonies which their own exorbitant privileges had impoverished. The realm of the crusaders was becoming the realm of merchants.

Organization of trade; fondouks and consulates

The merchants lived a life quite apart from the other Franks. Only if the need arose did most of them ever go to the Holy Land, where a small number of their compatriots resided the whole year round. The traders and shipowners of Western ports were thus at liberty to go about their business as they wished. The contracts they made show us how their transactions worked.[17] (This is not the place to analyse the complex legal questions raised by such contracts.) The complicated charter agreements go into every detail, specify the nature of the goods embarked and contain valuable information on the equipment of the vessels. Investors did not generally charter a boat themselves, although in 1248 Guy of Tripoli, Giles Jehan and Vivaldus of Jerusalem chartered the *Sicarde-du-Saint-Esprit*, with a cargo of 450 quintals and a crew of forty; usually they took an agent into partnership and paid over to him a certain sum of money, the profits from which would then be shared between the investor and the agent. Thus in 1243 a certain merchant received 140 *livres* in *royaux coronats*, and used this to procure 400 Acre bezants and a bale of Châlons cloth, with which he embarked on the *New Paradise* to go and trade in Syria. These goods would be used overseas to obtain spices and other produce, or even money, and out of this the investor would be paid when the ship returned.[18] A whole network of money-changers and bankers lived by this trade. They sometimes received large sums in deposit, but these were more often entrusted to the Templars and the Hospitallers. Originally these orders helped crusaders to obtain cash in the East; a man would, for instance, pledge an estate in France to them, travel to Syria, and there receive the equivalent of the revenues of the estate from the order. From this kind of thing to acting as bankers for merchants was only a small step which was soon taken. The Templars revived the letter of exchange, well known to certain ancient civilizations, which spared merchants the inconvenience of carrying large sums of cash about with them. Furthermore the Temple and the Hospital had their own ships, which competed with those of the mercantile cities for the transport of traders and pilgrims.[19]

Ships from these cities did not set out singly across the Mediterranean; they travelled in convoys, 'caravans',[20] under the command of one or more 'consuls at sea' chosen from among the merchants, not from the ships' captains. The consul settled all the disputes that arose during the voyage. These voyages generally took place twice a year, the autumn voyage setting sail in the middle of August and the spring voyage soon after Easter.[21] One curious point is that, except for the Venetians, who were entitled to use Venetian measures at Tyre, the ships' tonnages were reckoned differently on the outward and the return journeys. Outward, it was "by the cantar of Genoa" or Pisa or

Marseilles; on the way back it was by the cantar of Acre or of Syria, which was between 725 and 740 *livres*, about 230 kilograms.[22]

Once in Syria, the merchants no longer came under the jurisdiction of the consul at sea but under that of the local consul of their own nation. His functions and competence are revealed in the reports sent by merchants from Genoa and Venice to their home cities and by the statutes of Marseilles of 1255. Like the consul at sea, he was appointed, at Marseilles, by the head of the commune, with the agreement of the majority of the town council, as were also his advisers. If a particular place lacked a consul, one could be elected by the men of Marseilles there, provided they numbered at least ten. The consul swore to do justice "in good faith, without deceit or fraud, without respect to hatred, love, fear, to prayer or to corruption". The consul's decisions could only be taken in session with his two advisers and his clerk, the clerk preferably a notary public from Marseilles or, if none were available, a sworn ship's scribe, and were subject to review by the home city's council. The council also punished infringements of the consular oath with a fine of twenty-five *royaux coronats*, and refusal to accept the post of consul with a fine of ten *royaux coronats*. The consul had to send to the council one half of the profits of justice, which came to a tenth of the sum in dispute, and kept the other half himself. When he returned to Marseilles he could be challenged by those he had banished or sentenced, and he had to deposit in the city archives a 'cartulary' giving an account of his administration. It is clear, then, that although the consul on taking office swore an oath to the king of Jerusalem, in fact he depended solely on the mother city. Some crimes were outside his competence, but the *bayle* of Venice bears witness that in certain cases theft and murder were tried by the consular court (Pisa, Venice and Genoa had "consuls and viscounts") sitting in the presence of the castellan and the king's viscount. This was the case at Tyre, where the jurisdiction of the Venetians extended also over the Jews and Syrians of the Venetian quarter. The *bayle* Marsilio Giorgio recorded an instance when the lord of Beirut sent a Venetian from Cyprus accused of theft for trial by the Venetian tribunal, and another when the castellan of Tyre did the same.[23]

The consul had other duties besides the exercise of civil and occasionally criminal jurisdiction over his fellow citizens. He managed the commune's property; we possess some of the administrative reports written by the Genoese consuls of Tyre and Acre.

In 1249 rents from houses, warehouses and shops belonging to the Genoese in Acre came to 1,003 bezants 18 *caroubles*, of which the consuls rendered an account. They also had certain police duties, about which we can learn from the statutes of Marseilles. They were to check prostitution in the *fondouks* of their cities, and prevent the sale of white women.[24] They supervised the work of the *fondiguiers*, to whom the town farmed the *fondouk*, and if these did not act according to the oath they had taken to the mother city, the consuls dismissed them. The *fondiguier*, none the less, was protected against any arbitrary decisions on the consul's part; the latter could not, for instance, compel him to buy wine or other goods at a higher price than was current locally. As in the mother city, there was a *banvin*, a monopoly of the sale of wine, enforced by the consul; only wines brought by the men of Marseilles could be sold in the *fondouk*; when these were finished, other wine could be sold. Lastly, no one but a Marseillais could rent a shop in the *fondouk*, except for some special cases which the consul and the *fondiguier* would decide.[25]

Thus when merchants arrived at a port, its *fondouk* did not seem unlike the market of their native city. In their nation's own quarter they found houses and warehouses to rent by the year or "by the voyage", shops where they could display their merchandise, money-changers ready to give them bezants or *dirhems* for their Western coin, taverns close to the shops in the *fondouk* in which they could sell their wine, bathing establishments and bakehouses. When the convoy arrived, houses and shops were rented to the highest bidders, and during the whole of their stay the *fondouk* of their nation hummed with an activity which ceased almost entirely once the convoy set sail again, leaving in Syria only those Pisans, Genoese, Venetians, Marseillais or others who had come to stay for a longer period.[26] Nothing gives so clear an idea of the lives led by these merchants as do some of the tales in the *Arabian nights entertainment*, which vividly evoke the similar existence of their Moslem counterparts.

The role of the Syrians

Thus the officials of the king, or of the 'lordship of Acre', had no control whatever over a whole section of the kingdom's economy, and that the most important, indeed almost the only section, since now the kingdom's territory was likely to consist of a few *casals* and the gardens around Acre and Tyre. The country's whole wealth resided in these merchants, drawn thither by so many exemptions. As well as Western merchants, many of Acre's own citizens, both Frankish and Syrian, also carried on trade. Less is known about their activities, as almost all documents about them have perished. We know, however, that Abraghinus (Ibrahim?), money-changer of Acre, received in about 1280 by order of Pope Hadrian V a sum exceeding 6,000 *livres tournois*. Jews worked as money-changers; in 1274 Agnes of Scandelion owed 2,000 bezants to a Jew called Eli. And we have some information about wealthy Syrians in the will of one Saliba, "burgess of Acre", of Syrian race (his sister was called Nayma, his brother Bedr, his nephew Sarkis), drawn up in September 1264. Saliba left the greater part of his property to the Temple, a house to the Hospital, twenty-five bezants to the fabric of Acre, five for work at the church of St Laurence, an endowment of thirty-five bezants a year for a mass in the same church, legacies to relatives and to several churches in Acre, both Latin (Dominicans, Franciscans, Carmelites, St Agnes, Holy Trinity, St Bridget, the *Repenties*, the Magdalene, the Lepers of St Lazarus, the hospitals of the Holy Spirit and of St Anthony) and Greek (the hospital of St Catherine, a dependency of Mount Sinai). This interesting document shows how close was the association between Frankish and native-born citizens, for the executors of Saliba's will were a Genoese and a Pisan. A little later Saliba appears among other Acre merchants, Armenians, and men from Damascus and Mosul, as one of the owners of goods aboard a galley captured by the Genoese privateer Lucheto Grimaldi. Although their goods were captured aboard an enemy ship, they were not confiscated, since medieval maritime law differed from that current later and expressed by the maxim that "the flag covers the goods", and in 1271 Genoa paid the merchants the value of their property: 22,797 bezants, 7 carats, a figure that indicates the wealth of these merchants of Acre. No doubt these were the 'Syrians' whom King John exempted from payment of customs at Tyre.[27]

None the less, the real holders of economic power in the kingdom of Acre were "the men of the communes", Catalans, Marseillais, Languedociens and above all Italians. Their presence had not been a danger while strong royal authority was able to enforce respect of its laws, but now that the king's authority had all but vanished the Italian colonies became true political powers. It is significant that at the time of the fall of Tyre the Venetian *bayle* Marsilio Giorgio altered the wording of the consular oath: these judges now had not only to promise to deliver justice faithfully, but also to swear fidelity and obedience to the Signoria of Venice.[28] Something similar happened in the Pisan commune in 1257; its consuls at Acre, who thought they were free to act as they judged best, were called to order by the parent city and compelled to conform to its general policy. Wealth was in the hands of the Italians, who became ever more powerful as the barons of the realm became constantly poorer, so that the Italians were able to enlist the support of the barons for their own policies. From now on one can fairly speak of the mercantile republics' protectorate over Frankish Syria.

CHAPTER 5

The all-powerful communes

Conflicts between the commercial quarters

The establishment of an Italian protectorate over the Holy Land was hastened by the quarrels between the mercantile cities, quarrels that fill the pages of histories of the late thirteenth century. It was of course these quarrels that made the protectorate so damaging; instead of being supported by the ready aid of the powerful merchant republics, Frankish Syria was torn by their rivalries and divided between their zones of influence even more grievously than it had been between Guelfs and Ghibellines.

This is not to say that the Guelf-Ghibelline contest was over by 1250. Conrad II remained king of Jerusalem until his death on 21 May 1255, and after him young Conradin was recognized by the pope as duke of Swabia and inheritor of the kingdom of Jerusalem. In 1258 he granted a charter to the Hospital using the title of king of Jerusalem. But when in 1266 the young king tried to assert Hohenstaufen claims to the kingdom of Sicily, Clement IV threatened to deprive him of his crown of Jerusalem. Conrad III persisted, and on 5 April 1268 Clement IV stripped him of the kingdom of Jerusalem and released his vassals from their oath of fealty.[1] On 23 August of the same year Conrad was captured at Tagliacozzo by Charles of Anjou, and on 31 October he was beheaded at Naples.[2] It was the end of the Hohenstaufens; the kingdom of Jerusalem was at last without a king and could hope to find a resident one. Till then matters had gone on as if the throne were vacant, but with the rights of Conrad II and III always protected. The kingdom was administered from Cyprus by the Cyprus Lusignans as "lords of the kingdom" and by a *bayle* who acted as regent in Syria in their name. These were not circumstances likely to promote royal control of the mercantile republics.

There had long been trouble between these republics, especially between Genoa and Pisa, hereditary enemies who bitterly contested the supremacy of the Tyrrhenian sea. Venice rarely intervened, except, as in 1222, when she did so as mediator. This, however, was changing, as the commercial rivalry of Venice and Genoa now moved to the battlefield, thus beginning a struggle that lasted a century. Pisa did not stay long in the ring; its faithfulness to the Ghibelline cause brought it several sentences of excommunication, one in 1268 when the Pisans were supporting Conrad III, and other kinds of punishment, such as the reduction of its metropolitan see to the status of an ordinary bishopric, deprived of its Sardinian suffragans. Eventually the treachery of Count Ugolino, later to figure in one of the most terrible passages of Dante's *Divine Comedy*, delivered Pisa to its enemies. The city recovered in due course, but was never again a principal contender in the struggle for supremacy. This war, in which the Tuscan port fought for the Ghibelline cause, had its repercussions in the Holy Land; on 10 June 1247 Innocent IV abolished the privilege granted in 1200 by Theobald, bishop of Acre, and reduced the church of St Peter of the Pisans to a chapel, withdrawing its parochial jurisdiction over the Pisans in Acre. Soon afterwards, on 25 May 1248, Pisan ships were forbidden to enter Acre under the imperial flag. Perhaps it was this that caused war to break out between the Pisans and the Genoese in the winter of 1248–1249, depriving St Louis of ships and forcing King Henry I of Cyprus to dismiss John Fanon from the post of *bayle*; he may have been too closely involved with one of the parties. Henry gave the post to John of Arsuf, who with the help of the burgesses of Acre, of the Temple and the Hospital, succeeded in restoring peace. The campaign lasted twenty-eight days, and saw in action all the siege weapons of the time, mangonels, catapults and trebuchets, the better to bring destruction to the streets of Acre.[3]

The other communes were not usually so turbulent, but none the less Marseilles and Montpellier also began a struggle in the streets of this great Syrian town which was to develop into a general war. As long as both these cities owed allegiance to the king of Aragon, their property was managed and their 'caravan' commanded by a single consul.[4] But then Aragon lost Provence, and yet Marseilles still claimed the right to control the men of Montpellier. The latter wished to recover their autonomy and establish a consulate of their own, and thus the war began. It ended in 1257.[5]

Up to this point the Holy Land had only suffered in a limited way from these conflicts. They did not spread beyond the Genoese, Pisan or Provençal quarters, and were riots rather than actual war. The affray of 1249 was more serious because it continued longer. Soon there was to be a state of constant war, with all the different forces of the Frankish state called into battle and lined up against each other, reawakening the enmities of the Guelf-Ghibelline conflict.

Genoa and Venice had begun to strive for commercial supremacy. The role played by the great Adriatic port in the dismemberment of the Byzantine Empire aroused her rival's jealousy, and although the two cities fought as allies under the papal flag against Frederick II, who had ordered a blockade of Genoa, the Venetians gave only half-hearted support to the Guelf party, so as to avoid Ghibelline reprisals, should that party be victorious. There was not the same hatred between Pisa and Venice as there was between Pisa and Genoa. But a serious danger existed in the Latin East, an endless source of friction, in the way the Italian colonies' territories were inextricably mingled with each other. In Acre, the Pisans occupied the quays nearest to St Andrew's church, in the south-west part of the town. Between their quarter and that of the Venetians, which lay to the east, beyond the inner harbour, was to be found the street of the Provençals and the church of Our Lady. The Genoese quarter lay north of the Pisans', and west of the Venetians' quarter, and its two towers defied the Pisan towers. Enmities smouldered in the narrow streets bristling with turrets and fortified houses just as they did in the cities of Italy in the fourteenth century.

The authority of the king, or of the *bayle* who represented the representative of Conrad II or Conrad III, could not penetrate into the islands formed by the communes' quarters: the street of the Pisans, of the Venetians, or of the Genoese. It was unwise for the bearers of this authority to hazard themselves in an attempt to make the men of the communes respect the king's justice, even when the offences in question were ones that the Italian republics had agreed by treaty to be punishable by the king's officials. John of Ibelin, count of Jaffa, found this out. He ordered the arrest of a "dishonest youth", a Genoese convicted of theft, and in accordance with custom had his hand cut off. He was acting as *bayle* of the kingdom and the punishment of theft was his proper task. The national feeling of the

offender's compatriots was aroused, and they waited until the count
of Jaffa ceased to hold the office of *bayle*. On the very day in 1256 that
he laid it down, he and his escort were attacked by a number of
Genoese. The count's men were scattered and he himself barely
escaped with his life. He neither forgot nor forgave this attack.

Criminals could easily find shelter in Acre. Besides the many
sympathizers to be found in this great city's very mixed population,
there were sanctuaries almost everywhere. The Templars, the Hospitallers and the Teutonic Knights all exercised the right of offering
sanctuary; Pope Gregory IX rebuked the orders for the abuse of it in
1238. But the Genoese, Pisan and Venetian quarters claimed the same
right too; after a crime as infamous as the murder of the bishop of
Famagusta in 1259 the murderer took refuge with the Pisans, and
everyone was amazed when in 1261 the then *bayle*, Geoffrey of
Sergines, had him arrested right in the very *rue des Pisans*.[6]

The war of St Sabas

Until 1256 the Venetian and Genoese quarters were separated by a
stretch of neutral ground, coveted by both republics, an enclave in the
part of the town occupied by Italian, Provençal and Catalan colonies.
It consisted of a house and its appurtenances in the *rue de la Chaîne*
and belonged to the monastery of St Sabas. It stood at the top of
Montjoie hill, near a Genoese tower also called Montjoie. By an odd
chance, both colonies simultaneously asked the pope to grant them
this monastery, and although there is no such record in the registers
of Alexander IV, it was alleged that the papal chancery granted the
required bulls both to Genoa and to Venice.[7] In 1256, therefore, the
Venetian *bayle* Marco Giustiniani went to the patriarch with letters
from the pope ordering him to put the Venetian colony in possession
of St Sabas, while at the same time the Genoese colony was presenting its papal letters to the prior of the Hospital. A serious outbreak of
violence ensued; aided, amazingly enough, by the Pisans, the Genoese invaded the Venetian quarter, reaching St Mark's and wounding
every Venetian they met. The conflict may have been sparked off by
the death of a Genoese at the hands of a Venetian, a very likely event
in the tense atmosphere then prevailing in the Italian quarter.[8]

This affray turned into a regular war; the Venetians were besieged in their quarter by the Genoese and their Pisan allies and were also under attack elsewhere from Syrian barons such as Philip of Montfort, who was at that time expelling them from their quarter in Tyre, one third of the city. But they extricated themselves from this dangerous situation, and on 18 July 1257 a treaty with Pisa ensured them Pisan support. The mother city in Tuscany was at war with Genoa over the town of Santa Gilia in Sardinia, and learning with annoyance that its nationals were assisting the enemy, Pisa sent to call them to order. The treaty settled the local disputes which had set Pisans and Venetians against each other, especially questions over the use of public weights and measures, and it announced a twenty-year alliance of offence and defence, directed specifically against Genoa, throughout the eastern Mediterranean, from Crete to Syria.[9] In response to this treaty the Genoese made an alliance with the lordship of Acre, that is to say with the *bayle*, John of Arsuf, whose cousin John of Ibelin-Jaffa was supporting the Pisans. With the *bayle*'s aid they succeeded in capturing the tower of the Pisans.[10]

That was the last of their successes. Venice sent Lorenzo Tiepolo to the East, and he broke the Genoese blockade of the port – the Genoese had captured several Venetian ships, in reprisal for the seizure of a Venetian vessel previously captured by them, and so taken control of the harbour – and burned numerous Genoese ships. He landed his troops, and they attacked and took the house of St Sabas, which the Genoese had turned into a fortress. Marco Giustiniani, the Venetian *bayle*, recaptured a street of the Venetian quarter which their enemies had occupied. Acre was in the hands of the Venetians and their Pisan allies; a Genoese fleet from Tyre was defeated outside the harbour. It was now the Genoese who were under siege in their quarter, with no respite apart from such truces as their enemies would grant them.

By the end of 1257 the whole population was involved in this Italian war. John of Arsuf no longer supported the Genoese; the Temple was on the side of the Venetians, the Hospital on that of the Genoese. But it was after an attempt at reconciliation that the conflict reached its greatest extent. On 1 February 1258 Bohemond VI, prince of Antioch, brother of Plaisance, queen of Cyprus and widow of Henry I, arrived in Acre with his sister and her little son Hughet, Hugh II, heir of the lordship of the kingdom of Jerusalem. Bohemond asked for recognition as lord of the kingdom during his nephew's minority, but this was refused by the Genoese and their allies, the

Catalans, the Hospitallers and the men of Ancona. Bohemond had in fact been sent for by the grand master of the Temple and the count of Jaffa, both Venetian sympathizers, in the hope that he might bring peace, and this was enough to throw Genoa and the Hospital into the opposite party and make them decide that they would recognize no lord but King Conrad III.

Annoyed by this opposition, Bohemond then instructed John of Arsuf, whom he had just appointed *bayle* at Acre, that "if the Hospitallers and the commune of Genoa and the Spaniards did not sue for mercy, he should do them all the harm he could, and that he should not spare the prince's money, for he would see that he had sufficient". Bohemond did not merely open his treasury for this purpose, but also provided John with a troop of 800 French mercenaries, and they too fought in this civil war.[11]

It was not only the communes who were at war. Men of Marseilles and Provençals supported the Pisans and Venetians; Catalans and men from Ancona fought for the Genoese. The fraternities of Acre, those turbulent brotherhoods, which had already played their part in the Guelf revolt, took sides in the conflict. For the fraternities were enfeoffed to the great military orders; we still possess the text of the oath of fealty sworn to the Hospital in the name of the brotherhood of St James by its priors, Matthew of Piva and Ximenez ('Exemene') of Sandave in 1254.[12] Thus the brotherhood of St James organized the Spaniards and led them to battle against "all the brotherhoods of the land" leagued against Genoa.[13] Similarly, in spite of the official ban on aid to the Genoese, they received help from indigenous Christians, both from the Maronites sent by the Genoese lord of Jebail and from the brotherhood of St George, which was also linked to the Hospital, so that the Genoese too had their Syrian infantry.[14]

To this conflict was added a struggle between the barons. The count of Jaffa supported the Venetians and Pisans, as did almost all the barons of the land, including John of Arsuf the *bayle* and Prince Bohemond, but at Tyre Philip of Montfort welcomed Genoese ships, and sent men and victuals to Acre, through the officially neutral Hospital quarter, to the *rue des Gênois*. Perhaps it was this that drew the lord of Tyre into a war with his nephew Julian of Sidon in the years 1258 to 1260. Further north the county of Tripoli responded to the call of the lord of Jebail and plunged into full scale civil war. In Acre, every tower and turret bore an engine of war, except for the houses of the military orders, although these too were exposed to bombard-

THE ALL-POWERFUL COMMUNES

ment and the grand master of the Hospital had to retire to Montmusard from his dangerously situated castle near the harbour. Huge blocks of stone shook and shattered the buildings. The greater part of the strongholds of the city were destroyed in the course of this 'war of St Sabas', in which, according to the manuscript of Rothelin, the improbable figure of almost 20,000 were killed and eighty laden ships burned in the harbour.[15]

The war at last ended with the disaster that struck the Genoese fleet of Rosso della Turca on 24 June 1259. The army of the Hospitallers and Philip of Montfort, concentrated at Vigne Neuve at the gates of Acre, was to move in once the Genoese had taken over the harbour. But the Venetians, the Pisans and the count of Jaffa managed to obtain the aid of the grand master of the Temple, who put his Templars to guard the town while the allies hastily gathered a fleet, which captured twenty-four out of thirty-nine enemy ships between Acre and Cayphas; 1,700 Genoese were killed or made prisoner. Marco Giustiniani held the Genoese in Acre quiet while Tiepolo wiped out their fleet, and the besieged could do nothing but surrender. They gave up their street and their towers and took refuge in Tyre, promising that no ship of their nation should enter Acre without dipping its flag and acknowledging that Genoa had no further jurisdiction in the town, *ni cour ni bâton,* "neither court nor staff".[16] Even so they were not allowed to leave the city, which they did through the Hospital quarter, without passing between their enemies' swords, a new kind of Caudine Forks.

The papacy intervened to put a stop to this disgraceful conflict. On 6 July 1258 Alexander IV wrote to the three communes, deploring the struggle "which, with other things, may bring the wretched kingdom of Jerusalem, afflicted and broken by so many agonies and distresses, to utter desolation". He commanded that a truce be announced at Pisa, Genoa and Venice within three days, and that the order to lay down arms should be sent to Syria by the autumn voyage, or sooner if possible. An apostolic legate was to set off urgently for Outremer (he arrived early in 1259), and meanwhile no fighting ships were to set sail for Syria.[17] But it was too late. The Genoese in their refuge at Tyre, from which their enemies had been expelled, clamoured for the return of their quarter in Acre, which the Pisans and Venetians in January 1261 refused. The legate was unable to restore peace.

Genoese Tyre against Venetian Acre

From that time on there was fighting with every voyage. In August 1259 a Genoese fleet under Benedetto Zaccaria was preparing to attack Acre when the Venetians surprised and defeated it at Tyre. However, to make sure of victory, the Pisans and Genoese obtained permission from the rulers of Acre to fortify their quarter, which they did with stone taken from the Genoese quarter. The Italians did not merely make their streets bristle with towers modelled on their communes' belfry towers, they turned them into fortified enclosures, taking in other buildings which the owners were compelled to cede to them. The church of St Demetrius was enclosed within the walls built by Venice around the square of the Genoese and the street of the Provençals, and the bishop of Acre could do nothing but yield it to the triumphant Venetians in return for an annual rent.[18]

These were necessary precautions, for the Genoese were intent on taking their revenge. When Michael Palaeologus recaptured Constantinople from its Latin emperor on 25 July 1261, Genoa saw it as a success for herself, since Venice thus lost her privileges in ancient Byzantium, and indeed Michael did shower the Genoese with all kinds of advantages.[19] In the Holy Land, Genoa was accused of also being allied with the enemies of Christendom; an Arab historian asserts that the Genoese party called in the Mamluks against Acre in 1263, but there is no evidence to confirm this. There was another expedition in the same year: Simon Grill was sailing with twenty-one galleys to Tyre when he encountered a Venetian convoy, which he captured and took back to Genoa. His change of route had an unexpected result, for the Venetians had sent a fleet twice the size of Grill's in pursuit of him. Missing him, it sailed on to Syria, where instead of defending Acre it took the offensive. On 7 September the Venetian ships arrived off Tyre at dawn and two of them, with a kind of floating tower built on them, were brought close up against the walls between the St Catherine and the Chain towers. Crossbow fire from this raised crow's-nest rendered the ramparts untenable, and the assault was about to begin when the Genoese consul Milian of Marin came up. Although he was wounded by enemy fire, he quickly had another 'cage' built, using ships' masts; it commanded that of the attackers, and so it was their turn to be under fire. Milian thus gave Philip of Montfort time to arm "the villeins from his lands" and to summon his supporters from Acre. 2,000 men came from Acre, and the sixty-two Venetian vessels had to retreat. They remained another fortnight at Acre, still without sighting Grill's fleet.[20]

The only result of this sudden attack was the strengthening of the ties between Philip of Montfort and the Genoese. The treaty agreed between them in 1264[21] gave Genoa the right to trade freely in Tyre, one third of the revenue from harbour dues and the right to use the water brought by aqueduct to drive their sugar-cane mills. Genoa undertook to use the lord of Tyre's measures in the *rue des Gênois*, the cantar and quintal, the *buze* for wine and the *muid* for corn, and to defend the lord and his town against all comers. Various exemptions completed the treaty.

On 16 August 1267 Lucheto Grimaldi's twenty-five Genoese galleys attacked Acre, took the tower of the Flies which commanded the harbour, burned two Pisan ships and blockaded the roadstead. On 28 August a fleet of twenty-eight Venetian ships raised the blockade and forced Lucheto Grimaldi to take flight to Tyre, capturing five of his galleys. Next day the victorious fleet made a demonstration off Tyre, but did not draw Grimaldi into an unequal fight.

After more than ten years of conflict, a conflict enormously damaging to the Holy Land which was then engaged in a desperate war against the Moslems, Charles of Anjou suggested that a treaty might be made between Genoa and Venice, but his attempt at reconciliation was in vain. Not until three years later, 1270, did the two towns consent to make peace at the instigation of St Louis. But although the Genoese returned at last to the ruins of their street in Acre, they were only able to reoccupy part of their quarter. Pisa did not lay down her arms, in spite of the troubles she was then experiencing from the renewal of the Ghibelline war in Italy; nothing but the destruction of the Pisan fleet at Meloria in 1284 at last compelled the proud Tuscan city to submit. The Genoese of Acre then took their revenge for the humiliation they had endured in 1282 when, in spite of the Genoese distress, the Pisans celebrated in their own quarter the defeat of the lord of Jebail, traditional ally of the Genoese. The Pisans were at that time supporting Bohemond VII, prince of Antioch, against his vassal in revolt. In 1282 Thomas Spinola swore that he would revenge this cruel mockery, and now on 24 May 1287 he attacked the Pisan ships in Acre harbour. The Venetians then took up arms again to defend their Pisan allies, but were defeated. The Genoese were even on the point of landing in force, risking the reopening of the St Sabas war, and this only four years before the fall of Acre. At last the treaty which Pisa had to agree to sign in 1288 put an end to these dissensions; the Pisans eventually restored to Genoa that part of the former Genoese quarter that they conquered in 1258, and it was now their turn to raze the tower of the Pisans, as their opponents had had to do thirty years before.[22]

The tedious narrative of these dissensions shows how powerless was the holder of the lordship of Acre, and even the king, when the throne of Jerusalem ceased to be vacant, to make the Italian republics respect his authority. Not only were the Pisan, Genoese and Venetian residents able to devote themselves wholeheartedly to their private wars, but they dragged the entire kingdom of Acre into a civil war, with far-reaching consequences. The fraternities fought among themselves, the Temple and the Hospital took up old quarrels, the Genoese party raised the Ghibelline flag so as to avoid acknowledging a sovereign they thought inclined to favour their opponents. More serious still was the division of the Holy Land. Philip of Montfort and his son and heir John, who became lord of Tyre in 1269, protectors of the Genoese, adopted a pro-Genoese policy that brought them close to the lords of Jebail and opposed them to the princes of Antioch-Tripoli, determinedly hostile as these were to the great Ligurian port.[23] Acre in consequence became a Venetian protectorate, as we can see from events in 1273 when John of Montfort wanted to go through Acre on his way back to Tyre. Pietro Zeno, the Venetian *bayle*, refused to allow him into the town, and in order to preserve the decencies, for the unity of the Frankish kingdom still existed in theory, the barons of Acre persuaded John to make a pilgrimage to Nazareth, from which he returned to Tyre without going through Acre. Even after John of Montfort decided to restore to the Venetians the privileges his father had taken from them,[24] Tyre remained the Genoese base, where, for example, Spinola's fleet was stationed in 1287.

A further consequence of the Italians' capture of Frankish Syrian trade were the frequent appeals to the Moslems made by the citizens of one commune against the protectorate of another. In 1263 Genoa is thought to have called in the sultan Baibars against Acre; in 1288, just as Tripoli had given its adherence to Genoa, two merchants based in Alexandria, Pisans or Venetians, are said to have asked the sultan Qalawun to destroy this Genoese base, from which ships could easily be sent to interrupt Egyptian trade.[25] The problem in future was no longer one of defending Frankish Syria against Islam, but of preventing a rival, based securely on her business houses, which had by now become a true colony, from establishing her supremacy throughout the eastern Mediterranean. Venice tried to oust Genoa from Syrian ports, and Genoa did the same for Venice, with the result that thirty years after the war of St Sabas, the whole Syrian coast was occupied by the Mamluks. As for the Franks, who killed each other in order to win victory for whichever mercantile republic supported their fraternity or their party, nothing was to remain of them on the coasts of Syria where they had hung on so tenaciously since 1099.

CHAPTER 6

The kingdom in tutelage

Insecurity and poverty

The Italian republics' protectorate over the Holy Land, the subjection of Syria's trading cities to the mercantile powers of the
West, and that of the Frankish barons to the Italian communes, are
but one aspect of the decay suffered in the second half of the
thirteenth century by the very idea of a state of Jerusalem. To
Western eyes it seemed as if the former kingdom of Jerusalem,
precariously situated, shattered by one disaster after another, must
inevitably fall to the Moslems' attacks. The lack of a resident monarchy, of even a generally accepted representative of that monarchy
apart from the *bayles*, the increasingly less respected leaders of
feudal anarchy, meant that the Syrian Franks had no means of
pursuing a policy of their own. Nor was it possible since the disasters
of 1244 to 1248, lacking any territorial base, to adopt any policy other
than one of avoiding all friction with the Moslems, whose power was
so much greater than that of the Franks that any Mamluk or Ayubid
sultan must have felt he could throw them into the sea whenever he
pleased.

Everyone in the kingdom of Acre was aware of their danger. It is
not by chance that the deeds of this period commonly take a future
Moslem reconquest into account. Whereas in 1163 those who took a
twenty-five year lease of a *casal* in Galilee from its monastic pro-
prietors undertook to pay a rent of 100 bezants a year but reserved
the right not to pay this if the houses, vines or olives were damaged
by an enemy raid, from now on it was necessary to envisage more
permanent trouble.[1] When the bishop of Acre ceded the church of St

374 THE KINGDOM OF ACRE

Demetrius to the Venetians in 1260, he laid it down that the rent due to him need not be paid if Acre was lost.[2] John of Ibelin-Beirut, too, transferring Casal Humbert, his father Balian's fief, to the Teutonic Knights in 1261, stated that in the event of the capture of Acre by the infidels, the annual rent of 13,000 bezants should not be paid. He went a step further, however, requiring an acknowledgement of his right to receive this rent again if the town should be recaptured.[3]

These transactions also demonstrate the kingdom's poverty, the financial ruin now pressing on the proud Frankish barons. Agnes of Scandelion, inheritor of that lordship and wife of William of La Mandelée, owed 17,000 bezants in 1280 to Jewish and Sienese bankers.[4] John of Ibelin, count of Jaffa, could not afford to fortify his castle of Jaffa at his sole expense. Julian of Sidon, although enriched by his marriage in 1252 to the king of Armenia's daughter, was so heavily in debt, much of it his own gambling debts, that he had to sell his entire domain piecemeal: Casal Robert to the Hospital in 1254, the Schouf and the Gezin with the Cave of Tyron for 23,500 bezants to the Teutonic Knights in 1256–1257, and then three more *casals* near Sidon for 5,000 bezants. The destruction of Sidon by the Mongols completed his ruin. In 1260 he sold the whole of his fief of Sidon and Beaufort to his principal creditor, the Temple, and did it so pre-cipitately that he omitted either to consult his father-in-law the king of Armenia or to obtain permission from the king to make the sale. This constituted treason, but Julian's financial distress was such that the king forgave him, only insisting that he undertake to furnish him with the service of several knights.[5] Balian of Ibelin-Arsuf, son of the *bayle* John of Arsuf, could not provide for the defence of his domains, and in 1261 he gradually pledged larger and larger sections of his lordship to the Hospitallers.[6]

As well as this shortage of money, there was a severe shortage of men. Never had there been so few knights settled in the Holy Land. And even if the men had been available, what lands could have been given them in fief? Land was in shorter and shorter supply, and many fiefs were no more than a memory. Galilee was lost, but John of Fleury still called himself marshal of Tiberias.[7] In the fourteenth century there would be princes of Antioch and counts of Tripoli and Edessa in the kingdom of Cyprus; as well as prelates *in partibus* there were now lords *in partibus* too. This state of affairs was not likely to attract new immigrants, and those who now came to the Holy Land were seen not as men seeking their fortunes but as crusading heroes worthy of all praise.[8]

Thus the numbers of the defenders of Frankish Syria constantly shrank. The *devises* of olden days, long lists of knights owing military service to the king, were a thing of the past. The registers of the papal chancery provide a telling indication in the high number of marriage dispensations granted to members of the Frankish nobility. The preambles to these dispensations point out how difficult it was for Syrian nobles to marry within their own rank because there were so few families, and those were already linked by ties of kinship. Marriages therefore took place between spouses related in the third or fourth canonical degree, and there were very few marriages, especially among the upper nobility, which did not need a dispensation from Rome. We may wonder whether this inbreeding did not make for the weakening of the Frankish race and cause the heirs of the conquerors of the Holy Land to degenerate from their forbears' vigour.

Lacking men and money, more and more lacking local supplies, for famine had reappeared and in 1269 a *muid* of wheat cost eight bezants,[9] Syria relied increasingly on what could be sent from the West, both for men, money and food. The government in Acre did not have the money in its treasury with which to pay, and therefore depended on the charity of the Western powers. Like all medieval states, the kingdom had never been rich, but in spite of its financial difficulties the first kingdom of Jerusalem had been able to provide for its own defence. It sent appeals often enough to the princes of Christendom, but on the whole, and not counting unduly expensive campaigns, it paid its own way from day to day. But from this time onwards the lordship of Acre was seriously impoverished. Moslem conquests were about to strip it of its agricultural resources, and the revenues from taxes on industry and commerce were greatly reduced by the exemptions granted to Italians, Syrians and the churches. Furthermore, there was now no *parlement* able to impose a general levy. This had been tried in 1243[10] at the pope's suggestion, but it only aroused opposition from the Templars and the Hospitallers, jealous of their privileges and not inclined to give away their wealth, and from the Italians, who were not subject to the kingdom's jurisdiction.

Help from Europe

Appeals, therefore, to the generosity of the West followed one upon another. Sometimes, rare windfall, a monarch bequeathed a substantial sum to the Holy Land, as did Henry II of England, Philip Augustus and Frederick II, but smaller legacies were just as keenly sought.[11] The defence of Jerusalem was a work of piety, and the faithful felt it a duty to contribute to it. A regular tax for the benefit of Frankish Syria was instituted by the papacy in 1187, and this tended to become annual. It was the tithe, the "tenth of ecclesiastical revenues for the succour of the Holy Land". This tax was originally imposed to finance crusading expeditions, but eventually came to be raised for the general help of Syria, not for particular campaigns. It was levied on the revenues of ecclesiastical benefices, of which it took sometimes a tenth, sometimes a twentieth or a hundredth or even at times a fifth (the "double tithe"). Together with gifts, legacies, the redemption of their vows by crusaders who had sworn to cross the sea but changed their minds and had to pay a kind of fine, the tithe supplied the papacy with money for the upkeep of the Holy Land. Once collected, the tithe was sent to Syria, or else part of it would be paid out to barons preparing to set out for the East.[12] This tax was the first ever imposed by the papacy and was the origin of its famous fiscal system.

The kingdom of Acre shared in the levying of these tithes. Its bishops and archbishops went to Europe to set the collection of the tax on foot and to establish a centre for its receipt. One such collector was Walter, bishop of Beirut, who levied this tax in England in 1245. In 1265 a layman and a churchman, John of Valenciennes, lord of Cayphas, and the archbishop of Tyre were the collectors of the tithe in the West, *executores negotii crucis*.[13]

The Templars, international bankers, played an important part in the transfer of these sums of money. In 1249 we find them borrowing 10,000 bezants from the Genoese, and repaying them 3,750 *livres tournois*. In 1256 the pope wrote instructing the Temple at Acre to pay 1,000 marks of silver to the patriarch, and in 1257 another 100 marks to the same patriarch, on the 16,000 bezants deposited in their house by the previous patriarch, and 1,000 marks to the count of Jaffa. The treasurer of the Templars in Paris received letters of exchange, and tithe receipts were kept in the famous Temple tower (1267 and 1291).[14] Merchants of Genoa, Siena and Piacenza also took part in these operations; they made loans to the authorities in Acre, and indeed to the Temple and the Hospital as well, and were reimbursed by the commanderies in the West.[15]

The papacy played the principal part in this dispatch of funds. Hadrian V sent 12,000 *livres tournois* in 1276, the only notable deed of his short pontificate, and one which astonished the chroniclers of the Holy Land. In 1290 Nicholas IV sent 2,000 florins to the patriarch, Nicholas of Hanapes.[16] Others also contributed to the defence of the Frankish colonies in the Levant; in 1255 Alexander IV suggested to King Alfonso of Castile that he should consider the poverty of the Holy Land and show his generosity in supporting the fighting men. More than any others, the kings of France allocated considerable sums from their budget for use in the East. St Louis in 1265 promised to honour all letters of exchange presented to him in the name of the patriarch, the grand masters and his representatives, up to a total of 4,000 *livres tournois.* The merchants of Piacenza who lent the money lost the letters relating to a debt of 1,000 *livres* in a shipwreck and had to get new ones drawn up.[17]

More was needed than money. The holy king of France, struck by the Eastern kingdom's lack of men, and resolved to use every possible means of remedying it, resorted to a practice of which James of Vitry had long since noted the abuse, and which was also used by Frederick II in spite of the objections of the popes who deplored the transformation of the Promised Land into a convict settlement. St Louis gave condemned criminals a choice between receiving the punishment imposed on them or going to the Holy Land. He even extended the length of sentences of banishment to Syria passed on delinquents so as to provide recruits for the Frankish kingdom's forces.[18]

But the king of France provided other help, of higher moral value, for the Holy Land. When he took ship for the West in 1254 he left behind him a small troop of Frenchmen under the orders of the seneschal of the kingdom. In command of these 100 knights and 100 sergeants was a knight from Champagne, Geoffrey of Sergines. He had travelled to Syria before the crusade of 1248 and was with the king during his stay there. He was the principal "captain of the king of France's men", *capitaneus super gentem regis Francorum*, and for ten years he shone in French public opinion as the *chevalier sans peur et sans reproche*, the incarnation of all knightly virtues. The poet Rutebeuf said:

Ainz que j'eusse racontei	Before I could finish telling
sa grant valeur ne sa bontei,	of his great valour and worth,
sa cortoisie ne son sens,	his good breeding and good sense,
torneroit à anui, je pens.	it would become wearisome, I think.
Son seigneur lige tint tant chier	He held his liege lord so dear
qu'il ala avec lui vengier	that he went with him to avenge
la honte Dieu, outre !a meir ...	God's shame, beyond the sea ...
De ligier devra Dieu paier,	Easily will he pay what he owes God,
car il le paie chacun jour.	for he is paying Him now every day.
A Jasphes, où il fait séjour	At Jaffa, where he stays
(s'il at séjour de guerroier),	(if there is any stay in his warfare),
la vuet-il son tens emploier;	there he wishes to use his time;
félon voizin et envieuz	an ill neighbour and a terrible
et crueil et contralieuz	and cruel and pitiless
le truevent la gent sarrazine,	the Saracens find him,
car de guerroier ne les fine.	for he never ceases to make war on
	them.[19]

This is from the *Complainte de monseigneur Geoffroi de Sergines*, and other poems of Rutebeuf show us this courageous warrior making the presence of France felt on the Saracen borders in the face of the Mamluk threat, and remaining uncompromised in the civil wars. Geoffrey had great difficulty paying his small troop of men; a letter of 1267 from the patriarch of Jerusalem tells us that he had to pawn his personal property and borrow 3,000 *livres tournois* in order to raise the 10,000 *livres* needed for a year's pay.[20]

France was represented in the Holy Land by a small group of knights, Geoffrey of Sergines, Oliver of Termes, who died in Syria on 12 August 1275, and Erard of Valéry.[21] Geoffrey never returned to France. When he died, on 11 April 1269, Oliver of Termes took over command of the French contingent. Thus in 1273 Oliver took to Syria twenty-five knights and 100 crossbowmen in the pay of King Philip III; in October 1275 his successor William of Roussillon led another contingent to Syria, where he too died, in 1277. The French garrison, then under Miles of Cayphas, received a new commander in the person of Odo Poilechien in 1286; he was followed in 1287 by John of Grailly, ancestor of Du Guesclin's famous opponent, the Captal de Buch. John of Grailly was also seneschal of the kingdom from 1272 to 1278, and was present at the siege of Tripoli in 1289 and of Acre in 1291, during which he was wounded. The French contingent varied in strength, but was one of the most highly esteemed in the army of Acre.

The French king was not the only person to be concerned about the defence of Acre; England, especially under Edward I, did not neglect it, and a detachment under Otto of Grandson was financed by the London treasury. The papacy, too, maintained mercenaries in the Holy Land; in 1267 its representative, the patriarch of Jerusalem, was busy hiring fifty knights who had arrived with Odo of Burgundy, count of Nevers, and Erard of Valéry, for the defence of Acre, no doubt for a six month period, for they were to be paid sixty *livres* each, and a knight's annual pay according to the same text was over 120 *livres*. He also hired forty-eight other knights for five months, and crossbowmen. In 1272 the patriarch brought fifty men-at-arms paid by the church across the sea, and in the following year Giles of Santy and Peter of Amiens arrived with 700 crossbowmen paid jointly by the pope and the king of France. Assistance of this kind was supplied liberally by Nicholas IV just as Acre was about to fall.[22]

The aid sent by the West, then, was considerable. It was also supplemented by minor crusades such as those of the count of Nevers, Edward of England and King James I of Aragon, even though there was no general crusade such as was almost launched in 1270 and after the council of 1274. Without this aid from the West the *poulains* would never have been able to hold out against the Mamluk attacks. Opinion in the West sometimes found it burdensome, as is shown in Rutebeuf's *Dit du Croisé et du Décroisé*. He and other poets, however, were active in producing propaganda for the Holy Land. Rutebeuf, for instance, wrote the *Complainte d'Outre-mer*, in which he laments, "Messire Geoffrey of Sergines, over here I can see no sign that anyone will help you now".[23] Several others wrote *Chansons de Croisade*, rekindling the zeal of Western knights, who were deeply discouraged by the failure of the crusade of 1248. St Louis led fewer men to Tunis than had gone with him to Egypt.

Government from the West

But this invaluable assistance carried with it certain drawbacks. There was no king of Jerusalem to send it to, and the high court was split into parties, so that whereas at Tripoli Prince Bohemond VII used the contingent sent him by St Louis as he thought fit, in the kingdom of Acre forces had to be placed under the command of the seneschal, as the French troops were, or of the patriarch. Naturally therefore the seneschal chosen tended to be a representative of the king of France; thus Geoffrey of Sergines (1254–1267?), John of Grailly (1272–1277) and Odo Poilechien (1277–1286) succeeded each other in this post.[24] One of the great offices of the crown ceased to depend upon the king and went instead to knights from across the sea, who represented other monarchs, as it were residents-general in the Frankish colony of the Levant. As for the role of the patriarch, it was he who was ordered in 1290 by Nicholas IV to appoint commanders to the army and the Christian fleet, in consultation with the bishop of Tripoli, the lord of Tyre, at that time *bayle* of Acre, the Pisan and Venetian consuls, the grand masters of the orders, Otto of Grandson and John of Grailly.[25] Royal authority had at last totally disappeared. At the moment of the kingdom's final collapse it was the patriarch, not the crowned and consecrated king, who assumed the burden of government, assisted by a council of war in which the *bayle* of the kingdom, the officially appointed viceroy, was merely one in a group of men who were not even subordinate to him.

Money and troops were not all that the West sent to Syria. The Templars, the Hospitallers and the Teutonic Knights, from now on completely independent of the king, can also be counted as help from the West, though they were permanently installed in the East. As well as assistance, the West sent commands. At Acre the *bayle*, or the king, was nothing more than "the lieutenant of the kings beyond the sea" as Conrad of Montferrat had once put it. The very crown depended on Western rulers, and above all on the pope. Despite the protests of King Hugh III of Cyprus and of the lieges of the kingdom, the dispute between Hugh and his cousin Mary of Antioch over their claims to the throne was tried in a Roman court. The Holy See took up the affair in 1269, and it was the help of a part of the curia that enabled Charles of Anjou to obtain possession of the throne in 1277. As for the rights of the high court, Charles of Anjou never dreamed of respecting them. Once the papacy had dethroned Conradin (Conrad III) the kingdom of Jerusalem was obviously vacant, a piece of property ready to be taken by anyone that could get it. The decision was no longer made in the kingdom, but in the curia at Rome and in the courts of the West.

Syria's close dependence on the West was now a fact, and one that the Mongols were well aware of. They did not send their ambassadors to Acre or Nicosia; they knew that no decisions would be taken in Syria or Cyprus, and they went straight to the council of Lyons, to

Rome, Paris, Naples, Barcelona, London, and even, if the French or English monarchs were away from their capitals, to Tunis, as in 1270, or to Gascony.[26] The Latin kingdom was too weak to settle a question of peace or war on its own; this was decided for it in England, in Sicily, Aragon or the curia. The narrative of the journey of the Nestorian bishop Barsauma, who was sent to the Western courts by the khan Arghun, is very informative: the Mongol prelate, lamenting the lack of response his mission had met with in Paris and London, said, "Those whose hearts are harder than rock seek to capture Jerusalem, and those to whom she belongs take no interest in the matter".[27] The subjection of the Holy Land to the courts of Europe was beyond dispute.

This subjection was evident in matters of the smallest detail. Ever since they captured Tyre, Acre and Tripoli from the Fatimids, the men of the kingdom of Jerusalem continued to mint dinars (bezants) and *dirhems* in these cities without any alteration, endlessly reproducing the coinage of the eleventh- and twelfth-century caliphates. Eastern commerce knew no other money and did not use the *deniers* and other silver and copper pieces struck in the royal mints.[28]

Belatedly the papacy took note of the shocking fact that coins issued in the cities of the Holy Land bore invocations to Allah and were dated from the Hegira. In this most Christian of all lands, the currency recalled Mohammed's foundation of the Moslem faith. Innocent IV therefore ordered on 8 February 1253 that these issues should cease and that future coins should bear a Christian legend instead of an Islamic one. Acre made the change before Tripoli, and from then on the bezant always bore an invocation to the Holy Trinity in Arabic script, followed by a date according to the Christian era.[29]

Thus the care of the princes of the West for their colony of the Holy Land extended even to details of the currency. The former kingdom of Jerusalem was now the dependency of a mother country. Once an independent state, deferential, perhaps, to the papacy and, as Amalric's letters to Louis VII show, to the king of France, but none the less independent, it was now a colony. At the head of the barons of Jerusalem, beside their natural leader, were the representatives of the Western powers. As soon as important decisions were to be made, the latter had their say. Delays were long, though, between the Holy Land and the Italian coast; it was noted as remarkable when a

messenger from Acre reached London in one month.[30] At least twenty
days were needed for the journey to Rome. When siege was laid to
Acre in 1291 news of this had only just reached the West when the
town fell. No help could arrive in time. Furthermore, help was not
utilized as it might have been had royal authority existed in the Holy
Land; in a letter of 1273 Gregory X noted with sorrow that 60,000
livres tournois sent by St Louis had been wasted.[31]

The role of the patriarch

The papacy's care did not make up for the lack of a strong and
respected government. It was not enough to negotiate endlessly with
the princes of the West in order to obtain their help, to reconcile them
with each other, to prepare expeditions;[32] it was also necessary that
all this effort should not be wasted at the other end through apathy,
carelessness or stupidity. The theory maintained long ago by Daim-
bert of Pisa triumphed in this century of theocracy in the papacy's
domination of the kingdom of Acre. Jerusalem became another
patrimony of St Peter in which the patriarch, vicar of the pope, quite
overshadowed the king of Cyprus and Jerusalem. He, as once
formerly, was now no more than the Advocate of the Holy Sepulchre,
or rather of the church of the Holy Cross at Acre. But no patriarch,
not even the excellent Thomas Agni of Lentino, at first bishop of
Bethlehem and then raised to the see of Jerusalem, could be a war
leader. All the thirteenth-century patriarchs were good and holy men,
but this did not make them competent in military matters. In 1273
Gregory X had to acknowledge that the choice of Thomas of Lentino
to conduct mercenaries to Syria had been an unfortunate one; the
men he recruited were poor soldiers, and after that the pope entrusted
this task to Oliver of Termes, an experienced captain.[33] The patriarch
was, in the words of John of Ibelin, the spiritual lord of the kingdom.
Now, through force of circumstance and for lack of a king, he took
upon himself the functions of a temporal lord as well.
    Frankish Syria's situation was one of paradox: the existence of this
colony, now a heavy burden upon the West (except for the Italian
cities which drew huge profits from their business houses), could not
be justified by the need to protect the pilgrimage to the Holy Sepulchre, for Jerusalem was in the hands of the Moslems and there was

certainly no hope of recovering it. Yet no sacrifice was too great that might prolong the life of the remnant of the Latin kingdom until some unforeseeable change should occur. As it was, for over thirty-five years, from 1254 to 1291, Europe's strength stood firm against the waves of Mamluk attack.

The normal working of Frankish institutions was paralysed by Syria's situation. The conflict between Christendom and Islam was too great for its theatre of war, the kingdom of Acre, and the kingdom was too severely shaken by the civil wars that followed one upon another from 1231 onwards and by the disasters of 1244 and 1249 to be able to recover. A vigorous king, Hugh of Lusignan, was to try to revive it, but the close grip of the West's control, the price paid for its assistance, compelled him to relinquish his attempt. In conflict with the greed of a Charles of Anjou, king of Sicily, uncle of the king of France, master more or less of the papacy, and able to block the supplies of men and foodstuffs so essential to the Holy Land,[34] Hugh could only yield. The West had reduced its annexe in Syria to the status of a colony, in the modern sense of the word, and there was no question of the kingdom of Acre's having a policy of its own. The kingdom had ceased to be a nation, the Holy Land would henceforth depend closely on events in Europe, and the inexorable result of the Sicilian Vespers and their sequel was the fall of Acre.[35]

CHAPTER 7

Between the Mongols and the Mamluks

The Mongol danger

The increased interest in Frankish Syria shown by the Western powers after St Louis' crusade came at a good time, for in the twenty years subsequent to that crusade the Latin colonies of the East had to contend with a very great danger. An event affecting the whole known world took place, and its aftermath all but overwhelmed the kingdom of Acre. The expansion of the Mongols begun by Genghis Khan, who died in 1227, ceased for a while and then recommenced under his son Ogodai; Iran was conquered, Georgia subjugated, Seljuq Turkey crushed in 1243, Russia and the Ukraine occupied and Hungary and Poland devastated in 1241. Then the Tartar conquest paused again during the troubles over the succession with which the regent Turakina struggled and during the brief reign of the Great Khan Guyuk. Attempts were made to reach an understanding between Franks and Mongols at the time of St Louis' crusade, but they came to nothing, and the Mongol Empire was not then ready for war. After Guyuk's death the Gengiskhanid armies were poised to break out once more, this time under the Great Khan Mongka, conqueror of China. Hulagu, Mongka's brother, was appointed to govern Iran, and the Moslem East trembled with fear, for the Mongol conquest was clearly about to receive a fresh impetus. And indeed Baghdad was taken and sacked on 10 February 1258, and Hulagu immediately launched his attack upon Syria.[1]

The Franks of Syria have been blamed for failing to see the necessity of making an alliance with the Mongols, an alliance found acceptable only by Bohemond VI, prince of Antioch-Tripoli. But we should remember that for the Christians 'Mongol' had for two decades been a name of hatred and terror. Poland, Bohemia, Hungary and Croatia had seen these horsemen from the steppes sweep through their countries, burning their towns and slaughtering their peoples with terrifying method and calm. A general crusade was preached against them in 1241, and the liveliest dread in the minds of the popes in the thick of their war against Frederick II was that he, the "enemy of Christendom", might call in the Tartars against his fellow Christians. Danger from the Kipchak Mongols continued to threaten Europe's eastern frontiers; the missions of John of Pian del Carpine and of Ascelin between 1245 and 1248 were intended to reduce this threat by converting the Mongols to Christianity. Both embassies failed; Guyuk gave Pian del Carpine a letter addressed to the pope in which he expressed amazement at the pope's suggestion and commanded the pope and the Christian kings to submit to the Mongol Empire, if they did not wish to bring upon themselves a terrible war (11 November 1246).[2] In 1251 Andrew of Longjumeau, St Louis' envoy, brought the king of France an order to pay tribute, and the same order was given to William of Rubruck in 1253. Westerners had to resign themselves to seeing in the descendants of the fabled Prester John only enemies poised to attack them. And so in 1253 Innocent IV had a crusade preached against the Mongols in Bohemia, Moravia, Serbia and Pomerania. In the following year the Tartars' designs upon Livonia, Esthonia and Prussia were realized, and a crusade in these lands was preached. In 1259 fear of the Mongols was such that the abbots of Poland, Hungary and Livonia did not attend the general chapter at Cîteaux, and Alexander IV preached resistance against the invaders. His successor Urban IV on 9 June 1262 begged the king of Norway to help in this struggle, and Clement IV on 25 June 1265 preached a crusade against the Mongols in Hungary, Bohemia, Poland, Styria, Austria, Carinthia and the marquisate of Brandenburg.[3] Exceptional political insight would have been needed to see the Tartars, foes of Christendom on the Hungarian and Polish frontiers, as God-given allies in the East. Hethoum, king of Armenia, well informed by Eastern Christians, did realize how vital was the alliance with the Tartars, and in 1246, to the bewilderment of the West, he went and made submission to Guyuk. He also persuaded his son-in-law Bohemond VI of the wisdom of this attitude. Public opinion was horrified to see Bohemond among the Mongols; the bishop of Bethlehem excommunicated him, disgusted at his shameful submission, and all the more so since it had been necessary at the Khan's orders to enthrone a Greek patriarch at Antioch. But Bohemond appealed against the sentence, and on 26 May 1263 the pope suspended it; people were better informed in 1263 than they had been three years before.[4]

All this explains the panic caused in the Holy Land by the arrival of Hulagu to take up his governorship of Iran. Since 1255 men had been hoping that the situation in the Promised Land might improve, while they gave their attention to such matters as the endless lawsuit between the Hospital, which was demanding repayment for the cost of the defence of Ascalon in 1243–1247, and the titular count of that town, John of Ibelin-Jaffa. (In the end the count agreed in 1256 to give the Hospitallers fourteen *casals*, or 650 carucates, of his domain of Ascalon once the town was retaken.) But now they were sharply aware of the Mongol danger. There was no pause in work on the fortification of Jaffa for which in 1256 and 1257 the pope sent large sums of money to Count John,[5] but the patriarch left on 12 February 1257 to inform the pope of the urgency of the situation. Alexander IV at once took steps to have the walls of all the towns in Syria repaired, and had the necessary funds paid over to the patriarch.[6] He followed events in the East anxiously (while Acre was torn by the St Sabas war), and henceforth named the Holy Land alongside Hungary and Livonia in his letters concerning the Tartars (17 November 1260, 9 June 1262, etc).

The 1260 invasion and the Egyptian alliance

Meanwhile the Mongol invasion was launched. In 1256 it caused a sudden rapprochement between the Mamluks and the Ayubid princes of Syria, but no degree of co-operation between the Moslem rulers could enable them to make a united stand against these terrible horsemen. In February 1258 Baghdad was captured and the caliph slaughtered. The Seljuk Turks had been a second time defeated and forced to submit in 1256. Mosul yielded without resistance. Hulagu then sent a Mongol and Georgian force to besiege the Mesopotamian town of Maiyafariqin, called Montferanquin by the Franks. Hulagu himself moved against Aleppo, where the Ayubid al-Nasir Yusuf (who had annexed Damascus in 1250) had made an alliance with the

Mamluks. But Yusuf had taken care not to allow himself to be shut into Aleppo, and was still in southern Syria. The Mongol troops, reinforced by the king of Armenia and the prince of Antioch who joined them near Edessa, laid siege to the town on 18 January 1260; it fell to them at the end of February. Franks and Armenians entered the town with their allies, but the Mongol soldiers devastated Antiochene villages as well as Moslem ones. These ravages, and the enthronement of a Greek patriarch in Antioch, were a further reason for the Franks in Acre to fear the advent of the Mongols. Yet Hulagu, now recalled to Caucasia, left a Nestorian Christian general, Kitbuqa, as his representative in Syria. Such a choice might have induced the barons of Acre to assist the Mongols.

Before leaving, Hulagu had time to take Damascus, between 21 March and 6 April 1260, still with the help of the prince of Antioch. Bohemond VI had mass according to the Latin rite celebrated in a large mosque in Damascus, a former church, while his men desecrated some other mosques of the city. The Mongols had also given Bohemond all the former possessions of the principality of Antioch in Moslem occupation, and a text which is admittedly later, the *Flor des Estoires d'Orient* written about 1307 by the Armenian Hayton, tells us that Hulagu intended similarly to restore all the territories of the former kingdom of Jerusalem to the Franks.[7] This cannot be called a crusade, for the Mongols remained strictly neutral in matters of religion, but Hulagu and his Nestorian lieutenant Kitbuqa behaved as allies of the Latins against their common enemies the Moslems.

As Damascus was falling, the barons of Acre met to discuss the situation. They may already have sent an ambassador to Hulagu;[8] in any case they could not fail to see that they must either submit to the Mongol Empire or suffer at the hands of Kitbuqa's troops. Submission to the Mongols was far from attractive. Subjugated peoples, even those who yielded without resistance, were forced to pay heavy tribute in kind and in money as well as in slaves. As Urban IV put it:

This cruel race of Tartars, doomed to damnation, oppress the land they have enslaved with intolerable exactions; they torture and afflict the inhabitants so inhumanly that those who dwell under such tyranny prefer to die rather than endure such torments.[9]

The Mongols had certainly laid waste a number of Frankish villages during their conquest of Syria, and the arrival in Christian territory of Moslem refugees who preferred slavery among the Latins to certain death at the hands of invaders "whose cruel fury spares neither age nor sex" naturally increased the Franks' apprehension. It would probably have been wiser to take account of the newcomers' readiness to negotiate without paying too much attention to the atrocities which accompanied their advance and to make terms with them, as the prince of Antioch had done. But there was no leader in the Holy Land capable of conducting such negotiations or of understanding their importance; there was no king, and no regent, for despite the advent of Bohemond VI in 1258, he was not accepted by all. Geoffrey of Sergines, *bayle* of Acre, was a good knight but not a statesman. The patriarch James Pantaléon of Courpalais, the future Urban IV, had left for Rome upon the arrival of the legate Thomas of Lentino at the end of 1258.[10] Thomas was a newcomer, not conversant with Eastern politics. And as for the barons of Syria, all they could see was that their familiar world, the world in which they knew how to negotiate, was crumbling about them. The kingdom of Aleppo, the kingdom of Damascus, the small Ayubid principalities, all had gone. The letter the barons wrote to Charles of Anjou on 22 April 1260 gives voice to their stupefaction and alarm; they even went so far as to regret the collapse of their age-old enemies, the Moslem principalities. The waves of savage 'Tartar' tribesmen were now breaking against their own frontiers, and the prince of Antioch's alliance with these terrible Mongols seemed to them to be sheer treachery. Bishop Thomas instantly excommunicated him.[11]

The choice they made in these circumstances was not unheroic, with a heroism of despair. The manuscript of Rothelin, written under the influence of these events, for its narrative ceases at about this date, shows that only a small group of Christians remained to oppose the Tartars: "These few Christians took counsel together and said that never, so please it God, would they be subject to them. They said that almost all the land was lost except for some strong castles, for the Tartars had already almost reached them." The castles were hurriedly put into a state of defence; the Templars equipped seven fortresses, the Hospitallers two, the Teutonic Knights one, and Tyre and Acre were *garnies du commun*, that is, made ready at shared expense. Terror of the Tartars, however, made it hard to find troops for the garrisons. At last they prepared for a siege, cutting down the trees in the orchards around Acre, razing the towers built in these orchards, and even removing the stones from the cemetery and from buildings, ready-made missiles for the enemy's siege engines.[12] The little 'republic of Acre' was preparing to take on the Great Khan, master of Asia, singlehanded.

This decision may have been affected by the Sidon affair. Just at the time when Kitbuqa was clearly showing his friendship for the Christians, who during the seven-months occupation of Damascus were able to persecute the Moslems there just as the Moslems had persecuted them for centuries, a Frankish baron went out of his way to annoy the Tartars. Julian of Sidon, the lord who had gambled away all his wealth, "a dull, feather-witted baron" as Grousset calls him, saw nothing in the collapse of Moslem Syria but the chance to go out raiding. From his castle of Beaufort he led a wide-ranging foray into the Marj Ayun and brought back a considerable booty. The newly appointed keeper of the frontier over against Sidon was Kitbuqa's nephew, who had no intention of putting up with such a violation of Mongol territory. He took a small body of men and pursued Julian, but was defeated and killed. Greatly angered, Kitbuqa sent his men to attack the lordship of Sidon. Julian held out for some time outside the town, long enough for its inhabitants to leave it, and then, thanks to the providential arrival of two Genoese galleys on their way from Tyre to Armenia, he withdrew into the citadel on the sea. The Mongols sacked the town, razing the walls and killing all they found, but did not attack the landward or the seaward castle, which seems to show that they did not mean to annex the coastal colonies. But from that time onwards Kitbuqa ceased to trust the Franks, perpetrators of an act of aggression which had touched him personally, and the Franks could never forget the sack of Sidon.[13]

The Mamluks now opened negotiations with the barons of Acre. Qutuz, the new sultan, had just rejected the Mongol ultimatum and was preparing an expedition against Syria, relying on the fact that Kitbuqa had only a small army of occupation with him. Qutuz' aim was to prevent the Franks making an alliance with the Mongols against him. The notables of Acre were quite ready to assist the Mamluks, and a treaty in these terms was all but concluded;[14] the grand master of the Teutonic Knights, however, succeeded in preventing it, pointing out that the Saracens were perfectly capable of turning on their new allies once the Mongols were defeated. It was settled, then, that they should adopt a policy of benevolent neutrality towards the Mamluks, allowing them to pass through Frankish territory and even to enter Acre. At this, the most dangerous of the Franks' new allies, Baibars, planned to take the town by surprise, and very nearly put his plan into execution.

The Mongol army was thus taken in the rear. The 1,000 Mongols stationed at Gaza were thrust out of their positions and fell back on Kitbuqa's army. The Mamluks, travelling along the coast and victualled by the Franks, laid an ambush at Ain Jalud near Petit Gerin for the Nestorian general on 3 September 1260, into which he fell. His army was annihilated and he himself captured and beheaded. One of his lieutenants, Ilqa Noyan, managed to gather together the Tartar contingents that remained in Syria and led them into Anatolia. In the now masterless Syria, the Mamluk army had only to occupy all the strongholds, especially since the sultan of Aleppo and Damascus, Yusuf, who had surrendered to the Mongols, was dead. He had been executed on the orders of Hulagu, who at first gave him permission to return to Syria but then feared he would join forces with the Egyptians. Qutuz ruled a single empire stretching from Nubia to the Euphrates, an empire supported by a permanent army well supplied with bases, and possessing strong institutions, an empire that was to prove itself more powerful than Saladin's. The existence of a few vassal Ayubid kingdoms such as Hama and Homs was not going to enable the Latins to achieve anything through their usual tactics of diplomacy.

Qutuz did not rule long, being soon murdered by his lieutenant Baibars, who took his place on 17 January 1261, also disposing of a sultan who had been proclaimed at Damascus. The new Mamluk leader was a cruel Turk of amazing energy, flinching at nothing which would produce the result he desired, the unity of Syria and the expulsion from it of both Franks and Mongols. The Franks came immediately under Mamluk attack: as soon as Qutuz, who always kept his word, was dead, the emir of Jerusalem did not hesitate to break the truce and molest the numerous Christian pilgrims in Jerusalem in many different ways. They were forced to remain in the city, then to pay large ransoms, and then attacked on their way home. The observance of truces was at an end.[15]

Baibars did not, however, immediately open a campaign against the Franks in Acre; he began by containing the Mongols. These recaptured Aleppo at the end of 1260, but were defeated near Homs. Hulagu, the Ilkhan, was fighting a war against the Mongol khan of Saray, Barka, who was in alliance with Baibars, and so could not send a large army to Syria. The Mamluk sultan therefore turned upon Hulagu's ally, Bohemond VI, in 1261 and especially in 1262. Antioch was besieged, and was only saved by the intervention of the Mongol army of Anatolia.

The barons of Acre had still not grasped how mistaken they had been in 1260 when they decided to prefer their independence, and their weakness and isolation as well, to an alliance with the Tartars, which would have been humiliating, perhaps, but likely to bring them much unhoped for recovery of territory. Clearly, the rudimentary civilization of the Tartars must have reminded them of the Khwarismian hordes of 1244, but there did exist among the Tartars a considerable Christian element on which an understanding could have been based. In 1246 a highly placed prelate of Mongol race, Simeon Rabban Ata, a favourite of the khan, in a letter to the pope took under his protection the Nestorian bishop of Jerusalem and the other Eastern Christians "who are in Antioch, Tripoli, Acre and your other lands".[16] All that the barons could perceive in the 1260 campaign was the devastation of Moslem Syria, depopulated and without rulers. They tried to profit by this; not long after Ain Jalud, it seems, John II of Ibelin, the new lord of Beirut, together with the marshal of the kingdom and the Templars attacked a Turcoman tribe in Galilee. They were heavily defeated; the lord of Beirut, the marshal and many others remained captive in the hands of the Turcomans, who exacted a large ransom for their release. John of Ibelin had to sell his domain of Casal Humbert to the Teutonic Knights in 1261.[17]

This defeat still did not open the eyes of the Franks to the Mamluk danger. Baibars had already taken the offensive on 4 April 1263 when the bishop of Bethlehem, the leaders of the orders, and Geoffrey of Sergines were writing to the king of England to tell him that there could be no better time for recovering the Holy Land, the Tartars had killed off most of the Saracens and Syria was there for the taking. Even when Egypt and Syria became united, the Franks perceived it too late.[18] From 1257 to 1263 the only danger recognized in Acre, at a time when Antioch was being successfully defended by Mongols, was the Mongol danger. It was to seek reinforcements for the defence of the kingdom against the Mongol armies that John of Valenciennes, lord of Cayphas, and Giles of Touraine, archbishop of Tyre, travelled to the West, where in January 1263 Urban IV authorized them to collect the tithes, or more precisely the hundredths, in the dioceses of the north of France for the benefit of the fortification of the Holy Land.[19] The destination of the sum was soon changed, for the collectors did not return to the East for two more years, by which time the situation was much altered.

Baibars' victories

Anxious to put an end to the insecurity of the pilgrim route and to the local irritations caused by the Moslem authorities, the Franks in Acre began talks with the sultan. The count of Jaffa and the lord of Beirut wanted the town of Petit Gerin returned, and suggested an exchange of prisoners. In 1262 Baibars refused to accept these suggestions as a basis of discussion. As the truce agreed in 1252–1255 was about to come to an end, negotiations were reopened. This time Baibars wanted an exchange of prisoners, and early in 1263 he obtained the agreement of John of Ibelin-Jaffa and the Hospitallers of Arsuf, who had just rented Balian of Ibelin-Arsuf's lordship from him. Then Baibars encamped his army between Nain and Mount Tabor and requested the return of Safed and Beaufort from the lordship of Acre, and an exchange of prisoners. The Templars and Hospitallers refused, because slaves were cheaper to employ than paid workmen. The sultan, who merely wanted a pretext for war, solemnly denounced the avarice of the two orders and attacked Galilee. Mount Tabor was pillaged and the church of Our Lord's Table between Capernaum and Cana demolished. The cathedral of Nazareth was destroyed and the Latin monastery at Bethlehem sacked. At the same time the sultan's army moved against Acre on 14 April 1263; here, although they took the defenders by surprise, they could do no more than destroy the orchards.[20] A Frankish counter-attack was repelled without difficulty, and Geoffrey of Sergines wounded. His attempt having failed, Baibars returned to Jerusalem and there, in order to show that his reoccupation of Judaea was to be permanent, he put in hand various building works, such as the construction of a caravanserai by the city gate.

The Franks were utterly taken aback by the Egyptian attack. "Those who thought they had escaped from the fearful threat of the Tartars are confounded by the fury of the Babylonians."[21] They wrote to tell the king of England and the pope of their state: they lacked money and food, and the sultan was demanding towns and castles, and occupying the Holy Land, despite the truce, right up to Acre itself. After these first appeals for help the Dominican William of Tripoli and then the bishop of Bethlehem took ship for Rome and informed Urban IV of the extent of the disaster.[22] In January 1264 the pope decided to continue the work of fortifying Jaffa, the fortress that defended the frontier with Egypt, but in view of the uncertainty of the sultan's intentions he had the necessary money paid over not to Count John but to the patriarch, so that he might use it according to the kingdom's most urgent need. In 1264 the Latins counter-attacked, and did so with the less trouble as the Egyptian army was not present in Syria. On 16 January the Templars and Hospitallers took Lyon, capturing 360 prisoners. Soon afterwards Geoffrey of Sergines and the knights of Acre set off from Jaffa to go and harry the lands of Ascalon in reprisal for the treacherous capture at Ramleh of the castellan of Jaffa; they defeated two emirs on 15 June 1264. On 5 November they raided the Beisan region again. But the following year Baibars returned to Syria, determined to have done with this problem. On 27 February 1265 he surprised and captured the town of Caesarea, and received the surrender of the citadel on 5 March. The men of Acre, alarmed, learning that the sultan was moving north, razed all their advanced defence posts such as the Tower of the Mills, and demolished the monastery of St Nicholas on a nearby hill.[23] Cayphas was evacuated at the same time, and was razed by Baibars on 15 March. Châtel Pèlerin, the Templar stronghold, resisted all attack. Continuing to sweep up the Franks' possessions, except for the well-defended Acre, Baibars next attacked Arsuf, which held out from 21 March to 29 April before surrendering. Despite his given word to allow the Hospitallers to retreat, Baibars had them put in irons. Then he returned to Egypt.

Help was beginning to arrive. The regent of Cyprus brought his contingents in March 1265; Oliver of Termes had arrived with the first French troops intended to relieve Geoffrey of Sergines in 1264. The pope had had the crusade preached in October 1263 without much result, but in October 1265 Odo of Burgundy, count of Nevers, arrived with some fifty knights. These reinforcements seem to have given Baibars pause: after a demonstration against Acre and Montfort he attacked Safed, the most important Frankish castle of the interior. The siege cost the Moslems dear, but the sultan succeeded in turning the Syrian sergeants against their Frankish masters, and one of them, a Syrian called Leon, a *casalier*[24] of the Temple, persuaded the knights to surrender. Violating the surrender terms, Baibars massacred the garrison. This massacre excited general horror, for it was carried out with the most elaborate forms of torture, some of the defenders being skinned alive and then whipped. Sustained in their resolve by a small number of Franciscans, the Templars refused to abjure their faith. This was a mere beginning of Mamluk atrocity, for when in July 1266 the men of Acre asked for permission to bury the dead of Safed, Baibars had Christians in the suburbs of Acre slaughtered, and replied that they now had martyrs within reach of the town.

Safed became the Moslems' stronghold, from which they could launch attacks towards Acre, and without too much difficulty, since Baibars had demolished Toron. On 28 October of this same year 1266 the Safed garrison inflicted a damaging defeat on a Frankish pillaging expedition returning from Tiberias. Acre was effectively blockaded, and Baibars was able to appoint Moslem officials to collect the revenues from the *casals* in the suburbs. In May 1267, in a now regular rhythm, the sultan appeared once more before Acre. He disguised his men by giving them Christian banners and endeavoured to take the town by surprise. Failing in this, he had the peasants and poor people outside the walls and in the fields slaughtered, not without first torturing them. Then he went back and laid waste the orchards and vineyards, cutting down the fruit trees and the vines, and after a stay at Safed he then made a sudden attack on 31 October on the stables of the Hospital. 200 horses and twenty squires were burned to death. Next year, in spite of the truce made with John of Ibelin, the Mamluk army surprised and occupied Jaffa, although they allowed part of the garrison to withdraw to Acre. At the same time the "land of St George" was annexed, together with Lydda. This private truce had done Jaffa no good. However, the lord of Beirut obtained a similar truce in May 1267, by paying a large sum and surrendering his prisoners, and so did Philip of Montfort, who renounced his claim to Toron and Châteauneuf. Baibars granted him provisional recognition of his possession of Tyre and of ninety-nine villages.

One month after Jaffa, Baibars laid siege to Beaufort, which surrendered ten days later on 15 April 1268. The lord of Beirut, fearing the sultan's approach, paid another ransom. At that, the terrible Mamluk went to annex the principality of Antioch, taking the town itself by storm in May 1268 and occupying the whole region. He then, at the earnest request of Hugh III of Cyprus, the *bayle*, granted the Franks of Acre a period of respite. This truce, made on 27 May 1268, recognized as belonging to the lordship of Acre only the district of Acre, Carmel, three villages near Cayphas, ten near Montfort, and five near Châtel Pèlerin. The remaining *casals* in the area were shared between Franks and Mamluks. Ratifying the truces made with Beirut and Tyre, Baibars granted another to the Templars of Sidon, who had to renounce all their possessions in the Lebanon, keeping only the villages of the narrow coastal plain.

Next year, 1269, Baibars broke the truce, although it had been made for ten years. Four Moslems had accepted baptism in Acre, and for this crime the conflict began again, as it also did with Tyre on a comparable pretext. Baibars began his campaign with harrying raids, especially into the hitherto intact county of Tripoli, where the prince was left with little besides a few coastal towns. The two great fortresses of the interior, Châtel Blanc and Krak des Chevaliers fell in 1271. On 12 June of the same year the principal stronghold of the Teutonic Knights in the Acre region, Montfort, also fell. In the eight years from 1263 to 1271 the terrible sultan took from the Franks western Galilee, the whole coastal region from Caesarea to Jaffa, the whole of the mountain country east and north of Acre, two-thirds of the county of Tripoli and the whole of the principality of Antioch except Lattakieh.

With the same astounding activity that he showed in Egypt, Baibars, the true founder of the Mamluk Empire, rebuilt the towns of Palestine which had lain deserted since 1187; Hebron and Jerusalem rose from their ruins. There was no single stronghold taken from the Franks on which the sultan's builders were not immediately set to work. The conquering lion emblems of Baibars are to be seen today on all the Frankish ruins, at Safed, at Beaufort, and at Krak des Chevaliers.[25] Aqueducts, bridges, mosques and other public works sprang up in the steps of the great sultan. Syria, for eighty years a kind of no man's land, was no longer deserted and began to bristle with fortresses. Acre was blockaded by the new Mamluk castles of Safed, Montfort, Caco, rebuilt in 1267, and Caesarea.

Baibars displayed no less energy in punishing those who had made alliances with the Franks. This was the case with the Bohtor emirs of Gharb, Arabs near Beirut who manoeuvred so cleverly between their formidable neighbours that they obtained successive charters of seisin from the *malik* of Damascus, al-Nasir, from the Mamluk sultan, Aibek, and from Hulagu himself, all the while remaining in perfect amity with the Frankish barons. In 1255 Julian of Sidon gave a property in his village of Damur on the coast to the emir Jamal al-Din, which in no way prevented the emir from keeping the Mamluks informed, as a kind of counter-insurance, of his neighbours' plans. One emir who was jealous of another Bohtor, Zain al-Din, accused the latter to Baibars of negotiating with the prince of Antioch; he had written, he said, in his enemy's name to Bohemond VI, and received a reply which he sent to the sultan. It seems simpler to suppose that Zain al-Din was acting as the prince's spy and that his correspondence was intercepted. The suspected Bohtor was imprisoned and not released until 1277 when Baibars was dead. He continued his dealings with the Franks, however, for there is another charter, described in a chronicle written by one of his descendants. It was granted in 1280 by the lord of Beirut, who was then Humphrey of Montfort, and gave another estate to Zain al-Din in exchange for a promise to refrain from all depredations in the lordship of Beirut and from harbouring Moslem fugitives from that lordship. But the Bohtors had further trouble with the Mamluks in 1283 and 1288 because of their connections with the Franks. It looks as if it was becoming difficult to keep up the game the Latins had played so well, themselves enfeoffing the Moslem princes' vassals and so making use of them against their lords.[26]

The Eighth Crusade

Christendom did not see its Eastern empire founder without attempting to save it. A crusade was organized under two powerful sovereigns. The first to set off, in 1269, was James I king of Aragon, but his fleet was thrown back onto the Spanish coast by a storm and the aged monarch refused to re-embark. Only two princes of Aragon arrived in Syria, in October 1269. All they could do was to observe the Moslem depredations, and they were not even able to prevent the enemy ambushing and killing the seneschal Robert of Créséques, successor of Geoffrey of Sergines, under the very walls of Acre. As for the king of France, he took the cross a second time in 1267 and set off in 1270, taking with him the kings of Navarre and Sicily. But the Eighth Crusade chose a different route,[27] and St Louis died before Tunis on 25 August 1270 with no result but that Baibars that year was not able to campaign in Syria.

A tiny fraction of the forces of the Eighth Crusade did, however, reach the Holy Land in 1271, with the English princes Edward, on May 9, and Edmund. Few though they were, the crusaders were commanded by one of the most remarkable statesmen of the period,

Edward Plantagenet, who had not long since rid his house at the battle of Evesham of one of its most formidable adversaries, Simon of Montfort. In Syria he tried to compel the Italian merchants to observe the blockade of Egypt, for contraband trade in war materials was prospering more and more. He hanged some offenders, but was confronted by the Venetian *bayle* with privileges preventing him from putting into effect either papal commands or conciliar prohibitions. Edward also tried to co-operate with the Mongols, but they were only able to make one short expedition in the Aleppo region. Edward had to rest content with two plundering expeditions, a raid against Saint-Georges in the Acre mountains in July 1271 and another against Caco in November, where it was too dangerous to besiege the castle. Much booty was won, but other results were minimal. None the less it seems to have been Edward's presence which induced Baibars to conclude a peace agreement, which he did on 22 May 1272; Charles of Anjou, king of Sicily, acted as mediator. The treaty was to last ten years and ten months; it acknowledged the Acre Franks' possession of the plain of Acre and the pilgrimage of Nazareth. The kingdom of Acre was reduced to a smaller extent than it had known under Aimery and John of Brienne. All the efforts made by the West in the thirteenth century were now seen to be useless.[28]

Alliance with the Mongols

The Franks had tried to find allies against the Mamluks. Baibars' first attacks produced a change of heart towards the Mongols, and in any case Mongol savagery could be no worse than Mamluk cruelty. And indeed as early as 1260 the legate sent his chaplain, the English Dominican David of Ashby, to get in touch with the Mongols, which shows that even then opinion in Acre was hesitating between resistance and submission to these enemies. David was well received by Hulagu. News came in 1263 that Hulagu had accepted baptism, and the Mongols sent ambassadors to Rome, who were intercepted by Manfred. Urban IV instructed the patriarch of Jerusalem to enquire into the genuineness of Hulagu's conversion.[29] Regular diplomatic exchanges soon followed, and the Mongol chancery even went so far as to lay aside its arrogant claims to universal sovereignty so as to facilitate negotiation. (In 1262, so some authors said, a large Mongol embassy was sent to demand St Louis' submission to the Great Khan.) Little by little the papacy came to think in terms of the wholesale conversion of the Mongols to Christianity, a gigantic project, and one doomed to fail, but at the military level a genuine alliance directed against the Mamluks did come about. Urban IV's letter to Hulagu asking him to accept Christianity also asked him to subjugate the Saracens, and in August 1263 the pope was describing the Tartars as the God-sent avengers of Moslem perfidy.[30]

Negotiations took a more active turn under Hulagu's successors, his son Abagha and his grandson Arghun. The Mongol princes showed a keen desire to work with the Franks towards the crushing of the Mamluks; almost every year ambassadors arrived in Europe from Iran or set off home for Tabriz. Unfortunately, the Mongol rulers were at war with the khans of Turkestan and of Saray and this prevented their taking any action in Syria. As for the kings of the West, they were fully occupied with the questions of Scotland, Wales, Sicily and Aragon. Matters were complicated, too, by delays: in 1267, for instance, the Latin secretary of the khan of Persia was away and a letter written in Mongol was received in Rome. No one could translate it, and negotiations paused for a year.[31] In 1269 James I of Aragon had prepared an expedition to be carried out jointly with the Tartars, and Edward of England had done the same; Abagha was not able to bring his army to the appointed rendezvous, and he sent several times to apologize to the English prince.[32] In 1280, when a Mongol army was about to descend on Syria from Turkey, Abagha asked the Franks of Acre to unite their army with his and to arrange for supplies of food. In that year, indeed, the Mongol army of Anatolia was to take the road, and its 80,000 Armenians and Mongols threatened to overwhelm the Mamluk empire.

The Frankish defection of 1280

But since 1277 the kingdom of Acre had been in the hands of Charles of Anjou, St Louis' brother, count of Provence and since 1266 king of Sicily.

Charles' *bayle* of Acre, Roger of San Severino, did not think it possible to assist the Mongol war effort. As in 1260, co-operation between Franks and Tartars failed through the fault of the Franks.

This time the cause lay in Angevin policy. Charles of Anjou had great plans, but Palestine held only a tiny place in them. He did indeed mean to crown his work with the deliverance of the Holy Sepulchre, but first he intended to conquer the Byzantine Empire, which had been restored by Michael Palaeologus. Charles' relations with Egypt were excellent; it was he who in 1272 had persuaded Baibars to make peace. His policy was that of Frederick II and Manfred; he was not at all inclined to damage his good relations with the sultan even in order to take the unexpected chance that was now offered, as it had been once before in 1260, of conquering Syria in alliance with the Tartars. On 5 October 1280 the bishop of Hebron, vicar of the patriarch of Jerusalem, wrote to Edward I in terms that showed how the rulers of Acre were thinking: they lacked supplies of food in the Holy Land, which made it very difficult to prepare a campaign, especially as the king of Sicily was busy with a war.[33] The *bayle* sent word to Sultan Qalawun, Baibars' successor, of a plot against his life, and concluded a new truce with him. And so on 30 October 1281 the armies of Prince Mangu Timur and King Hethoum of Armenia, beside his Mongol allies once more, were defeated near Homs without receiving any aid from the Franks. And a truce between the lordship of Acre and the Mamluks, ratified on 3 June 1283, left in the sultan's hands the whole of the former kingdom of Jerusalem: Hebron, Jerusalem, Gibelin, Nablus, Bethlehem, Toron des Chevaliers, Ascalon, Jaffa, Ramleh, Arsuf, Caesarea, Caco, Beisan, Toron, Grand Gerin, Ain Jalud, Safed, Beaufort, Caymont, Tiberias, Châteauneuf, Maron, half of Scandelion, the Cave of Tyron, and so on. To the seneschal, Odo Poilechien, representative of the king of Sicily, it gave Acre, Cayphas, Carmel, a total of seventy-three *casals*, also Sidon and fifteen *casals*, and the church of Nazareth with four houses for the lodging of clerks and pilgrims. The Christians gained nothing but the ruins of Cayphas, and were allowed to fortify no other strongholds than Sidon, Acre and Châtel Pèlerin. They undertook during the ten years, ten months, ten days and ten hours that the truce was to run to give the sultan two months advance warning of the arrival of a crusade. The other lordships also accepted this Mamluk protectorate, Beirut in 1272 and Tyre in 1285, where the lady of Tyre and 'Count Raymond Jaskend', her representative, made a similar treaty.[34]

Having to choose between alliance with the Mongols and submission to the Moslems, the men of Acre opted firmly for the second. Yet they had suffered before from the Mamluks' faithlessness, and they were soon to suffer from it again. Nevertheless, poorly supported by the West, compelled to obey directives from Sicily, they at last turned their back on the crusades. This was at a time when the papacy, the kings of France and England, and the new khan Arghun were planning a fresh expedition, with the rendezvous appointed for the plain of Damascus in 1290. It was even being said in the West that "the son of the late king of the Tartars meant to be in Jerusalem for Holy Thursday" and to be baptized in the Holy City, that his army, including Georgians and his other Christian allies, had been issued with standards and weapons bearing the cross, and that he had struck money bearing a representation of the Holy Sepulchre and an invocation to the Trinity.[35] It was just at the time when the Mongol conquest began to take on the aspect of a true crusade that Frankish Syria, without leader or resources, threw itself into the arms of the Mamluks. Their weakness may explain their decision, but they did not now have the same excuse as in 1260, for frequent contact with the Mongols had made the Latins familiar with the idea of accepting them as allies.

The spurning of this alliance, both in 1260 and in 1281, marked the end of Frankish Syria and its imminent destruction by the Egyptians. In 1260 the God-given allies from the depths of the Gobi desert, expected by the crusaders in 1219, by St Louis in 1248, at last arrived where they were needed in Syria. The prince of Antioch and the king of Armenia rallied to their side; the kingdom of Acre, then still a real power, preferred the Mamluks.[36] In 1281 the defection of the last Latins in Syria once again betrayed the Mongols. When in twenty years time the third Mongol campaign in Syria did at last conquer that land, there were no Franks left to make the conquest permanent or to reoccupy the now liberated kingdom of Jerusalem.

CHAPTER 8

The kingdom of the *Assises*

The eclipse of royal authority

The treaties with Baibars and his successor bear witness to a fact now clear to all observers, the irreparable fragmentation of the kingdom. Tyre, Acre, Jaffa, Sidon, Beirut and Arsuf were now just so many separate lordships which made their own truces with the Moslems, and even, as at Beirut, accepted a Mamluk protectorate in defiance of the king's rights. An Arab author could write, "If one treated with the Hospitallers, the Templars took arms; if one made peace with Acre, the king of Cyprus attacked."[1] Anarchy was now absolute in the former kingdom of Jerusalem.

We have seen how the sovereign authority came to be split up. In the name of the Hohenstaufen king, accepted as the true heir of the throne but prevented since 1243 from exercising his royal prerogative, the king's nearest relative exercised a regency or *baylie*, with the title of 'lord of the kingdom'. Alice of Champagne, younger daughter of Isabelle of Jerusalem and sister of Mary of Jerusalem-Montferrat, was the next heiress to the crown after her great-nephew Conrad II, Mary's grandson, and she was chosen as regent. When she died the regency went to her son Henry I, king of Cyprus, and after him as 'lords of the kingdom' came the kings of Cyprus Hugh II or Hughet (1253–1267) and Hugh III of Antioch-Lusignan (1267–1269). The matter was complicated by Hugh II's age; he did not live to reach his majority, dying on 5 December 1267, and so he himself, "heir of Cyprus and of the *baylie* of the kingdom of Jerusalem", needed a regent. This regency was exercised by his mother Plaisance of Antioch jointly with her second husband Balian of Ibelin and later with her brother Bohemond VI of Antioch. After Plaisance died on 27 September 1261, the regency for Hughet was exercised by the child's aunt, Isabelle of Lusignan, sister of Hughet's father, Henry I; she was assisted by her husband Henry 'du Prince' of Antioch. In 1263 she died and the regency for the adolescent king went to her and Henry of Antioch's son, Hugh of Antioch-Lusignan. Thus in addition to the Cypriot crown the kings of Cyprus possessed rights to the reversion of the crown of Jerusalem; they were the legitimate line of the royal house of Jerusalem.

But neither the 'lord of the kingdom' nor his guardian resided in the Holy Land. He lived in Cyprus and from there appointed a representative in Acre, as it were a governor and a head of the nobility of Syria. This man was also known as the *bayle*, and we shall reserve this description for him. The names of these *bayles* proclaim the triumph of the house of Ibelin; with the two exceptions of John Fanon, appointed in 1248–1249 on Philip of Montfort's advice, and of Geoffrey of Sergines (1259–1263), they all belonged to this famous family: Balian of Ibelin-Beirut (died 1247), John of Ibelin-Arsuf (dismissed September 1248 but reappointed in 1249), John of Ibelin-Jaffa, who replaced his cousin for a year, 1255–1256, then John of Ibelin-Arsuf again (1256–1258); and after John's death and the regencies of Geoffrey of Sergines and Henry 'du Prince', Balian of Ibelin (1268–1269). Except for short intervals the Ibelins were the effective rulers of Frankish Syria for twenty years. Their pride grew out of all bounds; one of them had the audacity to tell King Hugh III in 1271 that the chivalry of Cyprus had agreed to serve in Syria for the sake of the Ibelins, not for the king of Cyprus.[2]

One of them, Balian of Ibelin-Arsuf, even hoped to take the place of the king of Cyprus; when Henry I died he married Henry's widow, Plaisance, against the opposition of Prince Bohemond VI, and claimed the regency of the young king. He was supported in this by his father John of Arsuf, who was not reconciled with Bohemond until 1258. This marriage was performed without regard to canon law; the couple were related in the third degree and did not wait for the necessary dispensation before marrying. It was not long before Plaisance, not noted, it seems, for fidelity,[3] wanted a separation from Balian, who refused to give up the regency. The pope had to intervene, on 28 August 1255 forbidding all subjects of the realm to obey Balian, and on 27 March 1258 annulling the marriage.[4]

Nothing could be worse for royal authority than this kind of interregnum. In theory the *bayle*, the 'lord of the kingdom', was invested with all the prerogatives of royalty, but in practice his powers were very limited. In 1243 the barons refused to give the royal castles into the keeping of Queen Alice and her husband Ralph on the pretext that they might usurp the rights of the true heir, Conrad II, as William of Villehardouin had dispossessed the heirs of Prince William of Champlitte in the Morea. Castles and fortresses would be entrusted to "the guard and care of the barons and the men of the said realm"; it would be the regent's task to provision them, but castellans would be appointed and decisions made by the feudatories. This scrupulous loyalism forced Alice to entrust Tyre to Balian of Ibelin and Acre to Philip of Montfort and Nicholas Antiaume. In fact what happened was that Philip usurped Tyre, and was recognized as its holder by King Henry in 1246. Thus the king's representative could not even dispose of the castles of the royal domain.[5]

The clergy too were ready to profit by the vacancy of the throne to restrict the *bayle*'s powers over themselves. The customs of the Latin kingdom did not allow ecclesiastical courts to try cases dealing with landed property, especially property owing service to the king. In 1257 the clerks of the Holy Land claimed to have the right to try such cases when no point of feudal law was involved,

on the pretext that this kingdom has at present no king. For although the *bayle* acts as and replaces the king in many instances, according to the customs and *assises* of the realm, to use their own terms, this *bayle* is nevertheless unable to give judgement in the case of a royal fief.

The case was brought before Alexander IV and aimed at nothing less than freeing ecclesiastical courts from all the restrictions imposed on them by the monarchy. The pope was careful not to cut the case short.[6]

Under the imperfectly acknowledged authority of the 'chief lord', the feudal lords came increasingly to enjoy the exercise of power. By custom, the *bayle* of the kingdom should have been chosen by the 'lord of the kingdom', with the assent of the feudatories. In practice, according to a passage in John of Ibelin-Jaffa, the famous jurist, the feudatories themselves elected their leader.[7] The lordship, *seigneurie*, of Jerusalem was coming to look more and more like an Italian *signoria*, a kind of highly aristocratic feudal republic. Its aristocratic nature is shown by the number of Ibelin *bayles*. The lordship even appointed a syndic, strongly reminiscent of the officials of the great

patrician cities of Italy and Provence; on 10 August 1257 Stephen of
Sauvegny, a vassal of John of Ibelin-Arsuf, is described as "syndic
and procurator of the lordship of Jerusalem".[8]

Government of the kings of Cyprus; accession of Hugh III

As long as the last Hohenstaufens survived, unquestioned descendants of Queen Isabelle II, daughter of John of Brienne, the kings of
Cyprus although bearing the title of lords of the realm were unable to
stem the rising tide of anarchy. The oath taken by the *bayle* was even
more restrictive than that sworn by the king.[9] During the St Sabas war
the Genoese party, annoyed at the support given to its adversaries by
Bohemond VI, at once appealed to the uncontested and inactive
sovereignty of Conrad III. The kings of Cyprus, or those who acted
as regent on their behalf, did not even find it easy to gain acceptance
as 'lords of the kingdom'. They had to obtain recognition as the
nearest heir of the crown from a specially convoked assembly of the
"greater and better part", *major saniorque pars*, of the kingdom's
feudatories. King Henry I was accepted without difficulty, but when
he died in 1253 his son Hughet was too young. Balian of Ibelin was
regent then in Cyprus, but was his regency recognized in Acre?[10]
After the annulment of her marriage to Balian, Queen Plaisance
obtained a more securely based authority. In 1258 she left Cyprus for
Acre, accompanied by her son and her brother Bohemond VI. Bohemond attempted to have his nephew Hughet recognized as "heir of
Cyprus and of the *baylie* of the kingdom of Jerusalem",[11] and himself
as the child's guardian. But this was right in the middle of the St
Sabas war, and those who had invited the prince of Antioch to take
over the government, vacant in practice since 1253, were of the
Venetian and Pisan party – the Templars, the Teutonic Knights, John
of Ibelin-Jaffa, and the patriarch, James Pantaléon. The Genoese and
the Hospitallers refused to accept Bohemond's regency. He was,
however, acknowledged by the majority; he acted as 'lord of the
kingdom', and entrusted his *baylie* to John of Arsuf when he went
away. When John died, Plaisance was able to go to Acre without
trouble and give the post of *bayle* to Geoffrey of Sergines, the
seneschal.

On 27 September 1261, however, Plaisance died. Who was to

succeed her? The regency of Cyprus was given to Isabelle of Lusignan, the sole surviving aunt of young Hughet. In 1263 she arrived in
Acre to ask for the regency of Jerusalem for herself and her husband.
This was during the full onslaught of the Mamluk attack, but that did
not prevent the high court assembling and discussing some very fine
points of law. In the end the vassals decided that the regency should
properly go to Isabelle, but that as she had not brought the heir to the
baylie with her, they would not proceed to the customary ceremony
of homage. None the less Henry of Antioch remained in Acre in
power, while his wife returned to Cyprus, where she died the same
year. The regency was again discussed. Hugh of Antioch-Lusignan,
son of Isabelle and Henry, claimed it, and so did his first cousin Hugh
of Brienne, count of Lecce, on the grounds that his mother Mary had
been the elder sister of Isabelle. We still possess the lengthy pleadings
in which the contestants tried to justify their claims before the
assembly of their future vasals, now their judges.[12] Hugh of Antioch
won the day, and thus became *bayle* of Cyprus and Jerusalem. The
count of Lecce took part in the defence of the Holy Land against
Baibars, and then returned to the West, having become count of
Brienne through his brother's death. None the less in 1275 he prepared an expedition to assert his claim to the kingdom by force of
arms, and the pope had to intervene to prevent this fratricidal war.[13]

Hugh of Antioch-Lusignan was a conscientious *bayle.* During the
terrible years when Baibars prowled about Acre he summoned his
knights whenever he learned of the sultan's approach and did not
leave Acre until the enemy was back in Safed.[14] He launched counter-
attacks and gave himself up entirely to the defence of the Holy Land.
When his nephew Hughet died on 5 December 1267 he exchanged the
title of *bayle* of Cyprus for that of king of Cyprus and left Acre for
Nicosia, leaving the *baylie* of Acre in the hands of Balian of Ibelin,
son of John of Arsuf and his father's successor as constable of the
kingdom – after the tenure of William of Boutron, a Tripolitan baron
expelled by Bohemond VI (1258–1262).

And now on 31 October 1268 Conrad III was beheaded. Acre set
illuminations blazing in delight, but the lords must have been much
less pleased. The line of Isabelle of Brienne was extinct, and the
monarchy of Jerusalem would become a reality once again. There
would be no more regencies, no more regencies of regencies. But
Frankish Syria had become accustomed to this way of life. Barons,
prelates, military orders, communes and fraternities enjoyed a prac-

tical independence; they kept the supreme authority of the 'lord of the kingdom' in being, but it seems more than likely that this was only in order to allow their institutions to function. As long as the *bayle*, the viscounts and the castellans held their powers from a legitimate ruler, the juridical life of the kingdom, in which questions of law mattered so much, was able to continue. To have a sovereign present in the Holy Land would be another matter altogether, and there was every reason to fear that the jealously guarded independence of each element of the kingdom would suffer. Those who most dreaded such an event were the usurpers of the royal domain, and Philip of Montfort most of all. As long as there were only *bayles* in the Holy Land, the law of Jerusalem, which he had himself partly shaped, authorized him to remain master of Tyre in the name of King Conrad. The presence of the king would compel him to give up Tyre, and Philip, who had recently lost his lordship of Toron to Baibars, had behaved as the fully entitled lord of Tyre for a number of years.[15]

Hugh III managed this difficult restoration with great skill. In 1255 he had married Isabelle of Ibelin, granddaughter of John the Old of Ibelin,[16] and this ensured him the neutrality of that proud family. The military orders were not hostile to him, and he had as yet no conflict with his Cyprus knights. He managed to soothe the apprehensions of the lord of Tyre, recognizing his possession of the town upon precarious tenure. (In any case, Philip was soon to be murdered, on 17 August 1270 at the order of Baibars, who wanted to be rid of one of the most remarkable barons of Syria; and his son and successor John had recently married the king's sister, Margaret of Antioch-Lusignan.) Unfortunately, a rival claimant to the throne came forward. Hugh derived his claim from Alice, daughter of Queen Isabelle I of Jerusalem and Henry of Champagne. Now Mary of Antioch, the king's cousin, a maiden lady of sixty – strange adversary for Sultan Baibars – laid claim to the throne in the name of her mother Melisende, daughter of the same Isabelle I and of Aimery of Lusignan. This was not a new claim; Melisende herself had raised it in 1249, alleging that she was more closely related to Queen Isabelle than were Alice's descendants.[17] It was a specious argument, but provided a rallying point for opposition to Hugh. Attempts were made to arrive at a settlement, but Mary would yield no part of her claim. The case was heard before the high court in 1268 and 1269, and judgement given against Mary. She refused to accept the decision, and on 24 September 1269 during the first coronation of a king that had taken place in

Tyre for sixty years – a coronation with little pomp,[18] in view of the troubled times – a clerk and a notary stepped forward in the church and the clerk called out in the presence of the assembled crowd that he objected to the ceremony. He had to make his escape from the blows of the congregation amidst indescribable uproar, but Mary had made her point and reserved her claim to the throne.

We can only agree with Grousset's judgement: "The restoration of the monarchy attempted by Hugh of Antioch came too late. During the thirty and more years that the throne had in practice been vacant, the barons and burgesses of Acre had come to relish independence too much for them to be willing to learn obedience again."[19] Moslem conquest and the feudatories' usurpations had greatly reduced the royal domain. In its absence, Hugh had little on which to found a renewed royal authority such as had been enjoyed by Frederick II's predecessors. He tried to make use of the customs of the country to establish his authority; for instance, Julian of Sidon sold his fief to the Templars without the king's permission, but Hugh none the less compelled him to guarantee his military service, granting him (on the money from the sale?) a money fief of some 10,000 bezants, to be held after him by his sons Balian II and John.[20] But since the beginning of the thirteenth century the laws of Jerusalem had developed in a different direction from that of the previous period.

The compilation of the Assises

The great event of the thirteenth century in the kingdom of Jerusalem was the flowering of a whole literature of the law which, if not unique in that century, is the most complete and the most interesting for an understanding of the feudal system. The jurists began work early in our period, originally with the purpose of preserving the customs of the first kingdom and the laws expressed in the *Lettres du Sépulchre*. Aimery thus tried to codify the principles of the king's authority. But after him the 'wise men' had a different end in view. Contending with Ghibelline arbitrariness and Frederick II's authoritarianism, the feudatories in a natural defensive reflex set up their own laws in opposition to the king's. Instead of a *Livre au roi*, they wanted a Book of the Vassals. Feudatories with a knowledge of ancient customs, Ralph of Tiberias, Renaud of Sidon, John the Old of Ibelin, had been careful to preserve and pass on to their sons the *assises* favourable to the vassals. Applying their own theories to this body of knowledge, the great jurists of the thirteenth century, Philip of Novara, John of Ibelin, count of Jaffa, Geoffrey Le Tort, and burgesses such as Philip Béduin, Balian and Nicholas Antiaume, tried to build up the law of Jerusalem into a scientifically structured edifice.[21] One of these men may have been the author of the *Assises de la Cour aux Bourgeois*, drawn up perhaps between 1229 and 1244, which attempts to fit the customs of Jerusalem into the framework of a manual of Roman law.[22] Philip of Novara's *Livre en forme de plait*, post-1260 in its final version,[23] still resembles a customary, but the *Livre de Jean d'Ibelin*, written about 1265, is a genuine treatise of jurisprudence, which inspired all the subsequent studies of the law, beginning with the *Livre de Jacques d'Ibelin* of 1271-1286.[24]

John of Ibelin, count of Jaffa, son of Philip of Ibelin and grandson of Balian II of Ibelin, lord of Nablus, is one of the most interesting figures of the Latin East in the thirteenth century. He was a good knight, deservedly enjoying the esteem of St Louis and the affection of Joinville, and appears, by the same title as his cousin John of Arsuf, as the head of the Frankish nobility. But he appears too as a "subtle litigant" – the praise of being cunning in the law was the highest that this law-struck society could bestow on one of its peers – and his subtlety at times comes near to guile. "Why does he say such fine things about the duty of a litigant to be honest, and at the same time cynically advise dishonesty?"[25]

As the origin of the law of Jerusalem, with its mutual obligations, John of Ibelin's constitutional theory presupposes a kind of feudal contract, rather as Rousseau presupposes a social contract. For the barons of the thirteenth century, the king was the man they elected, and the choice of Godfrey of Bouillon by the great barons of the First Crusade had become for them the election of a baron of Jerusalem by his peers, the other barons of the realm; as it happens this was a far from accurate view.[26] The undertakings which they believed Godfrey to have made formed the foundation for their whole juridical construction. Balian of Sidon addressing himself to Filangieri in 1231 summed up the baronial theory thus:

When this land was conquered, it was not conquered by any chief lord but by crusading and by pilgrims. And when they had conquered it they made a lord by agreement and by election and gave him the lordship of the realm, and afterwards, by agreement and with the knowledge of the valiant and honest men, they made enactments and *assises* which they wished to be kept and used, and then they swore to keep them and made the lord swear also.[27]

The king or regent upon his accession always had to swear that he would maintain the *assises* of the kingdom and ensure the observance of privileges granted by his predecessors.

Loyalty to the lord of the kingdom, whom John of Ibelin writing before the restoration of King Hugh always calls the *chief seignor*, was not an essential condition of liege homage but a consequence of the lord's respect of his vassals' rights. Thus in the thirteenth century kingdom the king's feudatories refused him their service when they considered he had injured them, and by common agreement withdrew from their fiefs. "The jurists saw homage as a kind of bilateral contract involving reciprocal and parallel obligations for vassal and lord. Through this they profoundly altered their respective situations."[28] Despite the impartiality displayed by the count of Jaffa in his exposition and discussion of constitutional theories,[29] his *Livre* reflects an advanced stage of the dissolution of monarchical law. It is interesting to compare his list of reasons for the confiscation of a fief with that given in the *Livre au roi* and based on the *assise* of Baldwin II.[30] The vassal whose fief may properly be confiscated is one who is a heretic, or has abjured his faith and gone over to the Moslems, or who "lays his hand on the body of his lord . . . goes in arms against his lord in the field . . . seeks the death and disinheritance of his lord and of this is attainted and convicted . . . sells his fief contrary to the *assise* . . . is appealed of treason and defeated in the field [namely in trial by combat]", and also one who surrenders to the enemy a castle which he could still defend, or who betrays his lord and delivers him to the enemy. This is a much shorter list than that in the old customary of Aimery, and each instance given is also much more narrowly defined. If "a man who refuses to obey his lord for a thing which it is reasonable to do" is no longer held to be at fault, then the only revolt to be punished is armed encounter between lord and vassal in the field.

Above all the *Livre de Jean d'Ibelin* and similar works develop a theory dear to feudal law, of which Amalric's *Assise sur la Ligèce* had already established the principles, the vassal's power to protect himself against his lord's arbitrary decisions. This was not peculiar to the Latin kingdom:

This well known 'right of resistance' [existing in embryo in Carolingian times] was proclaimed in the thirteenth and fourteenth centuries from one end of the Western world to the other . . . : Magna Carta in England in 1215, the Golden Bull in Hungary in 1222, the customary of the kingdom of Jerusalem, the privileges of the nobles of Brandenburg, the Aragonese Act of Union of 1287[31] are all instances of it. The right to withdraw service from and indeed openly to resist a lord guilty of making a decision against his vassal's interest "without consideration and knowledge of the court" was a recognized right of the feudal community which it did not hesitate to put into practice.

Another characteristic of the *Assises de Jérusalem* as set out by John of Ibelin is their formalism. The rules of jurisprudence display an amazing respect for correct form, one which would have delighted Beaumarchais' Brid'oison. Moreover, this formalism was carefully cherished by the jurists of the East, anxious to deal with every constitutional problem by procedural methods.[32] This is not the place to analyse the huge compilation amassed by the count of Jaffa and his emulators. Suffice it to say that constitutional law as expressed by the *Assises* delivered the sovereign bound hand and foot to the mercy of his barons and their instrument, the high court. The vacancy of the throne had allowed the barons to develop to their utmost extent the theories of law that could be deduced from what had originally been nothing more than a desire to protect the vassals against the arbitrary power of the king, and to subordinate the suzerain to those who owed him faith and homage.

The king's disillusionment

Hugh III of Antioch-Lusignan soon found this out. His knights in Cyprus began it in 1271 by refusing to serve overseas, being weary of crossing the sea each year to defend the Holy Land. More precisely, they reproached the king with requiring this service by virtue of the feudal contract, assuring him, however, that if he only knew how to win his knights' devotion they would ask nothing better than to accompany him on his expeditions. The lawsuit dragged on for some years, beginning at the time of the arrival of Prince Edward of England, and in 1273 the period of service outside the kingdom was fixed at four months per year. In 1279 the Cypriot knights, their four months' service done, abandoned their sovereign in the middle of a campaign.[33]

Indiscipline was still more marked in Hugh's Syrian kingdom. Although in 1264 "the court of the kingdom and my lord Geoffrey of Sergines and the legate and the masters and the communes and the fraternities" all supported his candidature,[34] no one meant to obey any orders given by the new king. The fraternities carried on their quarrels in the very streets of Acre; two of them, that of Bethlehem, perhaps the Melchites of the St George brotherhood in Bethlehem Street, near Montmusard, and the 'Mosserins' (merchants of Mosul?) even fought a regular battle, the Bethlehem group being enfeoffed to the Hospital and the Mosserins to the Temple. The Templars accused the king of complicity with the Bethlehem fraternity.[35] Nor had the local lordships learned to give up their independence; Tyre, indeed, was now Hugh III's faithful vassal, but Sidon, now in the hands of the Templars, behaved as if it were an independent domain. And as for Beirut, here Isabelle of Ibelin, Beirut's heiress, widowed of her second husband the Englishman Edmund L'Estrange, had been entrusted by Edmund at some date after 1272 not to the king, as custom required, but to the sultan Baibars. Hugh III occupied the lordship and removed Isabelle to Cyprus; Baibars insisted that Beirut be returned to him and Isabelle allowed to choose which protectorate she preferred, and thus the Frankish lordship of 'Baruth' became a Frankish emirate and a vassal of the Mamluk empire. Isabelle married Nicholas L'Aleman, lord of Caesarea, then William Barlais, and died before long. Her sister Eschiva, another daughter of John II of Ibelin-Beirut, in 1280 brought Beirut to a more faithful subject of King Hugh, Humphrey of Montfort, and then to the king's son, Guy.[36]

But Hugh's more serious problem was the stubborn opposition he encountered from the Templars. In 1274, with John of Grailly as mediator, an early dispute between the king and William of Beaujeu, the new grand master of the Temple, was settled, but William could not endure to take orders from the king. A politician with far-reaching views, an important baron of the realm of France, an able leader, hard and ambitious, he had joined forces with his kinsman Charles of Anjou and aimed at expelling the king of Cyprus from Syria. He began by systematically ignoring the rights of the crown; in October 1276 the order purchased the *casal* of La Fauconnerie near Acre from a certain knight. The *assises* of the kingdom required that William of Beaujeu should ask for the king's approval of this purchase, but he did not do so. Hugh III, who was grieving the recent loss of his father Henry 'du Prince', shipwrecked and drowned between Acre and Cyprus on 27 June 1276, could not put up with this fresh insult. He had been in conflict with the Templars since 1275 in the county of Tripoli, where he had been refused the regency for his cousin Bohemond VII; between 1278 and 1282 the Templars and the young Bohemond fought a bitter and bloody war, with ravages and atrocities on both sides. Exasperated by these problems, unable to restore royal authority, Hugh left Acre, on account of the La Fauconnerie matter and "of several other grounds of complaint he had against the orders, the communes, and the brotherhoods, whom he could not rule nor bring to his will".[37]

The people of Acre were distressed at their chief lord's desertion, and the orders, the fraternities and some of the Italians went to Tyre to ask Hugh to resume the government. The Venetians and William of Beaujeu refrained from joining in this request. Hugh could not, therefore, alter his decision, but he agreed to appoint officials in order to ensure the legal exercise of power. He once again made the constable Balian of Ibelin-Arsuf *bayle* of the kingdom, and then set sail for Cyprus, after writing to the pope and the kings of the West to explain that he was powerless to rule in such anarchy.

This was William of Beaujeu's moment. His envoys went to Rome to find Princess Mary, who had never laid aside her claim to the throne of Jerusalem. Not daring to appear before the high court of Jerusalem, she had taken her case to the Roman curia in 1272. Gregory X ordered an enquiry to be made into her case in October 1272, but it dragged on, with Hugh III's counsel maintaining that disputes over possession of the crown came under the jurisdiction of the court of the barons of Jerusalem. Mary did, however, in 1276 succeed in having the question called before the court of Rome. The near abdication of Hugh III was bound to benefit her cause.[38]

Accession of Charles of Anjou

Most important of all, Mary had joined forces with Charles of Anjou. He had taken Sicily from Manfred, Frederick II's bastard, and then adopted the ambitious schemes of the Hohenstaufens and the Italian-Norman kings both in Italy and in the East. He wanted the Empire of the East, and, moreover, he wanted too to bear his predecessors' title of king of Jerusalem. In 1275 he was to be found supporting the preparations of his vassal, Hugh of Lecce, count of Brienne, for a campaign against Cyprus.[39] As soon as Mary of Antioch managed to get her case reheard before the curia, during a vacancy of the papal throne, she set about preparing to cede her rights to Charles of Anjou. At the end of 1276, or rather early in 1277, on 15 January, in the presence of the greater part of the cardinals assembled together, she solemnly made over to the king of Sicily her rights to Jerusalem, as established by judges and lawyers, in return for an annuity. The authenticated deeds drawn up by the lawyers were the sole and highly disputable claim Charles of Anjou could put forward to the Latin kingdom, and rested on the seller's kinship to a queen of Jerusalem who had been dead for seventy years.[40]

William of Beaujeu's secretary, well informed about these events, implies that it was fear of finding himself in conflict with Charles of Anjou which inspired Hugh III to leave Acre; if it were so, he would thus have avoided being present in Acre when Charles' representative arrived there.[41] This was Roger of San Severino, count of Marsico, who reached the Holy Land in the spring of 1277 with a small fleet and some knights, and immediately installed himself in the Templars' castle. Balian of Arsuf, the *bayle* of Acre, summoned to deliver the king's castle to the count of Marsico, endeavoured to put up a show of resistance, but the barons of Acre, however much they might favour the Lusignans, did not dare oppose Charles of Anjou and the might of the Templars any more than King Hugh had done. Once the Templars had introduced Roger into the fortress, Balian had to withdraw, which he did on 7 June 1277. Obtaining the homage of the vassals of the crown and recognition as *bayle* was more difficult, but the feudatories had to do as they were bid when Roger threatened them with expulsion from the land and the confiscation of their fiefs and homes. Hugh III was unable to offer them any advice, despite his anger at being thus dispossessed. Even Bohemond VII of Antioch did homage to Charles of Anjou.

As in 1226 to 1231, the kingdom was once more under the control of the 'Longobards', led this time by Roger of San Severino, "royal *bayle* and vicar general of the kingdom of Jerusalem." The new *bayle*'s first care was to remove Frankish nobles from important posts and to replace them with devoted servants of the house of Anjou. The seneschalsy, vacant since John of Grailly had gone to be the king of England's seneschal in Gascony, was given to a knight from Champagne, Odo Poilechien, nephew of Simon of Brie, who as Pope Martin IV was to become Charles of Anjou's keen supporter. The constableship, held until then by Balian of Ibelin-Arsuf, or possibly by his son John from 1272, was entrusted to Richard of

Neublans, a knight from Burgundy who had probably reached Sicily in the retinue of Queen Margaret of Burgundy. The post of marshal went to a baron of Acre, James Vidal, who in 1269 had had the right of Hugh III to the crown in opposition to Princess Mary proclaimed in the high court; this post was the reward for his adherence.[42] As for the viscountcy of Acre, William of Fleury had to yield it to Gerard Le Raschas.

The new *bayle* was even able to make use of the French garrison. Like the patriarch and the grand master of the Hospital, its commander, William of Roussillon, refused to support Balian of Arsuf on 7 June 1277. San Severino himself appointed his replacement when William died in 1277 before Odo Poilechien arrived to take over command of the little troop. In order to bring all the nobles and citizens to his side Charles had his rights proclaimed from the pulpits, and got the pope to appoint one of his familiars, Hugh of Tours, bishop of Troja, to the see of Bethlehem. Hugh was to combat in the Holy Land the effect of the declarations made before the curia by the king of Cyprus. (The case was re-opened on 28 March 1279, and the bishop was translated to the see of Bethlehem on 5 October.)

Once again the Holy Land depended not on the poor but nearby kingdom of Cyprus, united to the Latin kingdom by common interests, but upon the distant throne of Sicily. The disastrous effect of this subordination was made clear during the Mongol expedition of 1281; in December 1280 Syria, although hoping to profit by the campaign in which Cyprus and Tripoli were preparing to help the Mongols, realized that the wars in which the king of Sicily was engaged would rob her of all assistance. The bishop of Hebron's letter to Edward I shows clearly what little use Angevin rule was for the defence of Acre.[43] The good relations existing between Charles of Anjou and the sultan of Cairo did not guarantee security for the Franks of Syria, as the letter just referred to shows, but they paralysed the Franks' action abroad. Charles was indeed considering a crusade, but postponed it while attending to other matters, and by the time he died on 7 January 1285, a few weeks before the death of Martin IV on 28 March, the Holy Land was in practice lost, in spite of the interest in its fate declared by so many people.

Charles' authority, however, had not met the same opposition as that of Frederick II, although it was not accepted with enthusiasm. The king of Sicily had the prestige of being the brother of St Louis and was the true head of France outside her borders, commanding the obedience of the former Norman kingdom of Sicily, already almost completely Italianized, the principality of the Morea and the remains of the Latin Empire of Constantinople. Nor was Roger of San Severino the active and brutal commander that Filangieri had been; he enjoyed the support of the Temple and the neutrality of the other orders, and with the exception of Genoa, the Italian communes also supported him. He was able in 1281 to give judgement in favour of the Hospital in a lawsuit between that order and the Pisans concerning the guard of a stretch of the walls of Acre, from the St Anthony to the Maupas Gate, without setting the Tuscan commune against him.[44] We may, however, wonder whether the king of Sicily's rule in Acre was not endured rather than welcomed; loyalty to Hugh III remained lively, and the Frankish nobility were slow in giving their adherence to Charles.

Return of the Lusignans

San Severino was not accepted by the whole of the former kingdom. Tyre seems to have remained faithful to the king of Cyprus; John of Montfort was Hugh III's brother-in-law. The Venetians at last consented on 1 July 1277 to be reconciled with the lord of Tyre, but it was thanks to the mediation of William of Beaujeu, not of the Angevin *bayle*. And Tyre was to be Hugh III's base of operations for the recovery of his kingdom. Hugh gathered a fine army of 700 knights and, disembarking at Tyre in 1278 or 1279, he entered into negotiations with the inhabitants of Acre, pouring out money like water. Many of his supporters, *poulains*, Pisans and others, prepared to come out on his side, but the Templars still stood by the Angevins, and the threat of intervention by these dreaded warriors prevented the pro-Lusignan movement breaking out. And then the knights of Cyprus informed the king that their four months' service outside the island was over, and they re-embarked. Bereft of part of his army, Hugh III had to abandon his attempt, and returned to Cyprus after them. He confiscated all the property of the Templars in the island and demolished their castles; a reconciliation was not reached until 1282.[45]

At this point came a dramatic turn of events. Not perhaps without the instigation of Michael Palaeologus, the people of Sicily rose against the Angevins on 30 March 1282 in the revolt and massacre of the Sicilian Vespers. They then appealed to Peter III, king of Aragon, and a ruthless war ensued between the new king, Peter, and Charles of Anjou, now king only of Naples. Martin IV launched the Aragonese crusade, during which Philip III king of France died. Charles, now at a military disadvantage, saw that he could not hope to maintain his power in the Holy Land, and recalled Roger of San Severino on 14 October 1282 and the bishop of Bethlehem in 1284, giving the post of *bayle* to Odo Poilechien, who still had the support of William of Beaujeu. Hugh III returned to Syria, disembarking on 1 August 1283 at Beirut, where Humphrey of Montfort readily acknowledged his authority. From Beirut he went to Tyre, but while he was travelling by sea, his army, which was marching along the coast, was attacked on 7 August by Saracens in a narrow pass not far from Sidon, between Châtellet and Damur.[46] He lost one knight and some infantry, and was certain the attack had been instigated by the Templars.

Hugh was never to leave Tyre. Ill omens marked his entry into the town: a banner bearing the arms of Lusignan fell into the sea, the leader of the Jewish community dropped dead as he presented the Torah to the king, and other such incidents occurred. And once again the attempt to restore a king to Acre met the opposition of the Templars, who succeeded in delaying it. None the less Hugh III prepared for a Lusignan take-over of Tyre; the death on 27 November 1283 of his brother-in-law John of Montfort, while deeply distressing him, allowed him to dictate terms to John's brother, Humphrey of Montfort, lord of Beirut. Humphrey did homage to the king for what was left of the lordship of Toron and undertook to deliver Tyre to Hugh if the latter paid him 150,000 bezants before the following May. Humphrey's death on 12 February 1284 enabled the king to enfeoff Tyre to his son Amalric of Lusignan.[47] But this final success in Hugh's campaign for his restoration was followed by his own death on 29 March. Angevin rule in Acre thus gained another two years' life, for the task interrupted by the king's death was not continued by his successor, John I, in his too short reign from 11 May 1284 to 20 May 1285, but by John's brother Henry II.

Henry was to complete the task of restoring the monarchy begun by his father. Barely fourteen years old and subject to epileptic attacks which later led to his being deposed by his brother Amalric (1306–1310), he worked for his accession with the same skill and the same desire to avoid civil war as Hugh III had shown. An envoy went from Cyprus to negotiate with the grand master of the Temple, the master of the Hospital acting as mediator, and an agreement was signed putting an end to the misunderstandings which from 1273 to 1284 had kept King Hugh and the order at odds with each other. Henry was then able to prepare for his return to Acre. On 24 June 1286 a fine fleet brought the king of Cyprus and his chivalry to the great city, and the people greeted their young king with acclamations. They came in procession to welcome him as he stepped ashore, and led him to the cathedral. The Angevin *bayle* had taken refuge in the castle, where he summoned the Neapolitan and French troops to him; being seneschal as well as *bayle*, Odo had command of these forces. Not all of them obeyed his summons. The siege of the royal castle lasted only a few days; the grand masters of the orders took a hand, and Henry II agreed to take up his residence in the palace of the lord of Tyre and to do no more than blockade Odo. At the same time he had it proclaimed that the French soldiers, although in the service of the king of Sicily, were not regarded as enemies, and that he undertook to submit his claim to the kingdom to the arbitration of the king of France.[48] Anjou's *bayle* therefore surrendered the fortress to the king of Cyprus as soon as he could do so without dishonour, that is, when supplies of food ran out, on 29 June.

The coronation of the young Henry II in the cathedral of Tyre on 15 August 1285 after half a century without a king marked the end of the anarchy in which the kingdom had floundered. The union of Cyprus and Jerusalem, aimed at in previous times by Aimery through the betrothal of his eldest son to Princess Mary of Jerusalem-Montferrat, was now at last firmly realized. Henceforth the lord of the kingdom and the king were one and the same. The nobles of Jerusalem and the military orders had at last come to see the need for a stronger power, now that the kingdom was under threat and consisted only of a few cities in a hostile land. The danger of war between the Italians that occurred in 1287 was averted, thanks to the efforts of all. But what hope had the Latin kingdom of withstanding the power of the Mamluk empire, now preparing its supreme assault? The fortnight's festivities that celebrated the last coronation in Acre were Acre's last festivities. The fall of Tripoli in 1288, following hard upon the fall of Lattakieh in 1287, marked the beginning of Frankish Syria's final collapse.

CHAPTER 9

The fall of Acre

Western Europe had long been aware of the desperate situation of its colonies in Syria. In 1274 the council of Lyons was summoned to take steps to avert the imminent catastrophe. But nothing was done. Various popes repeatedly preached a crusade, various kings took the cross with the firm intention of setting out for the East, but unfortunately the West was exceptionally disturbed at the end of the thirteenth century. The kings of Sicily, Aragon and France were in the throes of a terrible struggle, itself seen as a crusade, for the possession of Sicily, a conflict that had troubled the peace of Europe since the death of Frederick Barbarossa. While Charles of Anjou, Peter III of Aragon, Philip the Bold and after him Philip the Fair thus had to keep postponing their preparations for a crusade, and in so doing hindered the action of other monarchs such as the king of Castile, who began to gather a fleet in 1280,[1] the real leader of a future crusade, Edward I of England, was totally taken up with his struggle with Llewelyn ap Griffith and the great Welsh revolt. Edward was sincerely concerned for the Holy Land, and letters that he wrote to the pope are interesting: he approves of the preaching of the crusade and declares his intention of taking part, but each time asks for a further postponement because the urgency of affairs in his kingdom does not permit him to devote himself to the Syrian question as he wishes.[2] And when in 1287 and 1288 a Mongol bishop came from the khan of Persia to arouse the zeal of the princes of Christendom, he everywhere found understanding and good will, but was not able to take any positive result back to his sovereign.

Meanwhile the Mongol alliance repeatedly offered to the Christian princes was becoming more specific. Arghun appointed a rendezvous for the Christian armies to meet on about 20 February 1291 beneath the walls of Damascus, and promised the king of France horses for his knights if they had difficulty transporting their own mounts, and all necessary supplies of food. But the French and English armies did not set off.[3] Nicholas IV was doing all he could, but the papacy had not the resources to save the Holy Land by itself.

The fall of Tripoli and preparations for defence

The Holy Land was in no condition to oppose the Mamluks, who invaded the country in 1288, taking advantage of a revolt in Tripoli against the heiress of the county. In spite of the warnings of William of Beaujeu, no one had made any preparations to defend the town, although in 1285 the Mamluks conquered Margat and Maraclea, its defenders to the north, and in 1287 took Lattakieh, the last stronghold in the principality of Antioch. The king of Cyprus immediately sent his brother Amalric to Tripoli, and the marshals of the Temple and the Hospital together with John of Grailly, who had been restored to his command of the French garrison of Acre, also hastened thither, but they could not prevent the fall of the town on 26 April 1289. Henry II arrived in Acre on 24 April to defend his kingdom of Jerusalem against the coming Saracen attack.

   In Acre and in Cyprus men saw clearly that the end was approaching. The Frankish strongholds of the former kingdom of Jerusalem were now the only ones left; not only had they been cut off from Armenia and from the Mongols since 1268, but they did not even have secure communications among themselves. The Mamluk sultans' policy was systematically to reduce the Franks to the possession of the route along the coast and the *casals* of the plain; this was clearly shown in the sultan's treaty of 1283 with the lordship of Acre, Sidon and Châtel Pèlerin, belonging to the Templars and Acre, which recognized only the authority of Odo Poilechien the *bayle*; in the treaty of 1285 with Tyre, where the lady, widow of Humphrey of Montfort, acknowledged Hugh III as king; and in the treaty with Beirut. Except for Mount Carmel, all the hill country was in the hands of the Moslems, who were quick to intercept travellers along the coast; the passage of the Nahr Damur between Sidon and Beirut was dangerous, as Hugh III found in 1283. The district of Scandelion between Tyre and Casal Humbert was divided between Franks and Moslems; in 1280 thirty Christians were killed on this road in a short space of time.[4] War nearly broke out in 1289; the sultan, angered by the assistance given by the Templars, the Hospitallers and the king of Cyprus to the defenders of Tripoli, accused them of breaking the truce; the Franks managed to convince him, however, that the truce had been correctly observed in the kingdom itself, and Henry even obtained a renewal of the truce for ten years and ten months.[5]

The Franks of Syria needed to obtain the longest possible respite in the hope that a crusade would be launched. Henry II left Acre on 26 September 1289, his rescue mission accomplished, entrusting the *baylie* of the kingdom to his brother Amalric, prince of Tyre and constable of the kingdom of Jerusalem (the previous constable Baldwin of Ibelin had recently died), but before he left he sent the seneschal John of Grailly to the pope. Much disturbed, Nicholas IV wrote to tell the Christian kings of the deadly peril in which the Holy Land was placed, and began at once to send help; he made a loan of 4,000 *livres tournois* to the new patriarch Nicholas, to be spent on the fortifications of Acre, the building of war machines and the redemption of prisoners. On 13 September 1289 John of Grailly and the bishop of Tripoli were appointed to take twenty galleys to the Holy Land, to be stationed there for a year.[6]

The pope sought to send more help than this. He had a crusade preached and fixed the day of its departure for 24 June 1293, the date chosen by Edward I, who had taken the cross. He negotiated with Genoa, Venice and the other maritime cities for the dispatch of ships to the East. Contingents of Italian crusaders were already embarking under the command of Hugh Le Roux of Sully, a French captain in the service of the king of Naples. They were to stay in the Holy Land for a year, but they came home in 1290 on the pretext that Acre had not been attacked. Sicilian galleys obtained by John of Grailly from King James I of Sicily did the same. The pope even went to the length of seeking a reconciliation with James I in order to ensure the success of the crusade; by a treaty of July 1290 the Aragonese king of Sicily promised to send twenty galleys, 1,000 men-at-arms and 1,000 cross-bowmen in September 1291, and in 1292 these galleys and another twenty carried 400 knights, 1,000 other men-at-arms (*almugavares*) and 1,000 crossbowmen to Syria. In 1289 the king of England sent troops under Otto of Grandson. The pope supplied further sums of money, agreed to take the Sicilians onto his pay-roll and authorized the patriarch of Jerusalem to appoint commanders of the fleet and the crusading army.[7] At the same time more and more active negotiations with the Mongols were carried on, and the plan of the future campaign was carefully prepared. The Hospitallers drew up a detailed project for an invasion of Egypt, the *Devise des chemins de Babiloine*, a "list of the roads to Babylon", and a whole literature of recommendations and memoranda on the coming campaign sprang into existence.[8]

But Egyptian diplomacy was not idle; while the pope was negotiating with the maritime cities, the Mamluk sultan was entering into a treaty of friendship with the Genoese, who had made some reprisal raids after the fall of Tripoli. The treaty gave them advantages outweighing the damage done to their trade by the capture of Tripoli. And on 25 April 1290 King James of Sicily and King Alfonso of Aragon concluded a treaty of non-aggression with Egypt; it authorized the export of weapons and iron to Alexandria, and the Aragonese sovereigns promised not to support any crusade. In return, their nationals received permission to make the pilgrimage to Jerusalem without hindrance. James I therefore, when sending his ships and troops to the Holy Land, ordered that his galleys should do no more than repel any attacks made by Saracen craft, and his men should in no circumstances injure the lands or vassals of the sultan.[9] On 21 October 1290 the pope himself at the request of the merchants of Syria authorized trade with Egypt, even such trade as was normally forbidden, during the period of the truce, to avoid the destruction of the Holy Land.[10]

The war and siege of Acre

Probably the Mamluks only signed these treaties in order to detach possible enemies from the coalition now forming, and were merely waiting for a pretext on which to rid themselves of the dangerous Latin enclaves where the Mongols, their chief enemies, could always find allies. And this pretext was supplied by the very crusade sent by the West to protect Acre against possible attack. The crusaders who arrived in Acre in 1290 from central Italy and Lombardy were very ill spoken of by the chroniclers; one says that a "horde of pseudo-Christians arrived in the town, who had taken the cross to obtain pardon for their crimes". He speaks of their boastfulness, which melted like snow with the approach of the enemy, and of their idleness, spending their days in taverns and places of pleasure.[11] One day in August 1290 they posted themselves at the gates of Acre, the suburbs of which were all Moslem or Syriac, and began the extermination of the Saracens by massacring some thirty Arab peasants and a number of Melchite Syrians. They killed the latter because they did not like their beards, for Westerners in the thirteenth century were clean-shaven. Then they attacked a caravanserai, where the Moslem merchants had scarcely time to barricade themselves in. These merchants belonged to fraternities under the protection of the Temple and the Hospital, and knights of these orders came up in time to relieve the siege and conduct them in safety to the king's castle, although not before nineteen of them, it was said, had been killed in the market, near the Exchange.

The sultan took up this affair[12] and broadcast it to the world; it was even reported that Egyptian ambassadors had been killed in the massacre. He demanded that the authorities in Acre should surrender the murderers to him, knowing perfectly well that they could not deliver crusaders into the hands of Moslems. William of Beaujeu, grand master of the Temple and an astute politician, produced a scheme that the heads of the other two orders thought well of: could they not give the Mamluks the criminals in their jails? This idea, eloquent of the Templars' unscrupulous zeal (they paid for their sins twenty years later), was rejected by the other leaders meeting in the council of war. These were: the patriarch, the bishop of Tripoli, Amalric of Lusignan the *bayle*, Otto of Grandson the Swiss knight representing the king of England, John of Grailly the knight from Gascony representing the king of France, the Venetian *bayle* and the Pisan consul; and also perhaps the commanders of the Venetian fleet, Giacomo Tiepolo, and of the small squadron sent by the church, Roger of *Thodinis*.[13] They sent apologies to Cairo. The truce was broken.

The sultan put extensive preparations in hand, officially intended for a campaign in Africa. He did not deceive the grand master of the Temple, who had agents in Qalawun's entourage, but he duped all the other notables of Acre. The sultan died, but the expedition was not delayed; his successor the young al-Ashraf promptly gave orders for his troops and the vast quantities of siege material collected in Syria to be assembled in the plain of Acre, where the Franks were struck with fear at the Moslems' numbers. This young man, much the same age as Henry II, the twenty-year old king of Cyprus and Jerusalem, was to complete the task that Saladin had not been able to finish a hundred years before, the final expulsion of the Franks from Syria.[14]

The siege about to begin did not resemble the long blockade and slow operations of the siege of Acre in 1189–1191; the means employed by the Mamluks enabled them to finish with their adversaries speedily. To the 70,000 horsemen and 150,000 foot attributed to the Moslems, the whole population of Acre could only oppose some 40,000 inhabitants, 700 of whom were knights and squires and 800 infantry. Including the reinforcements brought by the crusading army, the Latins had some 15,000 fighting men.[15] It is true that the carefully maintained ramparts of Acre presented a formidable obstacle. Already very strong at the beginning of the thirteenth century, they had been constantly added to and improved. New work had been carried out by King Hugh III, by Prince Edward of England, by King Henry II and in 1287 by the countess of Blois. The town was enclosed by a double line of walls: the great wall, with its towers protected by barbicans, wooden outposts linked to the curtain wall by wooden or stone bridges, was itself defended by another wall bristling with strong towers and protected by yet more barbicans. Inside the town two quarters, the Bourg and the Town, each with its own viscount, were separated by the original twelfth-century wall, against which the king's castle stood.[16] Each block of buildings, with its towers and strongholds, could offer fresh resistance, and the headquarters of the Templars, the Hospitallers and the Teutonic Knights were particularly capable of holding out under attack.

But al-Ashraf had equally formidable means of attack at his disposal. In secret, and despite the snow winter had brought to the passes, he had had prepared and brought from all over Syria his war machines, the medium-sized catapults called *qara bugha* and two gigantic mangonels, Victorious and Furious, each of which needed 100 wagons to move it. Enormous missiles knocked down sections of the walls and towers. The sultan also relied upon mining; he allocated a team of 1,000 sappers to each of the towers under attack, Henry II's New Tower, King Hugh's barbican, the towers of the countess of Blois and of St Nicholas, in fact the whole projecting corner section of the walls, the most vulnerable part. The outlets of the town drains and the butchers' drain provided the sappers with a beginning for their tunnels. Attempts at negotiation failed in the face of the sultan's determination; the first envoys were thrown into prison, and those sent by William of Beaujeu were politely turned away. When King Henry arrived on 4 May accompanied by the archbishop of Nicosia and bringing 40 galleys, 200 knights and 500 infantrymen, he reopened the talks. Al-Ashraf replied that he intended to have the place whether or no, but out of respect for the king, who was his own age, he would be content with the stones of the town and would allow the Franks to depart with all their possessions. The king's envoys said that this would disgrace Henry in the eyes of the whole of the West. At this moment, enabling al-Ashraf to bring the interview to an end, a lump of stone accidentally released from a Frankish catapult struck the sultan's tent.[17] He drew his scimitar on the envoys, and although his courtiers intervened to prevent him striking, the momentary truce was over, the talks broken off, and the contest began again more bitterly than before. The Moslems' numerical superiority made any sortie impossible; an attempt at one by William of Beaujeu of 15 April had only slight success; the viscount of the Bourg was unable to reach the mangonel Victorious which he was supposed to set on fire, and another attempt was a total failure.

On 8 May King Hugh's barbican, linked to the wall by a wooden bridge, was set on fire by its defenders; Henry II had taken over command of this dangerous sector from his brother Amalric as soon as he arrived.[18] Moslem sappers were now working at the foot of the ramparts; on 15 May a section of the Round Tower, King Henry's New Tower, fell. The Cypriots were able to evacuate the tower while the Mamluks were filling up the fosse with gabions, and were at once replaced by a body of picked men. The space between the walls would soon become untenable and it was necessary to reckon with the imminent fall of the whole of the outer wall. It was decided to evacuate the women and children to Cyprus. This was feasible as the Frankish fleet had command of the sea, but on 17 May the sea was so stormy that the evacuees had to come ashore again. Meanwhile a wooden rampart was built behind the New Tower, while its last defenders held out to the death inside the tower. On 16 May a Moslem assault on the breach in the outer wall near the St Anthony Gate was thrown back and the breach filled by a palisade. But on 18 May the final assault was launched. The attackers burned down the wall surrounding the New Tower, and succeeded in capturing the stone barbican next to the Accursed Tower, which stood on the projecting corner of the inner wall corresponding to the New Tower on the outer wall, and they gained a footing on the curtain wall before the Latins could destroy the stone bridge which the attackers captured in their first rush. In response to this danger, for the Moslems were already attacking both southwards and westwards within the space between the two walls, the grand masters of the Temple and the Hospital in a valiant counter-attack attempted with a handful of men to retake the barbican and to drive the countless Moslems out of the first enceinte. The unceasing rain of enemy arrows and Greek fire frustrated this heroic attempt; William of Beaujeu was mortally wounded and John of Villiers, grand master of the Hospital, and John of Grailly were seriously injured and put aboard ship. The marshal of the Hospital continued to defend the St Anthony Gate and Otto of Grandson that of St Nicholas, but the defenders of the Accursed Tower were disheartened by William of Beaujeu's death and left their post. The Moslems could thus place their ladders against the wall unhindered and took the tower, rendering vain any further resistance from the adjacent sectors.[19]

The fight continued, however, in the streets of the city. Debouching from the Accursed Tower, the Mamluks took the St Romain quarter and the huge catapult set up there by the Pisans. After a violent struggle the quarter of the Teutonic Knights was taken, and the knights of St Thomas[20] stood and died in the approaches to the church of St Leonard. The St Nicholas Gate, the Legate's Tower and the St Anthony Gate fell in their turn, and gave admittance to the sultan's massed columns. The town was lost; it was impossible to hold out longer in the king's castle or in the Bourg or in the castle of the Hospitallers. The last defenders fell back towards the harbour. Matthew of Clermont, the marshal of the Hospital, although wounded, together with his brother knights held back the enemy at the harbour entrance so as to let as many Christians as possible make their escape. The last Hospitallers died with their brave leader in the rue des Gênois.

Unfortunately, the evacuation was not easy. There were plenty of boats available, but the low water prevented vessels of any size entering the harbour; only small boats could get in, and this need for transhipment proved disastrous. The wounded, the king of Cyprus and his brother, wrongly accused of being among the first to embark, for the king did not leave Acre until after the fall of the Genoese quarter, succeeded in reaching the ships, as did Otto of Grandson and a good number of other knights, but the mass of the refugees flung themselves on the boats in panic. The boat carrying the patriarch Nicholas,[21] the mainstay of the defence, sank beneath the weight of its occupants, as did several others. In the town, the Mamluks slew the Dominicans, singing *Salve Regina* as they waited for martydom, the Franciscans and many monks and laymen. Very soon the slaughter reached those who were waiting for the boats. Only those who had been able to take refuge in the Templars' stronghold near the harbour escaped death or enslavement. As long as the marshal of the Temple, Peter of Sevrey,[22] and his knights defended this five-towered fortress, the Christians' boats could continue the evacuation of the inhabitants. After several days of siege the Mamluks offered the Templars terms by which all those who had fled to the castle could depart freely. The small Moslem troop allowed into the enceinte fouled the chapel and raped women, and the agreement was cancelled. A second agreement was also broken and Peter of Sevrey killed by treachery. The last survivors then took up their arms again and in spite of the mines which brought their walls crashing down, fought to the end. In the assault of 28 May the undermined castle fell, crushing the few remaining Templars and many Mamluks.

Collapse of the kingdom

The impregnable fortress which had defied the assaults of Baibars had fallen, despite a glorious defence in which the Templars and the Hospitallers redeemed all the faults into which pride and greed had led them, a defence in which the royal house of Jerusalem shared, and despite all the efforts of the papacy "which had carefully provided for the needs of this city in ships, in warriors, in supplies of money; in forty-four days it fell."[23] The rest of the Holy Land did not show the same courage, so shattering was the effect of the fall of Acre. Adam of Cafran, castellan of Tyre, evacuated the second fortress of the kingdom, the fortress which had resisted Saladin's attacks from 1187 to 1189, just as for twenty years it had held the Frankish kings in check. In spite of its triple enceinte, its twelve great towers, its castles and its almost impregnable position, Adam did not think it his duty to defend Tyre and withdrew "out of terror" on the day the Saracens entered Acre. The Mamluks occupied Tyre on 19 May and enslaved those whom their unworthy commander had left behind.[24] Sidon, where Theobald Gaudin, commander of the Temple, took over command after leaving Acre, held out longer, but being quite without help it was completely evacuated on 14 July. Then it was Beirut's turn; despite the Moslem protectorate over this lordship, Beirut fell by treason on 21 July. Cayphas fell on 30 July, and the monks of Mount Carmel too sang *Salve Regina* as they died for their faith.[25] The Templars' last fortresses in Syria, Tortosa and Châtel Pèlerin, were evacuated on the 3 and 14 August 1291. No Franks but slaves or renegades were left in the Holy Land, and such as did manage to escape had many hardships to endure. Roger Blum, a Templar from Germany, embarked on a strange career in which he became successively a banished man, then, as Roger of Flor, captain of the Catalan Company, a son-in-law of the tsar of the Bulgars and a Byzantine Caesar, before he died murdered in 1305; now he was busy making appalling profits from the ladies who embarked on his Frankish ship the *Falcon*. He had to flee in consequence, but took the money with him.[26]

Al-Ashraf went to hold triumph at Damascus, after having slaughtered the prisoners who were not being kept for slavery and who would not abjure their faith. He had the town of Acre and the castles of Sidon and Châtel Pèlerin demolished and the door of the cathedral of Holy Cross taken to Cairo to adorn the mosque and tomb of the sultan al-Nasir.[27] And he made plans for future campaigns against the Armenians (he captured the fort of Hromgla in 1292) and perhaps against Cyprus. Death, however, prevented him from fulfilling his intentions; he died assassinated in 1293 and Christians saw in his death the hand of God.

Once again Frankish Syria had crumbled at a blow, once again countless refugees were in flight, just as in 1187. In the West there was the same horrified amazement, and the same anger against those who were held to blame. For some, such as the author of the *Excidium Acconis*, Henry II, king of Jerusalem, was responsible, for others it was the papacy which had sacrificed Syria to its Sicilian policy; moralists blamed the foul sins of the great trading city, which recalled to the ageing Joinville the prophetic words of the legate Odo of Châteauroux forty years earlier, that they would be washed away in the blood of the inhabitants. Others blamed the quarrels of the Italians, others again the fratricidal strife of the Templars and the Hospitallers. All this bitterness, skilfully organized by Philip the

Fair's lawyers, gathered to a head in anger with the order of the Templars, betrayers of Christendom.[28] Without waiting to work out exactly what blame should be laid at whose door, Nicholas IV was preparing a major expedition to halt the Moslem conquest – Cyprus was already trembling – and to recover Acre and the Holy Land. With the Sicilian problem at last settled, he asked all Christian princes to take the cross, or at least to send money, ships and men to save the Latin East. Edward I, as usual, took the lead in the movement. To avoid the dissensions which had been fatal to Frankish Syria, provincial councils were to meet to study the problem of the recovery of the Holy Land. In August 1291 Nicholas IV repeated the suggestion made at the council of Lyons in 1274 that the Templars and Hospitallers should combine to form a single order. Lastly a total blockade of Egypt was promulgated.[29]

The pope took immediate steps to save Cyprus and Armenia, which were directly threatened. In January 1292 the troops sent by the papacy to the relief of Acre were ordered to Armenia, whose king had sent an appeal for help to the West by the hand of the Franciscan Thomas of Tolentino, who died a martyr some years later near Bombay.[30] Otto of Grandson went to help the Armenians in their struggle with the sultan, and a papal fleet headed for the Eastern Mediterranean where it attacked the Turkish fort of Candelore and then threatened Alexandria. And yet the crusade from the West never set off. Philip the Fair did not move, Edward I, more deeply involved than ever with the Welsh and the Scots, did not leave for the East. Greater reliance than before was placed on help from the Tartars for a joint action, but with the death of the khan Arghun their cooperation became less likely, and the Westerners only sent small, scrappy expeditions to the East. As for the Genoese and the Venetians, they began another war against each other in 1292.

The attempted reconquest of 1299

Yet one last chance offered an unexpected opportunity to make the Holy Land once again into a Latin kingdom of Jerusalem. Cyprus, although swamped by a flood of refugees and reduced to great need, still remained the base from which a fresh crusade might be launched. Armenia, vassal of the Mongols, had called the Mongols to her aid, and the new khan Ghazan, convert to Islam though he was, was preparing to help the king of Armenia. He opened negotiations with King Henry II for a new campaign in Syria. On 21 October 1299 his envoy 'Cariedin', a Christian, arrived and proposed to the king of Cyprus and the three grand masters a joint action first against Damascus and then against Egypt. The grand master of the Temple and the commander of the Hospital were unable to agree, and when another envoy arrived on 30 November, nothing was ready. The Tartars, the Armenians and the Georgians defeated the Mamluks at Homs on 24 December 1299 without help from the Cypriots.

However, while the vanquished fled before their enemies as far as Gaza, Henry II sent a landing force to the Syrian coast, where the Mamluks still remained. 400 knights and Turcopols, with sixty archers and crossbowmen, formed the vanguard; they had orders from the king to attack the coast of the county of Tripoli. They disembarked at Le Boutron, where they were to fortify the castle of Nephin while waiting for the royal army to arrive. Unfortunately, encouraged by the arrival of some Maronite contingents from the Lebanon, the Franks made an attack upon the new city of Tripoli, which had been built inland so that no future crusading expedition could gain a footing on the peninsula. They were defeated and the Frankish commanders killed; the Lebanese troops dispersed and the rest re-embarked. Guy of Ibelin, count of Jaffa, did however capture Jebail with a Genoese fleet, but he could not maintain himself there. A small fleet under the admiral Baldwin of Picquigny set sail from Famagusta on 20 July 1300 carrying a landing party commanded by Raymond Visconti. Meanwhile the king, the prince of Tyre, the leaders of the two orders and Ghazan's ambassador Chiol failed to agree on a plan of campaign. Chiol sailed with the landing force and took part in the expedition. They landed at Rosetta, where they freed some Tartar captives,[31] and the 100 cavalry who had gone ashore laid waste a village. The ships made a demonstration off Alexandria and then sailed up the coast of Syria landing again at Acre and then at Tortosa, where they defeated some small Moslem detachments. A little further north at Maraclea the Hospitallers lost one knight and twenty infantrymen. The expedition returned to Cyprus with no very great results but able to confirm that the Moslems were in a state of disarray. The Cypriot army of 300 knights went with 300 Templars and the Hospitallers to take up a position on the coast of Tripoli and wait for Ghazan, who was to open a winter campaign against Egypt in November 1300. They occupied the island of Ruad, of which the

Templars were granted a part, and the town of Tortosa, but the Tartars did not come.

Next Guy of Ibelin-Jaffa and John, lord of Gibelet (Jebail), went to meet Qutlugh Shah, commander of the Mongol army of 40,000 horse which had at last arrived near Antioch in February 1301. Qutlugh Shah told them that Ghazan was ill, and that he, with his reduced forces, could not do more than raid the country round Aleppo; as for the Cypriots, they had had to evacuate Tortosa at the approach of a Mamluk force. The interior of Syria, however, remained in the hands of the Mongols, who appointed as governor of Damascus an Egyptian emir who had gone over to them. Qutlugh Shah had to leave for Iran, as the khan of Turkestan was attacking the eastern frontier of Ghazan's empire. He left 20,000 men in the Jordan valley under the command of Mulai.

Ghazan realized how difficult he would find it to keep his conquests and suggested to the Westerners that as Syria could easily be taken – there were only some small garrisons on the coast, scarcely strong enough to repel the weak Cypriot army – they should come and occupy the kingdom of Jerusalem. In May 1300 James II of Aragon offered galleys, ships, soldiers and mounts to the khan of Persia for the conquest of the Holy Land, asking for a fifth part of the territory for himself. As for Ghazan, he had declared to the king of Armenia early in 1300: "King of Armenia, we would gladly have delivered the lands of Syria to the Christians to hold, if they had come; and if they do come we leave our orders with Cotolossa [Qutlugh Shah] that he is to return the Holy Land to the Christians and give them counsel and aid in restoring the waste lands." And he wrote asking the pope towards the end of 1301 to send troops, prelates, clergy and also agricultural workers to repopulate the land and set up in it a network of colonists as strong as that of the twelfth century. The pope agreed to this, and in 1302 was doing what he could to fulfil Ghazan's request.

But it was already too late. Ghazan's long absence and the dila-toriness of the Westerners enabled the governor of Damascus to betray the Mongols, delivering his fortresses to the Mamluks in 1301, and Mulai's small army had to fall back on the Euphrates. That year, as we saw, Qutlugh Shah could bring only a small force which was unable even to effect a junction with the Cypriots at Tortosa. Ghazan returned in 1302, and the Tartar army reoccupied Hama and moved upon Damascus. On 3 May 1303 it was defeated before Damascus and the Euphrates became once again the frontier of the Mongol Empire.[32]

So this unlooked-for chance of reconquering the Holy Land was lost, and the precarious Christian hold on the coast of Syria at Ruad did not survive for long. The pope gave the island to the Templars in 1301, but they did not have time to build a castle there; in 1303, in the absence of a Frankish fleet, the sultan landed a small army on the island. The Templars held out bravely under the command of Brother Hugh of Ampurias, but their numbers were reduced by the departure of one of their commanders shortly before the attack, and a relief force failed to arrive. In Cyprus a fleet was fitted out to go to the island's help, but it was learned that the Saracens had brought the Templars to bay on a hill and offered Brother Hugh honourable terms of surrender which he accepted. In breach of their given word the Mamluks took the 120 knights captive to Cairo and beheaded the garrison's 500 Syrian archers.[33]

With the loss of Ruad, the Franks' last stronghold in Syria was gone. The Cypriots later made a few raids, but these could not restore Latin rule to the country. The kingdom of Acre had had its day, and it was in 1291 that it perished. Sapped by internal discords, the "blessed unity" produced by Baibars' attacks did not save it; help from the West never reached it in time; Angevin rule prevented it taking part in the Mongol campaign of 1281. Mongol aid itself was not always there when most needed. The opportunity offered in 1260 never came again, except when it was too late in 1299. Mongol khans and Christian princes, each preoccupied by troubles in Sicily, Aragon, Wales, wars of succession, wars in the Caucasus and Afghanistan, were unable to devote their full attention to Syria, or to co-ordinate their efforts, Left to itself, assisted only piecemeal, as small contingents arrived from time to time, the Holy Land had nothing with which to face the united Mamluk empire but a few hundred disunited knights. The restoration of the monarchy in 1286 came too late; the feverish efforts of the pope and the orders before the last attack produced nothing but promises. All that the last Frankish knights could do was to die fighting before the Accursed Tower; the last Templars, Hospitallers and Teutonic Knights died in the streets, in the towers, and before the gates of Acre, with courage as noble as that of the heroes of the old kingdom of Jerusalem. But nothing could save the Holy Land after it decreed its own damnation in 1244 and 1260, years when internal dissensions reached a peak while the increasing external danger was met in the kingdom of the *Assises* with the blankest incomprehension. After nearly two hundred years of life Frankish Syria finally ceased to exist, but no one could deny that it had had its moments of glory.

Notes to Part 3

Part 3

[1]Separate truces made between different lordships, now independent, and the Moslems, posed a serious threat to the kingdom. A letter from Urban IV (*Registres*, ed. J. Guiraud, ii. 867), dated 18 July 1264, emphasises the danger of this practice and rebukes those guilty of it. The form of this letter clearly shows the extent of the anarchy, then at its worst; it is addressed to all who hold authority in the kingdom, and the list is a long one: to the patriarch, to the prelates, "also to the masters of the houses of the militia of the Temple, of St John, of St Mary of the Teutonic Knights, and to Geoffrey of Sergines, seneschal, Henry, *bayle*, John of Jebail, marshal, John, count of Jaffa, John, lord of Beirut, and to the other nobles, to the consuls of the communes, to the rectors of the confraternities ..." Nothing could be more eloquent of the disappearance of the king's authority.

[2]The Guelf-Ghibelline wars in Syria were not solely an extension of those already long established in Italy, although the presence of numerous Italians in Syria did affect their development; they were principally the result of the same causes that operated in the peninsula. The accession of a foreign dynasty in the Syrian kingdom, as in the Lombard one, and the non-residence of the monarchs, inevitably produced a 'nationalist', Guelf party, and a 'loyalist', or Ghibelline one.

Chapter 1

[1]H. de Ziegler, *Vie de l'empereur Frédéric II*, Paris, 1935, 40. For the Guelf-Ghibelline war, see the studies by La Monte, John d'Ibelin, the Old Lord of Beirut, 1177–1236, in *Byzantion*, xii, 1937, 417–458; *The wars of Frederick II against the Ibelins*, translated from Philip of Novara, Columbia University Press; The communal movement in Syria in the thirteenth century, in *C.H. Haskins anniversary essays*, Boston-New York, 1929, 117.

[2]See above, page 265, *RR* 974, 1010.

[3]*RR* 1003; *Lois*, i. 325.

[4]*Lois*, ii. 399. Were Balian, Odo and Garnier at Frederick's side at Ravenna in December 1231? See Huillard-Bréholles, iv. 279.

[5]*Lois*, i. 325; *RR* 1003, 1056, 1073, 1120. In compensation Frederick gave Maron to the Teutonic Knights, and a rent of 7,000 bezants on the revenues of Acre, by virtue of Humphrey IV's cession of Toron to the king, by the terms of which these properties, ceded to Humphrey, were to revert to Count Joscelin if Toron were returned to Humphrey. This caused further problems with James of La Mandelée, ended only in 1244. See Riley-Smith, *The feudal nobility*, 171–173.

[6]Grousset, iii. 290–293. This is the meaning of John's declaration, "He is my lord; whatever he may do, we will keep our honours [fiefs]".

[7]*Lois*, i. 325.

[8]*Chiprois*, 700. The imperial forces certainly set off in 1231 and not, as was previously thought, in 1230. The news of their arrival reached Cyprus "in the heart of winter," 1231–1232. Riccardo Filangieri gathered his men and embarked in June–July 1231, according to a Sicilian chronicle, which at the same time mentions the confiscation of the Templars' and the Hospitallers' possessions in Sicily; *Richardi de S. Germano Chronicon* in Muratori, *Scriptores*, vii. col. 1027. The Temple's property was still sequestrated in 1250, when Frederick made his will. *Scriptores*, ix. col. 662.

[9]Ernoul, 460–461. Del Giudice, Riccardo Filangieri, in *Archivio storico per le provincie Napoletane*, xv–xvii.

[10]See *Registres de Grégoire IX*, i. 10 (1227). There was a canonical impediment to this marriage.

[11]*Chiprois*, 672–674. In this text Philip of Novara gives us a biased view of the facts. Baldwin of Belesme, a supporter of Queen Alice, was murdered by relatives of Philip of Ibelin; *Lois*, ii. 422. On familial relations between the members of the anti-Ibelin party and the Tripolitan nobility, cf. J. Richard, Le comté de Tripoli dans les chartes du fonds des Porcellet, 352ff.

[12]Grousset, iii. 327–330.

[13]This was a large number (the Syrio-Cypriot army at Agridi in 1232 only included 233 knights) and shows the size of the anti-Ibelin party in Cyprus, perhaps as much as a third of the nobility. See Amadi, 175. After their banishment from Cyprus, numerous knights and barons of the imperial party took refuge in Sicily. E. Bertaux, *De Gallis qui saeculo XIII° a partibus transmarinis in Apuliam se contulerunt*, Paris, 1903.

[14]The existence of an almonry in the brotherhood of St Andrew of Acre shows that this was still a charitable organization. Chandon de Briailles, Bulles de l'Orient latin, in *Syria*, 1950, 296–297.

[15]Rodenberg, *Epistolae Saeculi XIII*, i. 376. The patriarch may not have had the legation restored until 1237. See Delaville Le Roulx, ii. 509.

[16]Several important studies on the commune of Acre have been published in recent years, notably: H.E. Mayer, Zwei Kommunen in Akkon, in *Deutsches Archiv*, xxvi, 1970, 434–453; J. Prawer, *Estates, communities and the constitution of the kingdom* and *Histoire du royaume de Jérusalem*, ii. 233–256; J. Riley-Smith, The Assise sur la ligèce and the commune of Acre, in *Traditio*, xxvii, 1971, 179–204, reprinted in *The feudal nobility*. Riley-Smith thinks the formation of the commune of Acre was due to the Ibelin party's lack of success in attempting to put into operation the coalition of vassals laid down in the *Assise de la ligèce*, and that they failed mainly because Filangieri had

'Longobard' troops and did not depend on feudal service for a supply of men. This agrees well with our view set out above.

[17]See Grousset, iii. 339 and 344. Richard of San Germano (Muratori, vii. col. 1029) places John of Ibelin's takeover of Acre in April 1232.

[18]*Bartholomei Scribae Annales* in *MGH SS* xviii. 180–181; *RR* 1047, 1049.

[19]It took some time to pacify the island; note, for example, the dispute between the Rivets and the abbey of Belmont *propter turbacionem regni Cypri*; *Registres de Grégoire IX*, 1084.

[20]*Bartholomei Scribae Annales* in *MGH SS* xviii. 180–181. One of the leading Guelf barons, Rohard of Cayphas, gave extensive concessions to the Genoese in 1234; *RR* 1050.

[21]Grousset, iii. 350; Marino Sanudo, 214.

[22]H. de Ziegler, *Vie de l'empereur Frédéric II*, 142–143, "Many suspect [Sicilian] nobles were sent to the army in Syria". A Ghibelline party did exist in Acre (Richard of San Germano, 1232).

[23]Rodenberg, *Epistolae Saeculi XIII*, i. 471. Gregory IX had earlier required that the prisoners taken at Agridi should be freed, including among others Aymon of Aquino (*Registres*, 1037), which shows that negotiations continued in 1233. Huillard-Bréholles, *Historia diplomatica Frederici Secundi*, iv. 479, 483; v. 332.

[24]Rodenberg, 480, 548–549.

[25]Philip and Henry's first mission may be no more than a chronological error in the *Eracles*. The dates given by the pope's letters seem more reliable, and the treaty between the two negotiators and the grand master of the Teutonic Knights appears to belong to 1236. (See another chronology in La Monte, *The wars*, 49–50, 168; J. Prawer, *Histoire*, ii. 251, did not accept it.)

[26]Frederick did not second all the pope's attempts to find a settlement; he intended to put the Ibelins under the ban of the Empire and to punish the rebels. Thus on 20 April 1239 he blamed Gregory IX for granting dispensations for the marriages of two Guelf lords, Balian of Ibelin, son of John, and James of La Mandelée, whom he regarded as traitors; *RR* 1089.

[27]Grousset, iii. 358.

[28]*RR* 1036, 1038, 1063, 1065, 1107. An agreement between the abbeys of Jehosaphat and Mount Sion (Kohler, *Chartes de l'abbaye... de Josaphat*, 73) about a *casal* near Tyre, made by the castellan of Tyre and Philip Béduin, burgess of Acre, laying down recourse to the *secrète* of Tyre, then to that of Acre, shows that the judicial institutions of the country were functioning normally in spite of the divisions in the kingdom; and this was in April 1243.

Chapter 2

[1]Martene, *Thesaurus novus Anecdotorum*, i. col. 998; E. Petit, *Histoire des ducs de Bourgogne*, iv. 84–93. Huillard-Bréholles, v. 361, 426, 433, 474, 645–647 (assistance given to the crusaders by Frederick II).

[2]These infringements of the truce are confirmed by the *Eracles* and by letters from the pope warning the Templars that he would put the protection of pilgrims into Walter

of Brienne's hands if they could not ensure their safety; *Registres de Grégoire IX*, ii. 4129, 9 March 1238.

[3]Martene, *Thesaurus*, i. col. 1012.

[4]We have followed Maqrizi's account (*ROL* x. 323), which seems less biased than that of the *Eracles* (529–530); Grousset (iii. 374–376) thinks that Maqrizi is mistaken in saying that the Tower of David was besieged after the fall of the citadel.

[5]Grousset, iii. 378.

[6]*Histoire des patriarches d'Alexandrie* (in *ROL* x), 324–325. "The warfare that year between the Franks and the Moslems ended in the defeat of the Franks. This was because these Franks came from the West and knew nothing of the topography of the country, nor of Moslem fighting tactics.... The Franks who were established in the Sahel, and who wanted to keep the country for themselves, left them to get on as best they might, preferring, according to their custom, to ally themselves with their enemies against their co-religionists." This strange explanation echoes the violent disputes between crusaders and *poulains* after Gaza.

[7]For an account of what was now returned to the Franks, see P. Deschamps, Etude sur un texte latin énumérant les possessions musulmanes dans le royaume de Jérusalem vers l'année 1239, in *Syria*, xxiii, 1942–1943, 86.

[8]In a letter of 1244 Frederick II describes the treaty of 1240–1241 as *nostro regio foedere, quod nos una cum conventu et magistris domorum Sancti Johannis et Sanctae Mariae Theutonicorum nomine nostro contraxeramus*; Matthew Paris, iv. 300.

[9]Matthew Paris, iv. 138, 167, 290, 527. On Richard's expenditure in Syria, see the pope's letter giving him large sums in compensation (*Additamenta*, i. 91).

[10]*RR* 1104. The churches also benefited from the reconquest: the monks of Mount Tabor returned to their convent, and the nuns of Our Lady of Acre to their daughter house of Trois Ombres near Lydda. Du Cange-Rey, 835.

[11]P. Deschamps, *Le Crac des Chevaliers*, 100–101; see R.B.C. Huygens, Un nouveau texte du traité *De constructione castri Saphet*, in *Studi medievali*, 1965, 355–387.

[12]The lordship of Ibelin (*Lois*, i. 107) did not return to the Ibelins: the last holder had been Balian II, father of the Old Lord of Beirut. The laws of Jerusalem did not recognize inheritance 'by representation', namely the rule by which the descendants of a deceased person who, if he had lived, would have taken possession of some inheritance, could stand in his place. Balian's last surviving child was Margaret of Caesarea, mother of John of Caesarea. It was she who inherited Ibelin, and not her nephew Balian, lord of Beirut. As lady of Ibelin she was a vassal of Walter of Brienne, count of Jaffa.

[13]Matthew Paris, iv. 138.

[14]Perhaps Estrun, canton Cambrai, département Nord. Geoffrey is called "d'Estrueni" in the *Eracles*, when he rallied to John of Ibelin in 1232. The *Lignages* call him Geoffrey Poulain. He married Helvis, daughter of Rohard II and later the wife of García Alvarez, and had two sons by her, Giles and Robert. He died at Gaza in 1244. Possibly he was a son or grandson of Drogo of Estrun (*Estruen*), (Drogo died in Asia Minor after the Fourth Crusade; Villehardouin, ed. Faral, ii. 142) and was nicknamed 'Poulain'.

[15]Published by Röhricht in *AOL* i. 402–403.

[16]Simon was then in conflict with Henry III; see Bémont, *Simon de Montfort, earl of Leicester (1208–1265)*, Oxford, 1930, 64–65.

[17]Philip was born to Guy and Helvis, widow of Renaud of Sidon, between 1202 and

1204 at Sarepta, capital of the lordship of Sidon, of which Guy was no doubt *bayle* until Helvis died five years after Philip's birth; Amadi, 187.

[18]According to the *Historia Tartarorum* written about 1248 by the Dominican Simon of Saint-Quentin.

[19]Matthew Paris, iv. 167; Röhricht, *GKJ* 853–854. In 1238 there was almost a full scale war between the Temple and the Hospital over the ownership of two mills; Delaville Le Roulx, ii. 489 and iii. 59.

[20]Odo of Montbéliard was now the brother-in-law of the head of the house of Ibelin, Balian, who had married Odo's sister. See Les Montbéliard de Palestine, *Revue d'Alsace*, 1875.

[21]The *Livre au roi* laid down twelve as the age for coronation, but the king did not reach his majority until fifteen (Baldwin IV); queens did at twelve (Mary of Montferrat and Isabelle of Brienne); Dodu, 123–124. On the legal question, see J. Riley-Smith, *The feudal nobility*: the crown should go to the *plus dreit heir aparent* of the *derain saisi*, the last holder's nearest relative to appear; that is, the claimant had to be present in the East.

[22]But were the Ghibelline nobles there? The Pisans, supporters of the emperor, were not, although the Venetians, Genoese and Cypriots were summoned to attend. Ghibelline lords included Peter of Scandelion and Garnier l'Aleman the younger, who in May 1242 witnessed a deed of Filangieri; *RR* 1107. Raymond of Jebail (1240–1243), seneschal of the kingdom, was deprived of his office because he had been appointed by Frederick II, who had no right to do this; *Lois*, ii. 400.

[23]Alice had just returned from France, where she had gone to claim the county of Champagne. In 1189 Count Henry had made his vassals promise to recognize his brother Theobald as his heir, and the birth of two daughters, considered illegitimate, made no difference. But Erard of Brienne, with the help of John of Brienne, married Philippa, Henry's younger daughter, although the pope forbade it, and went to war in Champagne. The peace agreement made on 10 November 1221 left Champagne in Theobald's hands. Despite numerous papal bulls forbidding her such action, Alice adopted her sister's claim and took advantage of the enmity between Theobald IV and the other French barons, who objected to his loyalty towards the regent, Blanche of Castile (1230–1234). She only withdrew her claim in 1234/5, in return for an annual payment of 2,000 *livres* and a lump sum of 40,000 *livres*. To pay it, Theobald had to sell the feudal rights over his counties of Blois, Chartres, Sancerre and the viscountcy of Châteaudun to the king of France; d'Arbois de Jubainville, *Histoire des comtes et ducs de Champagne*, iv. 1. It is interesting that Erard of Brienne had the support of a Champenois prelate in the Holy Land, Clérembaut of Broyes, archbishop of Tyre; Chandon de Briailles in *Syria*, xxi, 1940, 82.

[24]Amadi, 192.

[25]*Barques de cantier* were the big longboats towed by galleys and used both as slave boats and as lifeboats. John of Gril did not dare risk this flimsy craft and the small Moslem vessel which picked up the rest of the crew, in the open sea; hence their return to harbour; *Chiprois*, 132.

[26]Balian of Ibelin, very angry at the brutal treatment inflicted on him by Filangieri when he was held hostage at Limassol by Frederick in 1228–1229, seriously hoped to kill his enemy.

[27]*RR* 1112. According to Richard of San Germano, the count of Acerra left in June 1242.

[28]Schlumberger, *Numismatique*: Philip struck copper coins as lord of Tyre (besides the gold Saracen bezants struck by the Tyre mint). His guardianship of Tyre was confirmed by King Henry I in 1246, while Balian of Ibelin obtained the grant of Casal Humbert, detached from the royal domain; Strehlke, *Tabulae*, 84. On the lordship of Philip at Tyre, cf. M. Chehab, *Tyr*, 498–541.

[29]The barons refused Marsilio Giorgio's demand that the Venetians should recover all their rights in Tyre, on the ground that the queen was not the lawful heiress of the kingdom, only Conrad being the true heir; Röhricht, *GKJ* 859.

[30]Mas-Latrie, *Les patriarches latins*, 22 (the new patriarch was Robert of Nantes). Rodenberg, ii. 6 (5 August 1243): *quam liberius et melius fieri potest, hoc tempore exorta discordia soldanorum.* Many Christians bequeathed their goods to rebuild the walls of Jerusalem and Ascalon; in 1257 these sums had to be used for the benefit of other cities; *Registres d'Alexandre IV*, no. 1939.

[31]Delaville Le Roulx, ii. 615ff. On 15 March 1244 he confirmed the grant of Ascalon to the Hospital in the presence of Bohemond V and nobles of Tripoli. In August or September he confirmed a grant to the same order of a *casal* in the Nablus region.

[32]New light has been thrown on this by M.L. Bulst-Thiele, in Zur Geschichte der Ritterorden und des Königreichs Jerusalem im 13 Jhdt bis zur Schlacht bei La Forbie am 13 Okt. 1244, in *Deutsches Archiv*, xxii, 1966. The author seeks to show that the Templars were not so much to blame for the breach of the truce and the consequent disaster as has been thought, and that Frederick II tried to put the blame on them. She also thinks that we are wrong to follow Matthew Paris in describing the Hospitallers as Ghibelline and the Templars as Guelf, although the Hospitallers assisted Filangieri in his attempts on Acre, and the Templars helped Balian of Ibelin to besiege the Hospitallers' headquarters. As for the Teutonic Knights, then divided over the succession to the grand mastership, they supported the Templars.

[33]The figures of the Forbie losses, given in a letter from the patriarch of Jerusalem (Muratori, *Scriptores*, viii. 1113): the Temple lost 312 knights out of 348, and 324 Turcopols; the Hospital 325 out of 351, and 224; the Teutonic Knights, 400. The knights of St Lazarus, the contingents of the lord of Cayphas, the archbishop of Tyre, the count of Jaffa, the bishop of Lydda, the prince of Antioch (300 knights), and the king of Cyprus (300 knights) were wiped out and their leaders killed or taken. The patriarch escaped from the disaster, and, well placed to inform us, put the total losses at 16,000 Franks and a large number of native auxiliaries, that is, the whole strength of the Frankish army in the field. The Franks' ally, the king of Homs, lost 1,720 Turks out of 2,000; Joinville, ed. N. de Wailly, 292.

[34]Frederick II sent an angry letter to Richard of Cornwall after the fall of Jerusalem: *Praeter id quod Templariorum superba religio et aborigenarum terrae baronum deliciis educata superbia soldanum Babiloniae ... per guerram improbam et improvidam coegerunt, nostro regio foedere parvipenso quod nos una cum conventu et magistris domorum S. Johannis et S. Mariae Theutonicorum nomine nostro contraxeramus....* Matthew Paris, iv. 100f; Huillard-Bréholles, vi. 236–240.

Chapter 3

[1]A letter from the "visitor of the East", Simeon Rabban-ata, to the pope; Rodenberg, ii. 200. See P. Pelliot, Les Mongols et la papauté, in *Revue de l'Orient Chrétien*, xxiv, 1924, 225.

[2]Frederick had again offered to lead the crusade, but Innocent IV did not believe him sincere; Röhricht, *GKJ* 871. Several Scottish barons took the cross; Dugdale, *Monasticon Anglicanum*, vi. 1155.

[3]Matthew Paris, iv. 339, 343.

[4]Canivez, *Statuta Capitularium generalium ordinis Cisterciensis*, ii. 294. Walter of Brienne, mentioned by name in this text, died in prison between 1245 and 1250. An unconfirmed rumour of his death was current in Champagne in July 1247; d'Arbois de Jubainville, *Histoire des comtes et ducs de Champagne*, v. 424. The county of Jaffa, which should have gone to his sons John and Hugh, was in 1247 in the hands of their nearest relative John of Ibelin, count of Jaffa and Ramleh; *RR* 1149. John of Brienne returned to the West; in 1248 King Henry of Cyprus ceded him the rights of Queen Alice, which he added to his county of Brienne (ceded in 1221 by King John of Brienne to his nephew Walter on his majority; *RR* 943). Another Brienne, John of Acre, son of King John, became butler of France and regent of Champagne.

[5]Matthew Paris, iv. 526. He calls the standard-bearer *Balcaniferum*.

[6]Rodenberg, ii. 87; Matthew Paris, iv. 556–559. Huillard-Bréholles, vi. 466–467.

[7]The pope refers to this letter from the sultan in the sentence of anathema pronounced against Frederick in July 1245.

[8]Rodenberg, ii. 218, 244, 299.

[9]Rodenberg, ii. 399, 400, 401.

[10]Legally speaking, the Holy Land was ruled by: a king, Conrad II; an hereditary *bayle* or regent, the king of Cyprus; and a second *bayle*, Balian of Ibelin or John of Arsuf, when the king of Cyprus was absent; not to mention Thomas of Acerra.

[11]Matthew Paris, iv. 559.

[12]Matthew Paris, iv. 559. It was now, according to a bull of 26 July 1248, that the hermits of Mount Carmel, who under St Burchard received their Rule from the patriarch Albert (died 1214), had to leave their mother house and began to swarm in the West. A second exodus took place at the time of the Mamluk invasion of 1263; bull of 31 October 1265. In 1254 the Carmelites established their earliest houses in England; *Bullarium Carmelitanum*, 1, 7, 32. Many Franks fled to Cyprus; La Monte, Register of the cartulary . . . of Santa Sophia of Nicosia, in *Byzantion*, v. 467; text of 1247.

[13]Grousset, iii. 427–428.

[14]Matthew Paris, iv. 490.

[15]P. Pelliot, Les Mongols et la Papauté, in *Revue de l'Orient Chrétien*, xxviii. 3ff. The duke of Burgundy wintered in the Burgundian-Champenois land of Morea.

[16]A war between the Pisans and the Genoese had for months made it impossible to find ships. John of Ibelin-Arsuf, *bayle* of the kingdom, had just restored peace.

[17]See J. Richard, La fondation d'une église latine d'Orient par saint Louis: Damiette, in *BEC* cxx, 1962, 39–54; La politique orientale de saint Louis: la croisade de 1248, in *Septième centenaire de la mort de saint Louis. Actes des colloques de Royaumont et de Paris (21-27 mai 1970)*, Paris, 1976, 197–207.

[18]This campaign, studied in E.J. Davis. *The invasion of Egypt by Louis IX of France*

and a history of the contemporary sultans of Egypt, London, 1897, is described in detail by J.R. Strayer, The crusades of Louis IX, in R.L. Wolff and H.W. Hazard, *The later crusades*, 2nd edn, Madison, 1969, 487–508, (*A history of the crusades*, ii), and by Grousset, iii. 436–485. Some boats bearing sick men – the duke of Burgundy, the legate Odo of Châteauroux, the patriarch and some prelates – reached Damietta; Matthew Paris, *Add.* i. 195.

[19]On the kind of feudalism the Mamluks practiced, cf. A.N. Poliak, *Feudalism in Egypt, Syria, Palestine and the Lebanon*, London, 1939, and E. Ashtor, *A social and economic history of the Near East in the Middle Ages*, London, 1976, 280–331.

[20]Joinville, ed. de Wailly, ch. 84 (see H.F. Delaborde, Joinville et le conseil tenu à Acre en 1250, *Romania*, xxxiii, 1893, 148–152).

[21]Delaville Le Roulx, ii. 673.

[22]Matthew Paris, *Add.* i. 195; *Eracles*, 437.

[23]See P. Deschamps, *Les châteaux des croisés en Terre Sainte*, ii, *La défense du royaume de Jérusalem*.

[24]*RR* 1216; *Registres d'Alexandre IV*, 1274. The existence of a suburb at Acre is attested in 1179; Jaffe, 13402a.

[25]On the very spectacular work done by the king at Caesarea, and the excavations which revealed the whole of the walls of this city, cf. M. Benvenisti, *The crusaders in the Holy Land*, 135–145, and J. Prawer, *Histoire du royaume latin de Jérusalem*, ii, 344–346.

[26]*RR* 1230, 1244.

[27]Julian of Sidon at about the same date ceded to the Hospital the small town of Casal Robert which he possessed in that region; *RR* 1217 (August 1254).

[28]Between 1256 and 1259. *RR* 1239, 1242, 1280, 1282; *Alexandre IV*, no. 1300.

[29]Balian of Ibelin, son of John of Arsuf, was supposed to receive a rent on the Nablus territory from King Henry between 1246 and 1253; Delaville Le Roulx, iii. 61.

[30]Matthew Paris, *Add.* i. 205 (letter from John of Caucy, treasurer of the Hospital), and Grousset, iii. 503. Matthew Paris records that Damietta was destroyed in 1251 by order of the sultan so that no future crusade should establish itself there; v. 254.

[31]Röhricht, *GKJ* 388. This order lost its whole contingent of knights, "leprous and healthy", at Forbie in 1244. We see here that the Moslems had recaptured Ramleh.

[32]Grousset, iii. 510.

[33]Röhricht, *GKJ* 874; Delaville Le Roulx, ii. 722, 739. The pope recognized the Hohenstaufen right to the crowns of Jerusalem and Sicily, but tried to prevent these kingdoms being united with the hereditary domains of the German Empire. Thus in 1247, although at war with Frederick, he tried to make Conrad II king of Sicily and of Jerusalem. See Wittmann, Urkundenbuch zur Geschichte des Hauses Wittelsbach, in *Quellen und Erörterungen zur Bayerische und Deutsche Geschichte*, v, 1857, 96.

[34]Röhricht, 883. Writing to the king of Castile in 1250, Frederick regretted that he had not had command of operations in Egypt, claiming that he would have prevented the disaster.

[35]In 1264 Philip of Montfort owed allegiance first to the king of France, then to the count of Montfort, lastly to the lord of the kingdom of Jerusalem. In 1268 he bequeathed to his eldest son the fiefs he held of the king in the districts of Albi, Carcassonne and Narbonne; *RR* 1331, 1357.

[36]Grousset, iii. 532; Grandclaude, 140.

[37]The 1255 treaty may have been made with Damascus alone, and that of 1256 with Egypt as well. The sources disagree on this point. Grousset, iii. 532.

Chapter 4

[1]Genoese and Venetians were trading in Syria in the twelfth century. As well as the classic works of Heyd and Schaube, readers should consult some of the many recent writers on economic history, such as R. Lopez. For Genoa, see the bibliography given by R.H. Bautier in Notes sur les sources de l'histoire économique médiévale dans les archives italiennes, in *Mélanges d'archéologie et d'histoire*, lx, 1948, 181–201.

[2]See C. Cahen, Orient latin et commerce du Levant, in *Bulletin de la Faculté des Lettres de Strasbourg*, 1952.

[3]See above page 149, n. 13. Cahen (Indigènes et Croisés, in *Syria*, xv, 1934, 359) quotes a passage from Ibn Jobaïr showing Frankish and Moslem merchants as quite indifferent to their rulers' wars.

[4]*Assises des Bourgeois*, section 237. On this text see J. Prawer, L'établissement des coutumes du marché à Saint-Jean d'Acre et la date de la composition du livre des Assises des Bourgeois, in *RHDF*, 4th series, xxix, 1951, 329–351; J. Richard, Colonies marchandes privilégiées et marché seigneurial, in *Moyen Age*, lix, 1953, 325–340; J. Riley-Smith, Government in Latin Syria and the commercial privileges of foreign merchants, in Baker, *Relations between East and West in the Middle Ages*, Edinburgh, 1973, 116–118.

[5]What were the *gelines dou Inde*, 'Indian hens', taxed at a tenth of their value? Not turkeys, still undiscovered in America, but perhaps pheasants or peacocks, both found in fifteenth-century princely menageries. See De Maulde, De l'origine des dindons, in *BEC* 1879.

[6]Kamel al Tevarikh (*RHC Hist. Orient*. i. 689). "They found in this town a great quantity of gold, pearls, *siglaton* (silk damask, according to Heyd), Venetian stuffs, sugar, weapons, and other goods; for this was the meeting place for merchants from France, Greece and elsewhere, from near and far"; this was an account of the capture of Acre in 1187. According to this text there were no goods left in Acre except those stored there by merchants who had gone away "because trade was at a standstill". Greek merchants began coming to the kingdom early in the twelfth century; Alb. Aq., viii. 45; xi. 27.

[7]Heyd, 686.

[8]*Assises*, no. 237. Goods exported to 'heathendom' usually paid one *carouble* per bezant, four percent.

[9]L. Blancard, *Documents inédits sur le commerce de Marseille au Moyen-Age*, Marseilles, 1885, ii. 102.

[10]In addition to Heyd (ii, supplement i, 555–711), we have used information from the Acre customs tariff, from Marino Sanudo, from Blancard, *Documents inédits*, and from E.H. Byrne, *Genoese shipping in the twelfth and thirteenth centuries*, Cambridge, Mass., 1930. Blancard and Byrne both publish contracts which set out the contents of cargoes. Sanudo, 53. See also Rey, *Colonies franques*, and the general survey of Eastern medieval trade in A.S. Atiya, *Crusade, commerce and culture*, Bloomington, 1962, 162–204.

[11]M. Bloch, Le problème de l'or au Moyen-Age, in *Annales d'histoire economique*, 1933, 21. See M. Lombard, L'or musulman, in the same journal, 1947, 143.

[12]Blancard, *Documents inédits*, i. 73, 102, 262, 273, 276–277, 315, 337, 338, 346, 351, 360, and ii. 9, 11, 13, 16, 22, 27, 37, 38, 39, 50, 52, 56, 61, 63, 78, 81, 82, 110, 133, 134, 160,

430, 436, 442, 443. H. Laurent, *La draperie des Pays-Bas en France et dans les pays méditerranéens*, *XIIe–XVe s.*, Paris, 1935, 66. Heyd, i. 91. These texts of 1248 show that the Holy Land's dangerous situation did not reduce the flow of trade.

[13]Sanudo, 42 and generally. These slaves came chiefly from southern Russia and even Asia Minor.

[14]*Assises des Bourgeois* no. 47.

[15]Heyd, i. 346.

[16]*RR* 1259; Rodenberg, ii. 94; *Registres d'Alexandre IV* no. 752.

[17]*RR* 1114, 1116; *Liber jurium*, ii. 405 (the Genoese only paid dues in the Tyre *funda* on goods from Egypt, Barbary and Constantinople; otherwise they were exempt. 1192).

[18]Byrne, *Genoese shipping*, 33; Blancard, i. 155 and ii. 9. See G. Fagniez, *Documents relatifs à l'histoire de l'industrie et du commerce*, Paris, 1898, i. 155ff.

[19]Blancard, i. 28, 73, 102, 120, 315; *RR* 889, 1339.

[20]In the seventeenth century the phrase *faire ses caravanes* was used of the escort voyages aboard Maltese galleys on which future naval officers were trained.

[21]L. Blancard, *Du consul de mer et du consul sur mer*, *BEC* 1857, 427.

[22]Byrne, *Genoese shipping*, 58; C. de la Roncière, *Histoire de la Marine française*, i. 244ff.

[23]G. Fagniez, *Documents relatifs*, i. 155ff; *RR* 1114. In order to control its consuls, Marseilles forbade the appointment of anyone whose personal status in Syria was likely to be higher than that of other Marseillais there.

[24]The papacy often expressed concern about the increase of prostitution in Syria; Gregory IX and Innocent IV (*Registres*, nos. 4134–4135 and 4106, March 1238 and May 1248) wrote exhorting the patriarchs to put a stop to this scandal which shocked pilgrims as soon as they arrived in the Holy Land. Innocent IV deplored the fact that at Acre even religious orders rented houses to these *meretrices*.

[25]Fagniez, *Documents relatifs*, i. 155ff. The consul must not be a *fondiguier*, nor one of the inn-keepers, wine-shop owners or craftsmen whom it was his duty to control.

[26]*RR* 1116, 1182.

[27]M. Prou, *Registres d'Honorius IV*, 183; *RR* 1114, 1334, 1362, 1381, 1399. Saliba left legacies to his freed slaves Marie and Marinet, and to his slaves Ahmed and Sophie for their baptism and enfranchisement.

[28]*RR* 1114.

Chapter 5

[1]Delaville Le Roulx, ii. 855; Rodenberg, iii, 667, 684, 685, 698.

[2]Illuminations blazed in Acre for several days at the news of Conrad's defeat; *Chiprois*, 771.

[3]Rodenberg, ii. 285, 400; iii. 702, etc.; *Eracles*, 437; Amadi, 199. Theobald's charter: Muller, *Documenti*, 82.

[4]This is shown by such deeds as *RR* 666 (1187) and 1014 (1229).

[5]Dom Devic and Dom Vaissette, *Histoire générale de Languedoc*, viii. 1417. The kings of Aragon were counts of Provence and lords of Montpellier.

[6]Delaville Le Roulx, ii. 523; Grousset, iii. 557.

[7]The monastery of St Sabas was a Melchite house between Jerusalem and the Dead

Sea; Saewulf (ed. Wright, 847) says it had 300 monks, who fled to Jerusalem in 1103. Innocent IV and Alexander IV several times suggested it should cede one of its houses to Genoa; *Liber jurium*, i. 1097. On the house in question, see J. Prawer, *Histoire du royaume latin*, ii. 363–364. It would have given the Genoese direct access to the harbour.

[8]Röhricht, *GKJ* 897–898.

[9]*Annales Januenses*, 238; Röhricht, *GKJ* 897–898; *Registres d'Alexandre IV*, 2611. *Annales Pisani* in Muratori, *Raccoltà*, vi, ii. 109.

[10]Amadi, 204; *Eracles*, 443. The confused chronology of this war (Grousset, iii. 540 n. i) can be established if we reckon the date of Bohemond of Antioch's arrival to be 1 February 1257 old style, but 1258 new style; the bitter war would have lasted a year, and the pope wrote to bring peace at the end of 1258.

[11]*RHC Hist. Occ.*, ii. 634–635 ('manuscript of Rothelin').

[12]Delaville Le Roulx, ii. 752; *Annales Januenses*, 238.

[13]Heyd, i. 346 n. 3.

[14]Grousset, iii. 539; Röhricht, *GKJ* 300. The Templars and Teutonic Knights received the reward of their support at Venice in 1260; Andrea Dandolo, *Chronicon*, 367–368.

[15]Dandolo, *Chronicon*, 367–368. In 1260 a Venetian, Renier Trevisan, made a declaration of the goods taken from him in Acre in the time of the *bayle* Giustiniani; Morozzo della Rocca, *Documenti*, ii. 380.

[16]Amadi, 205, wrote *ne haver torre ne bastion*, "tower nor bastion", but according to Rothelin, the *Eracles*, 443, and Sanudo it was *de cour et de baston*, the sergeant's *bâton* or staff.

[17]Rodenberg, iii. 446. Muller, *Documenti*, 455ff.

[18]*RR* 1285 (1260). *Eracles*, 443. The gates of the Genoese tower and the pillars of St Sabas were taken to Venice as trophies, where the pillars were affixed to the facade of the church of St Mark; Röhricht, 903 n. 5. But see Prawer, *Histoire du royaume latin*, ii. 562.

[19]In the 1261 treaty between Genoa and Michael, the Genoese excepted the city of Acre, the kingdoms of Cyprus and Jerusalem, Philip of Montfort and the other Syrian barons, the Hospital and the other orders, from those against whom the alliance was made. Officially the alliance was directed only against Venice (and Pisa).

[20]Röhricht, *GKJ* 923. Röhricht and Grousset date this campaign to 1264; medieval texts (Amadi, the *Annales*, etc.) give 1263, which would agree with the passage in Ibn Furat mentioning an unsuccessful Genoese attack on Acre (Grill's fleet?) and with the 1264 treaty between Tyre and Genoa. Nevertheless the *Eracles* gives 1264, and so do the *Chiprois*.

[21]*RR* 1331 (*AOL* ii. 225) – 5 March 1264 – see *RR* 1182, 1184.

[22]Heyd, i. 355; Röhricht, *GKJ* 991; Grousset, iii. 732. In 1280 a war between Venice and Ancona almost provoked the outbreak of a new war between the Venetians and the Genoese; *Archivio Veneto-Tridentino*, iv. 45–48.

[23]In 1282 when Bohemond VII captured and killed the lord of Jebail and took his lordship, the lord of Tyre and the Genoese hurried to the town's help, but were too late.

[24]*RR* 1413.

[25]Grousset, iii. 740. When the pope begged the Venetians to use their fleet against Baibars and drive him out of Syria, they refused, afraid of having their property in Alexandria confiscated; *Registres de Clément IV*, 1162 and 1412, 12 January 1267 and 17 September 1268.

Chapter 6

[1]*RR* 389.
[2]*RR* 1285.
[3]*RR* 1307.
[4]*RR* 1435.
[5]*Lois*, i. 530. *RR* 1217, 1252ff.; Grousset, iii. 594–597.
[6]*RR* 1313 (1261); Grousset, iii, 621; Delaville Le Roulx, iii. 61.
[7]*RR Add.* 1297a.
[8]See for example Rutebeuf's poems in praise of Geoffrey of Sergines.
[9]Sanudo, 223. In 1280 there was a famine resulting from a failure of supplies from Cyprus and Armenia, a war that hindered the arrival of goods from Sicily, and a plague of locusts; *RR* 1436. An example of these purchases of corn appears in the *Règle du Temple*, ed Maillard de Chambure, 471: the "commander of the Vault of Acre" bought a shipload of wheat and had it put into store in barns although it was "damp with sea water", against the advice of the brothers, who wanted to have it dried. The considerable loss that resulted led to the commander's expulsion from the order.
[10]Rodenberg, ii. 6 (rebuilding of the walls of Jerusalem).
[11]Richard of Cornwall bequeathed 8,000 marks before 1272; *Registres de Grégoire X*, 830.
[12]A. Gottlob, *Die päpstlichen Kreuzzugsteuern*, Heiligenstadt, 1892; Samaran and Mollat, *La fiscalité pontificale en France au XIVe siècle, Bibliothèque des Ecoles françaises d'Athènes et de Rome*, fasciscule 96, and M. Prou, *Les registres d'Honorius IV, Introduction*, p. lxiiff. The tithe was often paid "to merchants chosen by the Holy See who were thus reimbursed for advances they had made to the apostolic Chamber". The great development of this taxation system, which increased considerably in the fourteenth century, dates from the war between Frederick and the pope. In her *Papal crusading policy* 1244–1291, Leiden, 1975, Sister Maureen Purcell studies the "financial policy" of the popes with regard to the crusades pp. 137–157.
[13]*RR* 1137, 1338.
[14]*RR* 1183, 1347, 1509. *Registres d'Alexandre IV*, 1492, 1937, 1939, 2174.
[15]*Registres d'Honorius IV*, 183; *RR* 1339, 1347, 1509.
[16]Sanudo, 227; *Registres de Nicolas IV*, 4387.
[17]*Registres d'Alexandre IV*, 416; *RR* 1339. In 1272 Philip III advanced 25,000 marks for the Holy Land in connection with the contingents taken East by the patriarch and Oliver of Termes; *Registres de Grégoire X*, nos. 789–809.
[18]J. Bastin and E. Faral, *Onze poèmes de Rutebeuf concernant la croisade*, Paris, 1946, Documents relatifs à l'histoire des Croisades, i. 34; H. de Ziegler, *Vie de l'empereur Frédéric II*, 143; Prutz, 116ff.
[19]Bastin and Faral, *Onze poèmes*, 25. In February 1262 Urban IV granted a number of spiritual privileges to Geoffrey as a recompense for his services in Syria (*Registres* nos. 53–56). He is mentioned at Jaffa in 1244; *Chiprois*, 740.
[20]*RR* 1347. In the two and a half years between 1272 and 1275 John of Grailly expended 11,500 *livres tournois*; *Registres de Jean XXI*, no. 4.
[21]Geoffrey of Sergines and Oliver approved the Templars' and Hospitallers' expenditure of the 4,000 *livres* promised by St Louis in 1265. Erard of Valéry, then in France, paid 1,000 *livres* over to the *executores negotii crucis* the same year on the king's

behalf; *RR* 1338. For Erard, see Bastin and Faral, *Onze poèmes*, 67. Oliver was a passenger aboard the *St Victor* when this ship was arrested at Messina in 1250; he may have been one of the men of Languedoc who were suspected of heresy and compelled to go to the Holy Land; B.Z. Kedar, The passenger list of a crusader ship, in *Studi medievali*, 3rd series, xiii, 1972, 275–278.

[22]*RR* 1347. *Registres de Nicolas IV*, 2252, 2269–2270 (the pope even effected a reconciliation with the king of Sicily to expedite the sending of help), 6850. Otto of Grandson was given many privileges in 1289; *Registres de Nicolas IV*, 1862–1864, etc. See Esther R. Clifford, *A knight of great renown: the life and times of Othon de Grandson*, Chicago, 1961. Sanudo, 225.

[23]Bastin and Faral, *Onze poèmes*, 41; J. Bédier and P. Aubry, *Les Chansons de croisade*, Paris, 1909.

[24]La Monte, 252. John of Grailly appears, perhaps by mistake, as marshal of the realm in about 1273; *Registres de Grégoire X*, 810.

[25]*Registres de Nicolas IV*, 2252, 4385, 4387.

[26]Röhricht, *Etudes sur les derniers temps*, 650 n. 81.

[27]Chabot, Histoire de Mar Jaballaha III, in *ROL* 1894, 112.

[28]In the will made by the Syrian Saliba, referred to above, these coins are described as *livres de royaux d'Acre*, namely *deniers* struck in the king's name. See P. Balog and J. Yvon, Monnaies à légendes arabes de l'Orient latin, in *Revue numismatique*, 6th series, i, 1958, 133–168; also J. Yvon, Besants sarracénats du roi de Jérusalem, in *Bulletin Soc. franc. Numism.*, 1961; Orient latin, in *A survey of numismatic research* 1966–1971, New York, 1973, ii. 304ff.

[29]*Registres d'Innocent IV*, no. 6336; *bisantios et dragmas* are equivalent to *dinars* and *dirhems*. See Schlumberger, *Numismatique*, 139, and *Bulletin de la Société des Antiquaires de France*, 1878, 181 (type *Dragma Acconen*). The *drahans* mentioned in Cyprus in 1296 (*Lois*, ii. 359) with reference to the price of bread must be *dirhems*, not *deniers*.

[30]H.F. Delaborde in *ROL* ii. 208.

[31]*Registres de Grégoire X*, no. 797. On 27 May 1290 the court at Palermo received news sent from Acre on 23 April; Finke, *Acta Aragonensia*, iii. 12.

[32]*Registres de Grégoire X*, 789–809. The pope asks for money for the Holy Land from the kings of France and England, and raises troops with it. He asks the king of Sicily for food, the Venetians, Genoese, Marseillais and Charles of Anjou for the small fleet of twelve galleys, each with a crew of thirty, which will carry them, etc.

[33]*Registres de Grégoire X*, 797. Gregory's policy towards the Holy Land is studied by V. Laurent in La croisade et la question d'Orient sous le pontificat de Grégoire X, in *Revue hist. du sud-est Européen*, xxii, 1945. Gregory X visited the Holy Land shortly before being made pope, but Marco Polo is mistaken in calling him a papal legate; M.H. Laurent, Grégoire X et Marco Polo, in *Mélanges d'archéologie et d'histoire*, 1941–1946.

[34]Authorization of the dispatch of corn had always to be obtained from Sicily, whether it was in 1272 (M.H. Laurent, Grégoire X) or after the fall of Acre in 1295; Mas-Latrie, *Histoire de Chypre*, ii. 91.

[35]Perhaps we receive slightly too strong an impression of the colonial nature of the Latin kingdom, now the property of the West, because our main sources are the papal registers, which may exaggerate this aspect.

Chapter 7

[1]Grousset, iii. 563f; P. Pelliot, Les Mongols et la papauté, in *Revue de l'Orient Chrétien*, xviii. 55.

[2]P. Pelliot, Les Mongols et la papauté, in *Revue de l'Orient Chrétien*, xxiii. 23.

[3]See J. Richard, The Mongols and the Franks, in *Journal of Asian history*, iii, 1969, 45–57.

[4]*Registres d'Urbain IV*, 292. See *Claris et Laris*, ed. J. Alton, lines 40ff.

[5]*RR* 1245–1247: *Registres d'Alexandre IV*, 1492, 1937, 2174.

[6]Rodenberg, iii. 415; *Registres d'Alexandre IV*, 1939 (28 April 1257).

[7]*Chiprois*, 751; *Documents Arméniens*, ii. 171–172.

[8]Röhricht, *GKJ* 910; Matthew Paris, v. 654; J. Richard, Le début des relations entre la papauté et les Mongols de Perse, in *Journal asiatique*, 1949, 291.

[9]*Registres d'Urbain IV*, 373.

[10]According to the *Eracles*, p. 446, James left so as not to have to take orders from his suffragan, Thomas bishop of Bethlehem, now promoted legate.

[11]H.F. Delaborde, Lettre des chrétiens de Terre Sainte à Charles d'Anjou, in *ROL* ii. 207.

[12]*Hist. Occ.*, ii. 636; Sanudo, 221.

[13]On this affair and the whole Mongol campaign in Syria, see the excellent account in Grousset, iii. 594–597. The date of the sack is uncertain, probably mid-1260. For the part played in the Mongol campaign by Bohemond VI, who took Baalbek for Hulagu, see the final chapter of Cahen, *La Syrie du nord*.

[14]Grousset, iii. 601–603.

[15]*Hist. Occ.*, ii. 638.

[16]Rodenberg, ii. 200.

[17]*RR* 1307. The following passage from the *Règle du Temple*, ed. Maillard de Chambure, p. 471, seems to refer to a different episode: "It happened that brother James of Ravane was commander of the palace of Acre, and he took brothers and Turcopols and sergeants, ours and the town's, and led a raid to Casal Robert, and the Saracens of the land came forth crying their war cry and defeated them." James was put in irons "because he had made the raid without permission". In 1260 the commander was Matthew Sauvage, and if any official of the Temple was dismissed it was the marshal Stephen of Saisy, at the order of the pope, for being 'scandalous': he was accused of having attacked at the wrong moment out of hatred of the lord of Beirut, his rival in the graces of a lady of Acre; *Registres de Urbain IV*, no. 2858, *de Clément IV*, 21–23, 836. Fifteen captured Templars were ransomed, including the future grand masters William of Beaujeu and Theobald Gaudin, as were the marshal, John of Beirut and James Vidal.

[18]Rymer, *Foedera*, i, ii. 54. In 1280 it was still being said that Syria was to be had for the taking.

[19]*Registres d'Urbain IV*, 373–396.

[20]*Registres d'Urbain IV*, 344. It may have been at this time that the fine church of St Mary Magdalene at Magdala was turned into a stable; *AOL* ii. 278. Baibars demanded Safed and Beaufort on the pretext that the treaty of 1240 had been annulled by the defeat at Forbie, and he claimed reparations, more or less genuinely, for various violations of international law. See Röhricht, Etudes sur les derniers temps du royaume de Jérusalem, *AOL* ii. 375ff.

[21]*Registres d'Urbain IV*, 344 (20 August 1243).

[22]Rymer, i, ii. 54 (letter incorrectly dated 1260); *Registres*, 473 (7 January 1264).

[23]Amadi, 207. Templars and Hospitallers had made peace in 1262. Work was being done on the fortifications of Acre in 1264; *Registres d'Urbain IV*, 869, 17 July 1264.

[24]A *casalier* administered a *casal*. *Règle du Temple*, section 76: "The *casalier* brothers may have two beasts and one squire and the same quantity of barley as the masters, and they may give four *deniers* to a brother and a saddlegirth for the beasts they ride."

[25]P. Deschamps, *Les châteaux des croisés en Terre-Sainte*, generally. The lions also occur on the 1273 bridge at Lydda and elsewhere.

[26]K.S. Salibi, The Buhturids of the Gharb, in *Arabica*, viii, 1961, 74–97; Clermont-Ganneau, Deux chartes des croisés dans des archives arabes, in *Recueil d'archéologie orientale*, v. 1–30. (These charters were written in Arabic by a Syrian scribe, dated not from Christ but from Alexander, as was usual among indigenous Christians, and sealed by the Frankish lord.) See Cahen, La chronique de Kirlay, in *Journal asiatique*, 1937, 142–144.

[27]The detour to Tunis may have formed part of a plan to free the Holy Land by pressure on Egypt's west coast; see J. Richard, Saint Louis dans l'histoire des croisades, in *Bulletin de la Société d'émulation du Bourbonnais*, 1970, 238–240, reprinted in *Orient et Occident au Moyen Age. Contacts et relations*, London, 1976.

[28]Röhricht, *Etudes sur les derniers temps*, i, La croisade du prince Edouard d'Angleterre, in *AOL* i, 1881; iii, Les combats du sultan Bibars, *AOL* ii, 258–297 and Die Kreuzfahrt des königs Jacob I. v. Aragonien, in *Mittheilungen des Österreich. Instituts*, xii, 1890, 372; Grousset, iii. 621–663.

[29]For the dating of this letter, see J. Richard, Le début des relations entre la Papauté et les Mongols de Perse, in *Journal asiatique*, 1949, 291ff.

[30]*Registres d'Urbain IV*, 2814bis and 344.

[31]P. Pelliot, Mongols et Papes aux XIIIe et XIVe siècles, in *Revue bleue*, 1923, 111. G. Soranzo, *Il papato, l'Europa cristiana e gli Tartari*, Milano, 1930, 228–243. p. 165 n. 32.

[32]The council of Lyons in 1274 offered an opportunity for contemplating a very close alliance between Christianity and the Mongols. Cf. J. Richard, Chrétiens et Mongols au concile: la papauté et les Mongols de Perse dans la seconde moitié du XIIIe siècle, in *1274. Année charnière. Mutations et continuités*, Paris, 1977, 31–44.

[33]*RR* 1280. Grousset, iii. 692f. Röhricht, *Etudes sur les derniers temps*, ii, Les batailles de Hims, 1281 et 1299, in *AOL* 1881, 617–652. The prince of Antioch and the king of Cyprus were preparing to help the Tartars, as were other Syrian barons (the Hospital remaining neutral); but the Mamluk army moved rapidly between the coast and the Mongol army to prevent the expected junction; *Bulletin de la Société d'histoire de France*, i, ii, 1835, 1–10, and *BEC* lii, 1891, 58. These letters confirm the shortage of food and the king of Sicily's preoccupation with his expedition against the Greeks. See also Muratori, *Scriptores*, viii. 869–870.

[34]Grousset, iii, 666; *RR* 1485. According to the bishop of Hebron's letter the truce with Acre expired in March 1281; war was obviously feared; text in Rymer, i, ii. 189. This truce established a condominium in the districts left in Frankish hands; see J. Richard, Les 'casaux de Sur': un partage de seigneurie entre Francs et Mamelûks, in *Syria*, xxx, 1953, 72–82.

[35]Salimbene, *Chronique*, 537 (1284) (*MGH Scriptores*, xxxii).

[36]We must remember that the Franks of the Holy Land were kept informed from 1248 of Armenian negotiations with the Mongols. These resulted in 1254 in an Armenian-Mongol alliance. Sempad, the constable, King Hethoum's brother, wrote

from Samarkand to John of Ibelin and to King Henry I of Cyprus on 2 February 1248 (see Mosheim, *Historia ecclesiastica Tartarorum*, App. no. 12). Thus the barons of Acre in 1260 were not ignorant of Mongol intentions, but their civil wars must have prevented them paying heed to them. In any case, the decisive factor, their aid to the Mamluks in the 1260 campaign, is emphasized by Eastern historians, especially by the Armenian Grigor d'Akanc'; History of the nation of the archers, ed. Black and Frye, in *Harvard journal of asiatic studies*, xi, 1949, 349.

Chapter 8

[1]*GKJ* 919.

[2]*Lois*, ii. 434: "And still we declare certainly ... that the men of the kingdom of Cyprus have served the house of Ibelin outside this realm more than they have served my lord the king or his ancestors."

[3]Urban IV asked her to lead a more respectable life; the bull *Audi, filia*; *Registres*, 2808. Perhaps 'Count J', requested in letter 2807 to leave his life of dissipation and return to his wife, sister of the king of Armenia, was Julian of Sidon.

[4]*Registres d'Alexandre IV*, 741 and 2510.

[5]*Lois*, ii. 401; Amadi, 198. Similarly in 1185 the *bayle* Raymond III of Tripoli was entrusted with only one royal stronghold, Beirut. The *bayle*'s decisions were valid only for the duration of his own regency; G. Dodu, *Histoire des institutions*, 127.

[6]*Registres d'Alexandre IV*, 1936 (11 May 1257).

[7]*Lois*, ii. 401: "The liege men put the lord of Arsuf in possession of the lordship, and afterwards I went there for them. Then I had work to do at Jaffa against the enemies of the faith. Then we put the lord of Arsuf in possession of the lordship again."

[8]*RR* 1259 and 1269.

[9]*Lois*, i. 312 and 453–454.

[10]Was this why his father John of Arsuf, the *bayle*, was dismissed and replaced by the count of Jaffa?

[11]Amadi, 204: *Herede de Cypro et del baliazo del reame de Hierusalem*.

[12]*Lois*, ii. 401ff. The point of law was whether or not the *Assises* recognized inheritance by 'representation'. Mary had not been invested with the regency, so that her claim was inferior to that of her sister, who had, and of her sister's descendants.

[13]Martene, *Thesaurus novus anecdotorum*, i. c. 1013 (letter to the king of Navarre offering Hugh of Brienne's apologies for his delay in doing homage for Brienne). *Registres de Grégoire X*, 832. In fact Hugh left for the Morea with two ships and 180 knights; Filangieri, *Atti perduti*, i. 2, no. 966.

[14]Martene, *Thesaurus*, i. c. 1013 (27 May 1267). Also in 1265 (23 April), in August 1266, and in 1268 (22 April).

[15]He took the title in 1254 (*RR* 1221), although usually known as the lord of Toron. Before 1260 he gave the Hospital a *casal* in exchange for a gate of Tyre previously granted to this order (*RR* 1286).

[16]*Registres d'Alexandre IV*, 71 (dispensation for kinship).

[17]Rodenberg, ii. 482 (24 March 1249: Melisende, as nearest relative of King Conrad since the death of her half-sister Alice, asked the pope for the domain and *baylie* of the

kingdom of Jerusalem). *Lois*, ii. 416. Mary bases her case on her being the nearest kin to Isabelle I, *la deraine saisie dou royaume*, the last holder of the kingdom. See J. Riley-Smith, *The feudal nobility and the kingdom of Jerusalem*, 212–214, 220–223.

[18]Sanudo, 223, *parva, quantum extimo, solemnitate vel cordis laetitia*; Mas-Latrie, *Histoire de Chypre*, i. 430.

[19]Grousset, iii. 619.

[20]*Lois*, i. 530–531. Repenting after a dissolute life, Julian entered the order of the Temple. Balian II died in 1278 in a battle between Franks. He married Mary of Jebail and had by her two daughters, Femie and Isabelle; *Registres de Nicolas IV*, 2001.

[21]A group of works on the law relating to fiefs is represented by a treatise sometimes attributed to Peter of Belleperche which we hope to examine shortly.

[22]Grandclaude, *Essai critique*, 124. See J. Prawer, Etude préliminaire sur les sources et la composition du 'Livre des Assises des Bourgeois', in *RHDF* 4th series, xxxii, 1954, and Etude sur le droit des Assises de Jérusalem, in *RHDF* xxxix–xl, 1961–1962.

[23]Grandclaude, 130, dated the *Livre* of Philip of Novara, who died after 1264, to between 1252 and 1257. Philip's reference to the settling of Julian of Sidon's affair in 1260 and the fact that his work seems to be known to John of Ibelin, died 1266, allows us to place his *Livre* between these years.

[24]See Riley-Smith, *The feudal nobility*, 121–144 ("a school of feudal jurists").

[25]Grandclaude, 142.

[26]See above pages, 59–60.

[27]*Eracles*, 390.

[28]Grandclaude, 111.

[29]Grandclaude, 145 ("A profoundly original mind, but always practical . . . and always scrupulously fair"). John did not intend to write a customary but a work that should be at once a treatise and a book for the use of litigants; certain well known *assises*, such as that of Belbès, are not included in his collection.

[30]See above page 69. La Monte, 276.

[31]M. Bloch, *La société féodale: Les classes et le gouvernement des hommes*, Paris, 1940, 259.

[32]The strangest device of all was when Philip of Novara succeeded in withdrawing Syria from the authority of Conrad II by expelling the king's garrison from Tyre in the king's own name.

[33]Grousset, iii. 604.

[34]*Lois*, ii. 414.

[35]*Eracles*, 474; Grousset, iii. 671.

[36]Guy was not originally meant to marry Eschiva. A dispensation was requested for his brother Amalric, prince of Tyre, and a bull was sent which mistakenly bore the names of both Guy and Amalric. It was annulled and another issued with only Amalric's name on it. He, however, married Isabelle of Armenia, and Guy married Eschiva, and had by her a son, the future King Hugh IV of Cyprus; Guy died a year after his marriage; Amadi, 240; *Registres de Nicolas IV*, 4026 and 6276.

[37]*Eracles*, 474. Charles of Anjou mentions his kinship with the grand master in his deeds; Filangieri, *Atti perduti*, i, 1. 545.

[38]Sanudo, 227.

[39]Gregory X's letter (no. 832) asking the king of Sicily to put a stop to the count of Brienne's plans seems to show that it was in Charles' kingdom that the count was finding support. See Mas-Latrie, i. 451–452.

[40]Riant, *Eglise de Bethléem-Ascalon*, 387–391. For a detailed study of the agreement between Charles of Anjou and Mary of Antioch, see G. Hill, *A history of Cyprus*, Oxford, 1948, ii. 190–192.

[41]*Chiprois*, 783: "and this he did as a blind . . . and the king did not wish to be present in Acre". The *Eracles'* account is biassed and accuses Hugh III of calling in the sultan against Acre (p. 475).

[42]*Lois*, ii 415–419. For James Vidal, see *Familles d'Outre-mer*, 602–603. His predecessor as marshal was William of Canet, nephew of Oliver of Termes (1269–1273). Odo Poilechien, justiciar of Otranto, 1274–1277, was appointed vice-marshal of the kingdom of Jerusalem in 1278. Soon after his arrival he married the widow of Balian of Arsuf (died 29 September 1277) and was made seneschal. Angevin registers mention other officials: Geoffrey of Summesot, in 1278 vice-seneschal and master of the king's household, then in 1283 justiciar of Bari; William of Villers, Simon Ancelin and Thomas Vidal, promoted to other posts in 1283 (Filangieri, *Atti perduti*, i, 1, 574; i, 2, no. 853, 1204–1206, 1290). Richard of Neublans, former vice-constable of the kingdom of Sicily (Durrieu, *Les archives angevines de Naples*, ii. 357) is referred to in 1288 as an agent of Queen Margaret (*Registres de Nicolas IV*, 560) and in 1294–1307 became lord of Neublans (Jura, arr. Poligny). Which of these is meant in *Chiprois*, 789, where the marshal appointed by Charles of Anjou is described as a "knight of France"?

[43]Rymer, i, ii. 189.

[44]Delaville Le Roulx, Inventaire de pièces de l'ordre de l'Hôpital, in *ROL* iii. 105 (31 October 1281). The Venetian *bayle* Alberto Morosini gave wholehearted support to the Angevin officials; Andrea Dandolo, 393.

[45]*Chiprois*, 784; Sanudo, 228.

[46]This has been wrongly identified as the Châtellet at Jacob's Ford; it seems to have been a small castle built on the coast to protect this dangerous passage, possibly at Khan-el-Khaldé.

[47]Humphrey's sons Amalric and Rupin (died 1313) and Rupin's son Humphrey bore in turn the single title of lord of Beirut. Amalric of Lusignan is described as prince of Tyre in 1285.

Chapter 9

[1]On 18 May 1280, learning that the king of Castile was looking for ships for his expedition, Edward I ordered his officials in Gascony to facilitate the king's purchases. Alfonso X hoped to combine his and Edward's crusades, and was negotiating with the Mongols. But war between France and Aragon compelled him to attend first of all to Spanish affairs, and in 1282 Edward wrote to him that events in Wales prevented him for the time being from going on crusade; Rymer, i, ii. 177, 184, 202.

[2]Letters from Edward to the pope in 1286 carried by Otto of Grandson, and in 1288, in which the king asks for a postponement until 1293; Rymer, i, iii. 9, 43.

[3]Grousset, iii. 705–727.

[4]*RR* 1458, 1450; Rymer, i, ii. 189.

[5]*Chiprois*, 804. The Templars wanted to use this respite to build a new fortlet near Acre at *Castavilla*; *Registres de Nicolas IV*, no. 1291.

[6]*Chiprois*, 804 (the *bayle* of the kingdom before Amalric was Philip of Ibelin, seneschal of the kingdom). Amalric became prince of Tyre after 1285. Philip of Ibelin, like Baldwin, Henry II's uncle, became seneschal of Cyprus on the death of his brother Balian. Rymer, i, iii. 49. *RR* 1495, 1496; *Registres de Nicolas IV*, 2252.

[7]*Registres de Nicolas IV*, 2269, 2270, 4385, 4387, 6664, 6684. G. La Mantia, *Codice diplomatico dei re Aragonesi di Sicilia* (Palermo 1918), i. 493.

[8]C. Schefer in *AOL* ii. 89–107; Michelant and Raynaud, *Itinéraires*; Delaville Le Roulx, *La France en Orient au XIVe siècle*, i. 16, 19.

[9]*Liber jurium*, iv. 143; La Mantia, *Codice diplomatico*, 455, 493. (Sicilian policy did not alter.)

[10]*Registres*, no. 4403. Bratianu, Autour du projet de croisade de Nicolas IV: la guerre ou le commerce avec l'infidèle, in *Revue historique du Sud-Est européen*, xxii, 1945.

[11]Pipinus in Muratori, *Scriptores rerum Italicarum*, ix. 733; Sanudo, 230.

[12]The agents of the Aragonese king of Sicily had in fact reported the sultan's preparations against Acre as early as 22 April 1290, that is before the events of August. They ascribed this perfidy (*enguayn*) to the probable breach of the truce resulting from the arrival of the Venetian fleet on Easter day; Finke, *Acta Aragonensia*, iii. 12.

[13]The members of the defence council are listed in *Registres de Nicolas IV*, 4387; Roger of *Thodinis* may not have arrived until after the fall of Acre, with the galleys sent urgently by the pope at the news of the town's fall; *Registres*, no. 6850ff. The Italian crusaders numbered 3,540, all infantry, and arrived aboard Tiepolo's galleys; Amadi, 218.

[14]The siege lasted from 5 April to 18 May 1291. See G. Schlumberger, *La fin de la domination franque en Syrie*, Paris, 1914, and R. Röhricht, Die Eroberung Akkas durch die Muslimen, *Forschungen*, xx. 95–126.

[15]Other figures given are: Moslems, 60,000 cavalry and 160,000 infantry; and Henry's last reinforcements: 100 knights and 200 infantrymen; Sanudo, 230, and Amadi.

[16]*Chiprois*, 810: "a Provençal who was viscount of the Bourg at Acre". For the walls of Acre see Rey, 453f. King Hugh III built a barbican and a tower (perhaps one and the same; see Pipinus in Muratori, *Scriptores*, ix. 714), and the countess of Blois, who died in Acre on 2 August 1287, a tower added to the barbican near St Nicholas and a barbican between the St Thomas and the Maupas Gates; Sanudo, 229. The commune of Acre had no doubt long ceased to exist; La Monte, *The communal movement*, 128.

[17]This missile was launched by Italians in the Legate's Tower.

[18]Having command of the sea, the Franks could attack the Moslem flank from their ships. The tower of the countess of Blois fell at the same time as King Hugh's barbican; we think that both these were situated between the New Tower and the St Nicholas Gate.

[19]We are here following Sanudo, who is very clear; see also Rey, 459ff.

[20]*GKJ* 1020. The hospitaller order of St Thomas of Canterbury had its base at Acre and from 1257 a hospital in London (*Registres d'Alexandre IV*, 1553, 1664). It was transformed into a military order, specifically for Englishmen, when Prince Edward was in the Holy Land (Röhricht, *GKJ* 965, 1011). Another minor military order, that of St Laurence, possessed the church of Saint Laurent-des-Chevaliers in Acre. See *Procès des Templiers*, i. 140. Ludolf of Sudheim in *AOL* ii. 340.

[21]Nicholas of Hanapes acted as commander of the besieged stronghold; see the letters of Nicholas IV, and Muratori, *Scriptores*, xvi, 682.

[22]Peter of Sevrey (Sevrey, Saône et Loire, arr. Chalon-sur-Saône, where there was a

house of the Templars) was castellan of Tortosa, then *drapier* of the Temple; J. Michelet, *Procès des Templiers*, i. 208, 418; ii. 222. He is not to be confused with another man of the same name, preceptor of Bures in about 1298 and suspected of criminal practices.

[23]*Registres de Nicolas IV*, 6778 (23 August 1291; the pope's letter informing the king of France of the disaster).

[24]*Registres de Nicolas IV*, 6778. The concentric triple defences of Tyre were built before the crusades; they are described by Anna Comnena (*Alexiade*, xiv. 8) just as the pilgrim Burchard describes them in 1284 (*GKJ* 1025). Volumes ii and iii of M. Chehab, *Tyr à l'époque des croisades* (vol. i, Paris, 1975), will be devoted to description of the town and the excavations in it.

[25]For the interruption of the admission of a Templar in the chapel of Sidon by a Moslem attack, see *Procès des Templiers*, i. 259–260. The Carmelite monastery on Mount Carmel in the diocese of Caesarea, distinct from their house in Acre, was rebuilt in 1263; *Bull. Carmelitanum*, 23, 28.

[26]Schlumberger, *Fin de la domination franque*, 52.

[27]Röhricht, *GKJ* 1024. The gate was taken to Cairo in 1303. Hromgla fell on 28 June 1292. For the projects against Cyprus, see Amadi, 229.

[28]Nothing could be alleged against the order on this head in the case brought against it; it was recalled that William of Beaujeu and Matthew Sauvage had been accused of selling themselves to the sultan because they enforced strict observance of the truce (*Procès des Templiers*, i. 44–45, 209, 215; after 1250 some said: i. 196), but such rumours were disproved by the death of the grand master and 300 knights at Acre (i. 43, 143).

[29]*Registres de Nicolas IV*, 6778, 6782–6799, etcetera. Röhricht, *GKJ* 1026. Throughout the thirteenth century the papacy tried to combine several orders into one; this happened to the mendicant orders: the Brothers of the Sack and the Humiliati were united with the Franciscans, as were the Brothers of Penitence, by the decree *Religionum diversitatem nimiam* of the council of Lyons.

[30]*Registres de Nicolas IV*, 6850f. Cyprus continued to be seen as a base for a future crusade (Mas-Latrie, *Histoire de Chypre*, ii. 91, 99, 118). These crusading plans are studied in A.S. Atiya, *The crusade in the later Middle Ages*, London, 1938; see also F. Pall in *Revue historique du Sud-Est européen*, xix, 2. 527ff, and in the same volume, 291, G. Bratiano, Le conseil du roi Charles [Charles II of Sicily].

[31]Franks were released as well, for example the Englishman Geoffrey of Semary, captured at Acre in 1291; Rishanger, *Chron.*, ed. J.O. Halliwell, 442–444. For Chiol (Zolo Bofeto di Anastasio, a Pisan in high favour at the Mongol court), see Pelliot, "Isol le Pisan" in *Journal asiatique*, 1915, ii. 495, and J. Richard, Isol le Pisan: un aventurier latin gouverneur d'une province mongole?, in *Central Asiatic Journal*, xiv, 1970, 186–194.

[32]Röhricht, Les batailles de Hims, 1281 and 1299 in *AOL* i, 1881. *Chiprois*, 848; Amadi, 234–238; Hayton in *Documents Arméniens*, ii. 197; *MGH SS* xxii, 482–483; Finke, *Acta Aragonensia*, iii. 90 (confirmation of Ghazan's offer of the Holy Land, 23 March 1300). Amongst many other calumnies, King Henry II was accused of deliberately wrecking the Tortosa army's food supplies; *ROL* xi, 1907, 447–448. Abel Remusat, *Mémoires sur les relations politiques des princes Chrétiens avec les empereurs mongol*, ii, 386–388.

[33]Amadi, 238–239; *Chiprois*, 849; *Registres de Boniface VIII*, iii. 4199, 4383–4384; *Procès des Templiers*, i. 39.

CONCLUSION

Latin rule in the Holy Land: the balance of the account

The fate of the Frankish population

For over 190 years the Latin kingdom of Jerusalem attracted large numbers of Western pilgrims to Syria, many of whom remained in the East and settled in Palestine. Throughout the whole period a European, mainly French, element was superimposed on the native population. Far fewer than the Christian and Moslem Syrians, though perhaps reaching equal numbers in some towns,[1] these immigrants did not generally found stable rural settlements; the Latin colony was always one of masters, despite the attempts at more general settlement revealed in some twelfth-century franchise charters. None the less, when the fall of Acre sounded the death knell of the little Latin state so strangely flung by the crusades onto the shores of the East, there were tens of thousands of Franks in the Holy Land, some of whom had been settled there for generations.

Keen anxiety was felt for them in the West. What had happened to all those men and women who had gone to settle in the Levant? For many, the massacres and bloody defeats of 1187, 1244, 1263–1272 and 1291 were the end of the story. But there certainly remained a very great many Latins who had not been killed; what happened to them? Of those who managed to escape – at Acre in 1291 almost 10,000 took refuge in the Temple[2] – some returned to Europe. The lords of La Mandelée once again found shelter in Calabria, whence they had originally come to Jerusalem, and we have the list of nine noble Venetian families, *lignages*, who returned to Venice and in 1296 were restored to their places on the Great Council.[3]

Most of the refugees went to Cyprus, totally destitute; they arrived in such crowds that prices shot up, rents going from ten to 100 bezants a year, and any small sums they were able to bring vanished at once. The economic balance of Cyprus was destroyed for several years, and the problem of corn long remained difficult. The very relatives, said the chronicler, of refugees, pretended not to recognize them when they came to them for help, and it was only the personal distribution of alms by Henry II and his queen, who also took some of these poor people into their employment, that did anything to relieve their distress.[4] This influx of Syrian Franks reinforced the Latin element in the island's population and no doubt strengthened the Cypriot kingdom which continued to be a Frankish, chiefly French, state for two hundred years before becoming a dependency of Venice.

But many Franks were unable to escape, and we know what happened to them from an enquiry made by a Dominican missionary, Ricoldo of Monte Croce, who followed up the effects of the sack of Acre as far as Baghdad and collected all the information he could:

Monks and soldiers were killed; children were spared to become Moslems; women, both mothers of families, nuns and girls, were distributed among the Saracens as slaves and concubines. Christians were sold as far afield as Baghdad and in the furthest parts of the East because there was such an immense number of captives.

And Ricoldo laments the many acts of sacrilege, churches defiled, pages torn out of Gospels to make drumskins, and:

chalices and veils and other ornaments of the altar have passed from Christ's table to Saracen banquets . . . the books of the prophets and the gospels have been given to the dogs [Ricoldo managed to find and purchase some books from the cloister of the Dominicans at Acre, where his brothers were martyred at three in the afternoon of Saturday 19 May 1291],[5] and, sadder, than all the rest, of the nuns and virgins vowed to God, the most beautiful were chosen to be sent as gifts to Moslem kings and nobles, to give them children to be brought up in the beliefs of Islam; the others were sold and given to strolling players to take them about the world to the shame of Christians.[6]

Others were not thought worthy of slavery:

I see old men, young girls, children and infants, thin, pale, weak, begging their bread, and they long to be Saracen slaves rather than die of hunger . . . . Poor wives and old women weep at the foot of the cross, inconsolably mourning their sons and their husbands killed or enslaved by the Moslems.[7]

The 'slaves of Babylon' had long been one of the most pressing concerns of the popes, anxious to release from captivity those who had gone to fight for the faith, and after 1291 the matter became much more urgent. In 1279 Nicholas III sent a Franciscan to Cairo to provide spiritual consolation for the captives. This messenger reported in 1282 that the Christians were in chains, digging castle moats and carrying earth in baskets, and living on a scant ration of three small loaves a day. Other Franciscans sent to Cairo in the time of Boniface VIII obtained permission to visit the captives; they praised the zeal of the Copts who gave alms to buy food for the Frankish slaves and redeemed them from captivity when they were able to do so. In 1317 John XXII even lifted the prohibition on trade with Egypt in the hope of thus facilitating the redemption of the slaves. None the less a whole population of Frankish slaves and freedmen, referred to as *Gazani* by a traveller in 1329, still remained in Egypt. These Franks had two chapels, one at Babylon (Cairo) and the other at Alexandria. The traveller, an Irish Franciscan, spoke scathingly of the "fables of raving women" which depicted these captives as suffering extremes of cruelty; in spite of the maltreatment they received, especially from renegades of Ethiopian, Nubian and other races, the "slaves of the sultan" exercised various trades, such as masonry and carpentry, and were paid and fed according to their work. Many of them were materially better off than they had been in their own country. All, however, suffered from not being able to return home or to keep Sunday.[8]

These Latins in Egypt were soon absorbed into the Egyptian population. Many of them abandoned the Roman faith, which it was difficult for them to observe in isolation, without priests, and instead joined the Melchite or the Coptic churches. It is even possible that one of them became the Coptic patriarch of Alexandria; the list of the patriarchs of Abu'l Barakat includes "Theodore, son of Raphael, the Frank, six years and six months, from 10 *abib* 1010 to 5 *toubah* 1016 (14 July 1294–31 December 1299)". Could this be a descendant of Latin captives who had taken orders in the Jacobite church?[9]

Many of the Latins, however, had not the courage to retain their faith; Ricoldo noticed sadly that "many of the Christians who survived adopted the law, or rather the perfidy, of Mohammed".

It is well known [said the author of a plan for a crusade] that there are many renegades in pagan lands, and we must consider that they have not abandoned the Christian faith because they think the law of Mohammed better than that of Christ. Some have abjured from weakness, to escape the pains and torments of prison, others on the pretext of poverty, and all who adopt their perfidy are equipped by the Saracens with arms and horses. And if these men who have denied their faith could see that there was some powerful lord permanently established in that country [the author wanted to

found a military order in the East]... it is to be supposed that the majority of them
would gladly return to the Catholic faith. This would seriously weaken the pagans, for
these renegades are the best troops the Saracens have.[10]

At the end of the thirteenth century there were missionaries staying at
Cairo with renegades who held high positions at court or in the
sultan's army. One such was a Frenchman called John, captured at
Acre. Of three of the sultan's dragomans in 1329, all renegades "of
mouth but not of heart", one, Izz-al-Din, was a member of the Roman
church, the friend of a former Templar, now renegade and married,
and the other two were Italians who had adopted the Jacobite faith.
These missionaries brought other such renegade Christians back to
the faith, such as the converts made by the Friars Minor of Jerusalem.[11] Everyone knows of the success of the Frankish renegades in
the Moslem Mediterranean states, the most dreaded of the Barbary
pirates who dominated that sea from the sixteenth to the nineteenth
century.

Intellectual life

Fugitives, slaves or renegades; such became all that was left of the
Frankish stock planted in the kingdom of Jerusalem. Nothing
remained of the small French community of Syria but scattered
elements absorbed into the native population. Its work, however,
could not all be destroyed.

The Frankish Holy Land enjoyed an active intellectual life. Clerks
and even some laymen such as Renaud of Sidon took an interest in
Moslem culture. William of Tyre wrote a history of Moslem dynas-
ties. It does not, however, seem that Arab thought can have reached
the West by means of the kingdom of Jerusalem; Sicily and Spain
were much more important in this respect. A number of translations
of works of Eastern philosophy were made in Frankish Syria, but we
do not know how large this number was, nor whether it justifies our
speaking of real Franco-Moslem literary activity.[12] Deeper insights
were gained into Eastern Christian thought; discussions on uniting the
churches led to fruitful encounters. In 1237 the Friars Preachers of
the community of Jerusalem endeavoured to bring peace to the
discords of the monophysite Jacobite church, and in 1247 the patriarch of that church joined the church of Rome. Philip, prior of the
Dominican province of the Holy Land,[13] in 1237 sent the pope a

report which demonstrates the range of the conversations held between his colleagues and the Eastern prelates. Translations from Coptic and Syriac literature were published at the time of the Fifth Crusade. Western scholarship thus acquired a deeper understanding of the East, and this was one of the principal results of the crusades in the intellectual sphere.

But the most outstanding development in the Holy Land was the emergence of a literature written in French. Syrian barons kept in close touch with their peers in French countries, and were well informed about Western literary activity. The nobles of Syria and of Cyprus enjoyed the romances of the Round Table and of the heroes of classical antiquity. In 1286 festivities at Acre included dramatic scenes in which young nobles 'counterfeited', that is, enacted, passages from their favourite romances, presenting Lancelot, Tristram and Palomydes on stage. Philip of Novara, the Cypriot poet, wrote an account of the war between John of Ibelin and Aimery Barlais parodying the *Roman de Renart*, and this, like his other poems, was well received by the Frankish knights.[14] We possess hardly any *chansons* written by the barons of the Holy Land, but Philip cannot have been a solitary voice among them. The field in which the barons excelled, both Philip himself and John of Ibelin, Geoffrey Le Tort and many others, was jurisprudence. The *Assises de Jérusalem* stand high in the French literature of the law.

These lettered laymen even intruded into the literary domains of the clergy. The history of the Frankish conquest of the Holy Land was written by Fulcher of Chartres and continued many years later by William of Tyre. William's work was translated into French and was well known to the barons of the kingdom. James of Vitry, bishop of Acre, included a summary of it in his *Historia Hierosolymitana*, and others wrote continuations of it in French. After this, however, it was laymen who took on the task: in the first quarter of the thirteenth century Ernoul, a former squire of the Ibelins, wrote a narrative of events in his time in the Latin East; and this was later continued by Bernard the Treasurer.[15] Philip of Novara, more attached to Cyprus than to the Holy Land although not unimportant in the latter, recorded the events of the war between John of Ibelin, the Old Lord of Beirut, and Frederick II. A writer wrongly known as the Templar of Tyre began the *Gestes des Chiprois*. We are less certain of the Syrian origin of the historical romances based on the legend of Saladin, but their earliest written version, the *Estoires d'Outremer*, owes a great deal to the kingdom's historical writings.[16]

Buildings and art

The destruction of libraries and of most of the archives of the
communities of the kingdom, such as seigneurial chartularies,
prevents our knowing much about the Franks' literary activity in the
Holy Land. But a number of books, many of them illuminated ones,
were brought to the West before the fall of the Latin East. They
enable us to know the work carried out by scribes and illumin-
ators who produced in the towns of the Frankish kingdom such
manuscripts as those of the *History of Outremer* now preserved in the
Leningrad, Lyons, Paris and Brussels libraries. And modern scholars
are able to speak of an 'Acre school of illumination,' which was
active during the second half of the thirteenth century.[17]

The monuments the Franks raised on Syrian soil bear witness to
the vitality of the Western civilization planted by the crusaders in the
Levant. These are the countless castles, Montfort, Banyas, Kerak,
Beaufort, and so on, which are still after many centuries such
remarkable examples of medieval military architecture.[18] The two
citadels of Sidon and the walls of Caesarea are evidence of the
success of St Louis' endeavours in this field. The presence of these
mighty strongholds, combining as they do Western and local
influence, the latter often the stronger, recalls the stubbornness with
which the Franks defended their kingdom against the Moslem
reconquest.

As well as castles, Frankish builders erected many shrines in the
Holy Land. The pilgrim churches, usually built before the caliphs'
conquest of Syria, for the most part gave way to Romanesque and
gothic edifices whose plan came straight from the West. The French
masters of works who built these churches, many of them Romanesque buildings altered in the thirteenth century, brought the styles of
Burgundy and of the west and south-east of France to the Levant. It
seems as if the workshops were never idle; the great number of
pilgrims and their donations, and the wealth of abbeys and chapters
caused the work to prosper. France in the eleventh and twelfth
centuries was clad with a white robe of churches, and so too the Syria
of the twelfth and thirteenth centuries renewed her mantle of holy
places.

The architects had to cope with problems rarely encountered in the
West. They had to respect what was standing on the sites where they
built, as for example at Nazareth, and at the Holy Sepulchre, where

the remains of the ancient basilica of Constantine were preserved. But they overcame these difficulties and built churches which, if not perhaps markedly original (except for the Holy Sepulchre), can well stand comparison with those built in France at the time.

Unfortunately, the Moslem reaction which tore down a number of castles attacked the churches with particular fury. Baibars destroyed the shrines of the Table of Our Lord and of Nazareth; Ricoldo of Monte Croce deplores the transformation of the beautiful churches of St Mary Magdalen at Magdala and at Bethany into stables.[19] Nor did the destruction then cease; many travellers tell us of churches that were later to disappear. The cathedral of Tyre in which William of Tyre preached still stood in the eighteenth century; the pasha Jezzar had it partly demolished so as to take the pillars to Acre, and all that remained prior to the recent excavations was one pillar and a section of wall. The church built at La Mahomerie in the twelfth century was destroyed in 1915, as the abbey church of St Mary the Great at Jerusalem had been in 1901. St John's at Gaza, built by the Templars in the twelfth century, perished in the war in 1918. The church of Jacob's Well, the church of St John at Nablus and the church at Lydda, partly destroyed by Baibars in 1273 and later restored in the Greek style but still recognizable in the nineteenth century, all these have gone. St Andrew's at Acre was still standing in the eighteenth century, a great three-aisled church in which the famous brotherhood of St Andrew began, but nothing of it now remains.

Very few of the Frankish churches that were so numerous only two or three hundred years ago now survive. Some are mosques, like the church at Hebron, built about 1120, and the Romanesque cathedral of Ramleh which has been the Great Mosque since 1298. Some country churches are still standing, such as those of the Petite Mahomerie and of the Spring of Emmaus, Frankish colonies where churches were built for the Latin population in the twelfth century. The second of these, now Qariet-el-Enab, still belongs to French Benedictines; it was a fortified church, as churches needed to be in those small Frankish towns. The Great Mosque at Beirut is a former cathedral dedicated to St John, "a charming little colonial cathedral, not too costly, elegant, practical and solid," with a porch leading to an aisled nave, and three absides, the whole exterior strongly reminiscent of the choir of a romanesque church in the west of France. This cathedral was built between 1110 and 1187, and reconstructed in the gothic manner in the thirteenth century.[20] The ruins of the cathedral at Sabastya, where Usama was so struck by the fervour of the canons at prayer, also bear witness to the vigour with which romanesque architecture flourished in the Holy Land.

More archaeological traces of the Frankish period are to be found in Jerusalem than anywhere else. Thus at St Mary of the Latins the archivolt over the doorway bears the representation, so common in the West, of the signs of the zodiac and the figures of the months. St Anne's is almost intact, the cloister of the Temple remains, and so do the chapel of the Ascension and some other churches. Above all the Holy Sepulchre recalls its Frankish builders. Although damaged by fire in 1808, this sanctuary is still the building consecrated in 1149 by the Latin patriarch, replacing and as far as possible preserving the ancient basilica of Constantine. The Romanesque capitals and the lintels of the façade are clearly the work of a school of Frankish sculptors connected with that of the west of France. This school's most famous monuments are the capitals discovered in the ruins of the ancient basilica of Nazareth. In other arts, the Franks knew how to make use of local tradition; painting, it seems, was usually entrusted to artists of the Byzantine tradition, as for instance at the Spring of Emmaus and above all at Bethlehem, where the painters Basil and Ephraim were commissioned by Manuel Comnenus and by Amalric to execute works of art in which Western saints mingle strangely with Eastern ones, and the Latin with the Greek tongue.[21]

It was also artists of the Byzantine tradition who carved the ivory tablets of Queen Melisende's Psalter, and the marble tombs of the kings of Jerusalem. Although violated by the Khwarismians in 1244, these tombs still bore the epitaphs of Godfrey of Bouillon and Baldwin I until their destruction by the Greeks in 1810. Fragments of the tomb of Baldwin V showing clear Byzantine influence have been found incorporated in the Al-Aqsa Mosque.[22] We also know, for example from the evidence of Wilbrand of Oldenburg writing in about 1212, that Syrian artists were prized for ornamental work in houses and palaces, as their skill was greater than that of their Frankish rivals. "The Syrians, the Saracens and the Greeks excel in the decorative arts," noted Wilbrand, agreeing in this with the opinion of the Latins of Syria.[23]

Thus Frankish architects and sculptors collaborated with native painters, workers in mosaics, inlay and carving, to produce a Franco-Syrian art which prospered in the Latin colonies of the East for two hundred years.[24] This artistic and literary activity shows how inaccurate it would be to suppose that the Franks in Syria consisted of uneducated warriors who brutally enslaved a more civilized people without attempting to understand their culture. The efforts made to comprehend Arabic thought and history by William of Tyre, by the Dominicans and by the barons themselves, and the combination of Graeco-Syrian decorative arts with Frankish architecture, are enough to prove how successfully the Latins adapted to Eastern civilization. Western merchants carried Asia's rarest products to Europe by way of Syrian ports, and Syria, especially the coastal region, owed to the Franks its last period of splendour before it succumbed to the profound decay that came upon it at the fall of Acre, defeating the local attempts at restoration by men like Fakhr-al-Din and Jezzar, and persisting till the end of Ottoman rule.

Thus the history of the Latin kingdom of Jerusalem is not the history of a fruitless venture. The little state founded by the crusades to protect the pilgrimage to the Holy Sepulchre, still very popular even after 1291,[25] was not simply a garrison in a hostile land. In spite of the insecurity arising from the nearness of the Moslems, always ready to push the Franks into the sea, it succeeded thanks to a remarkable dynasty in creating a fresh and living political organism. Before it disappeared, victim of its divisions, of the weakness of its institutions resulting from the many vacancies of the throne, victim above all of the reconstitution of united Moslem empires of Egypt and inland Syria, the Latin kingdom had its time of glory. Nor did it perish through any fault in its institutions, which were stronger than is often realized. They enabled the kingdom to gather several nationalities together without oppressing them and to ensure the common life of Syrian Christians of different sects, of Moslems, Jews, Samaritans, Bedouins and Frankish colonists, all under the direction of an aristocracy of French origin which, despite its leanings towards a liberty sometimes verging on anarchy, provided the Latin settlements with a sturdy and effective structure. Clearly evident in the Latin kingdom of Jerusalem, the first attempt by Franks of the West to found colonies, are such qualities as the power to understand native thought, qualities which alone enabled the founders of the kingdom to build a work that would endure.

Notes to Conclusion

[1]We do not know the exact size of the Frankish population. From figures given for the army, 17,000 Latins in 1244, a larger number in 1187, we may suggest that it was between 100,000 and 200,000. The populations of Jerusalem (see above pages 179–180) and Acre must have been at least half Frankish.

[2]*Chiprois*, 814.

[3]Du Cange-Rey, 613; Vidal, *Registres de Benoît XII*, 1974 (1339: John, lord of La Mandelée). See also *Chronicon Parmense* in Muratori, *Raccoltà*, 62.

[4]Amadi, 227.

[5]Röhricht, Ricoldi de Monte Crucis, O.P. epistolae, V, in *AOL* ii, 2, 1883, 258–296. The martyrdom of the Dominicans is said to have taken place the day after the fall of Acre (p. 291).

[6]Röhricht, Ricoldi, 272, 281, 291. The Poor Clares disfigured themselves to escape slavery and were also martyred; *Archivum franciscanum historicum*, ii. 471.

[7]Röhricht, Ricoldi, 286.

[8]Golubovich, *Biblioteca bio-bibliografica della Terra Santa*, i. 275–276, ii. 60, iii. 68. *Registres de Jean XXII*, ed. Mollat, ii. 5742. *Itineraria Symonis Symeonis*, ed. J. Nasmith, Canterbury, 1778, 56.

[9]E. Tisserand and G. Wiet in Maspero, *Patriarches d'Alexandrie*, 358ff.

[10]Ricoldo, 270; C. Kohler, Deux projets de croisade, in *Mélanges*, 553.

[11]Golubovich, iii. 68; *Itineraria Symonis Symeonis*, 62.

[12]Franks like Renaud of Sidon and Humphrey of Montreal spoke Arabic, and we know of at least one translation made in Syria: Philip the deacon dedicated his translation of the *Secret of secrets*, *Sirr al Asrar*, to the bishop of Tripoli. Dominicans like Ricoldo of Monte Croce and William of Tripoli studied the Koran. Western works were translated into Arabic; see E. Cerulli, *Il libro etiopico dei miracoli di Maria*, Rome, 1945. "It would be interesting to study . . . Acre as a contact place between Islamic culture and the Western Christian world": U. Monneret de Villard, *Il libro della peregrinazione nelle parti d'Oriente di fra Ricoldo da Montecroce*, Rome, 1948, 102 n. 432. Acre as a cultural center: Jaroslav Folda, *Crusader manuscript illumination at Saint Jean d'Acre* 1275–1291, Princeton, 1976, 8–21.

[13]For this province see F. Balme, La Province dominicaine de Terre Sainte, in *ROL* i. 526, and B. Altaner, *Die Dominikanermissionen des 13 Jhdts*, Habelschwerdt, 1924.

[14]*Chiprois*, 793. L. Foulet, *Le Roman de Renart*, Paris, 1914, *BEHE* f. 211. 511ff.

[15]See M.R. Morgan, *The chronicle of Ernoul and the continuations of William of Tyre*, Oxford, 1973. The traditional identification of Ernoul with Arnéis of Jebail seems to us not to be proved.

[16]Saladin was not the only Moslem to figure in these thirteenth-century legendary tales. In *La fille du comte de Ponthieu*, in which Saladin is linked to a Western baronial family and is said to have been knighted by Humphrey of Toron, there appear as heroic figures and converts to Christianity both 'Corbaran' (Kerbogha) and 'Dodequin' (Tughtekin), the latter taking the name of Hugh of Tiberias. A parallel development occurs in the *geste* of the house of Ardennes, from the Godfrey poems of the *Chevalier au Cygne* to the *Bastart de Bouillon* and *Baudoin de Sebourc*. The final version of this series of legends has been studied by Robert F. Cook and Larry S. Crist in *Le second cycle de la croisade*, Geneva, 1972; its earliest version still awaits study.

[17]Several books from the bishopric of Sidon are preserved, mainly in the Vatican Library. See P. Gasnault, L'homiliaire de l'ecclesia Sydonensis, in *Bulletin de la Société nationale des Antiquaires de France*, 1967, 276–282 and A. Maier, Die Handschriften der Ecclesia Sidonensis, in *Manuscripta*, xi, 1967, 39–45. For the ornamentation of manuscripts written in the kingdom's scriptoria, see H. Buchtal, *Miniature painting in the Latin kingdom of Jerusalem*, Oxford, 1954 and J. Folda, *Crusader manuscript illumination*, quoted above. The only documents surviving from seigneurial chartularies are those preserved in church archives, but we know that some barons, including Amalric of Beisan and the lord of Jebail, deposited charters with the Hospitallers.

[18]Rey's *Etude sur l'architecture militaire des croisés* is now replaced by the very valuable: P. Deschamps, *Les châteaux des croisés en Terre Sainte*, ii, *La défense du royaume de Jérusalem*, Paris, 1939; T.S.R. Boase, *Castles and churches of the crusading kingdoms*, Oxford, 1967 and his *Kingdoms and strongholds of the crusaders*, London, 1971. The crusaders' buildings other than military are studied in M.M. Benvenisti's handsome *The crusaders in the Holy Land*, Jerusalem, 1970. See also P. Deschamps, *Terre Sainte romane*, La Pierre qui vire, Collection Zodiaque, 1964.

[19]Ricoldo, 278. For these churches see C. Enlart, *Les monuments des croisés dans le royaume de Jérusalem*, Paris, 1925, M. de Vogue, *Les églises de Terre Sainte*, Paris, 1860, and Père Abel's *Guide Bleu de Syrie-Palestine*. The most striking, the church of Our Lady at Tortosa, is outside our scope; see M. Pillet in *Syria*, x, 1929, 40.

[20]C. Enlart, *La cathédrale Saint-Jean de Beyrouth*, taken from the *Recueil de Mémoires* published for the centenary of the *Société des Antiquaires de France*, Paris, 1904.

[21]Vincent and Abel, *Bethléem, le Sanctuaire de la Nativité*, Paris, 1914, and *Jérus-alem, recherches d'archéologie et d'histoire*, Paris, 1914, ii (the Holy Sepulchre). P. Deschamps, La sculpture française en Palestine et en Syrie à l'époque des croisades, in *Fondation Eug. Piot, Monuments et Mémoires*, xxxi, 1930, 91. As well as the capitals of Nazareth, mention must be made of those of Sabastya; see David A. Walsh, Crusader sculpture from the Holy Land in Istanbul, in *Gesta*, viii, 2, 1969, 20–29. Among the icons preserved in the monastery of Mount Sinai, some were executed during the Frankish period and show the mingling of Latin iconography and Greek painting techniques.

[22]Du Sommerard, *Les arts du Moyen-Age, Album*, 2nd series, plate 29, the psalter's

binding. J. Strzygowski, Ruins of tombs of the Latin kings in the Haram of Jerusalem, in *Speculum*, xi, 1936, 499.

[23]Rey, 8. For the employment of local artists, see Nurith Kenaan, Local Christian art in twelfth century Jerusalem, in *Israel exploration journal*, xxiii, 1973, 167–175, 221–229 (especially for the ornamentation of the Holy Sepulchre). This article contains numerous references to artistic activity in the Latin kingdom.

[24]The Franks often made use of antique sculptures, expecially Roman capitals; this does not indicate lack of creative power among the artists but respect for the ancient stones of the shrine and for classical art.

[25]William Adam the Dominican (*De modo Sarracenos extirpandi* in *Documents Arméniens*, ii. 528) laments the large number of pilgrims who pay their thirty-five *gros tournois* a head to the sultan's treasury, and tries to think of a way of diverting them from the Holy Land.

Abbreviations used in the notes

AOL: Archives de l'Orient latin
BEC: Bibliothèque de l'École des Chartes
BEHE: Bibliothèque de l'École des Hautes Études
EHR: English historical review
GKJ: Röhricht, R., *Geschichte des Königreichs Jerusalem*
MGH: Monumenta Germaniae historica
PL: Migne, J.-L., Patrologiae latinae cursus completus
RHC: Recueil des historiens des croisades
RHDF: Revue historique de droit français et étranger
RHE: Revue d'histoire ecclésiastique
RHF: Recueil des historiens [des Gaules et] de la France
ROL: Revue de l'Orient latin
RR: Röhricht, R., *Regesta regni Hierosolymitani*
SATF: Société des anciens textes français
SOL: Schlumberger, G., et al., *Sigillographie de l'Orient latin*
WT: William of Tyre, in *RHC, Hist. Occ.,* i

Bibliography

The study of the history of the Latin states of the East now has excellent tools at its disposal:

Mayer, Hans Eberhard, *Bibliographie zur Geschichte der Kreuzzüge*, Hanover, 1960.

Mayer, Hans Eberhard, Literaturbericht über die Geschichte der Kreuzzüge, in *Historische Zeitschrift*, Sonderheft 3, 1969, 641–731 (for the years 1958–1967).

Atiya, Aziz Suryal, *The crusade. Historiography and bibliography*, Bloomington, 1962. This is not so full, but offers a useful introduction to the subject. As regards the kingdom of Jerusalem in particular, J. Prawer, *Histoire du royaume latin de Jerusalem*, 2^d ed., Paris 1977, has a very full bibliography.

I Sources

Lists of sources are given in the works mentioned above. Below will be found the titles of works referred to in our notes, with a note of their latest editions and most accessible translations.

First in importance is the great *Recueil des historiens des croisades* (referred to here as *RHC*) published by the Académie des Inscriptions et Belles Lettres in five series: *Historiens Occidentaux* (*Hist. Occ.*), *Historiens Orientaux* (*Hist. Or.*), *Historiens Grecs, Documents Arméniens* (*Doc. Arm.*) and *Lois*. A new series in this collection, *Documents relatifs à l'histoire des croisades*, began to appear in 1946.

A) Narrative sources

Albert d'Aix (Alb. Aq.), *Liber christianae expeditionis* (*Hist. Occ.*, iv).

Amadi, *Chroniques d'Amadi et de Strambaldi*, ed. R. de Mas-Latrie, Paris, 1891, in *Documents inédits sur l'histoire de France.*

Ambrose, *Estoire de la guerre sainte*, ed. G. Paris, Paris, 1907 in *Documents inédits sur l'histoire de France.* Translated by M.H. Hubert and J.L. La Monte as *The crusade of Richard Lion-Heart*, New York, 1941.

Andrea Dandolo, *Chronicon*, in Muratori, *Historiae patriae monumenta, Scriptores*, xii.
Aubri de Trois-Fontaines, *Chronicon*, ed. Scheffer-Boichorst in *MGH Scriptores*, xxiii.
Chiprois, see *Gestes*.
Ekkehard: *Ekkehardi . . . Hierosolymita*, ed. H. Hagenmayer, Tübingen, 1877.
Eracles: Estoire d'Eracles, empereur, in *RHC Hist. Occ.*, ii.
Ernoul, *Chronique d'Ernoul et de Bernard le Trésorier*, ed. L. de Mas-Latrie, Paris, 1871
in *Société de l'Histoire de France*. On these two texts, see M.R. Morgan, *The chronicle
of Ernoul and the continuators of William of Tyre*, Oxford, 1973.
Fulcher of Chartres, *Historia Hierosolymitana*, ed. H. Hagenmeyer, Heidelberg, 1913.
Translated by F. R. Ryan and ed. H.S. Fink, as *A history of the expedition to Jerusalem*,
Knoxville, 1969.
Gestes des Chiprois in *Doc. Arm.*, ii.
*Itinerarium peregrinorum (Das). Eine zeitgenössliche englische Chronik zum dritten
Kreuzzug*, ed. H.E. Mayer, Stuttgart, 1962 in *Schriften der MGH* 18.
James of Vitry, *Historia Hierosolymitana* in Bongars, *Gesta Dei per Francos*, Hanover,
1611, 1047ff. Translated by Aubrey Stewart as *The history of Jerusalem A.D. 1186 by
Jacques de Vitry*, London, 1896 in *Palestine Pilgrims' Text Society*.
James of Vitry, *Lettres de Jacques de Vitry*, ed. R.B.C. Huygens, Leyden, 1960.
Matthew Paris, *Chronica Majora*, ed. Luard, 7 vols., London, Rolls Series, 1872–1883.
Michelant, H. and Raynaud, G. *Itinéraires à Jérusalem rédigés en français*, Geneva,
1882 in *Société de l'Orient latin*.
Oliver of Paderborn, *Historia Damiatina*, ed. Hoogeweg, *Die Schriften des Oliverus*,
Tübingen, 1894.
Philip of Novara, *Mémoires de Philippe de Novare*, ed. C. Kohler, Paris, 1913.
Translated by J.L. La Monte and M.J. Hubert as *The Wars of Frederick II against the
Ibelins in Syria and Cyprus*, New York, 1936.
Rothelin: Continuation de Guillaume de Tyr dite du manuscrit de Rothelin in *RHC Hist.
Occ.*, ii.
Sanudo (Marino Sanudo the elder, called Torsello), *Secreta fidelium Crucis super Terrae
Sanctae recuperatione et conservatione*, in Bongars, *Gesta Dei per Francos* (reprinted
with a foreword by J. Prawer, Jerusalem, 1972).
Tobler, T. and Molinier, A. *Itinera Hierosolymitana*, 2 vols., Geneva, 1885 in *Société de
l'Orient latin*.
Villehardouin, *La conquête de Constantinople*, ed. and tr. E. Faral, 2 vols., Paris,
1938–1939.
William of Tyre (abbreviated *WT*), *Historia rerum in partibus transmarinis gestarum*,
in *RHC Hist. Occ.*, i, 2 vols. Translated by E.A. Babcock and A.C. Krey as *A history of
deeds done beyond the sea by William, archbishop of Tyre*, 2 vols., New York, 1943.

Arabic narrative sources. A collection of passages concerning contacts between
Moslems and crusaders was published as early as 1829; it forms the fourth volume of
the *Bibliothèque des croisades*, by M. Reinaud, Paris, 1829. Another such collection is
the *Storici arabi delle crociate* by F. Gabrieli, Turin, 1957, translated into German as *Die
Kreuzzüge aus arabischer Sicht*, Zurich and Munich, 1973.
The principal Moslem authors are:
Abu Shama, *Le Livre des Deux Jardins*, in *RHC Hist. Or*. iv.

Beha al Din, *Anecdotes et beaux traits de la vie du sultan Yousouf*, in *RHC Hist. Or.* iii.
Translated by Wilson and Conder as *The life of Saladin*, Lindon, 1897 in *Palestine Pilgrims' Text Society*.
Ibn al Athir, *Kamil al-tawarikh*, in *RHC Hist. Or.* i.
Ibn al Furat, *Târīkh al-Duwal wa'l Mulúk*. Extracts from this are published in *Ayyubids, Mamlukes and crusaders*, text and translation U. and M.C. Lyons, historical introduction and notes by J.S.C. Riley-Smith, 2 vols., Cambridge, 1971.
Ibn Jobaïr, *Voyages*, in *RHC Hist. Or.* iii; a later translation by M. Gaudefroy-Demombynes, 3 vols., Paris, 1942–1953 in *Documents relatifs à l'histoire des croisades*; translated into English by R.J.C. Broadhurst as *The travels of Ibn Jubayr*, London, 1952.
Ibn al Qalanisi, English translation: *The Damascus chronicle of the Crusades*, by H.A.R. Gibbs, London, 1932; French translation: *Damas de 1075 à 1145*, by R. Le Tourneau, Beirut, 1952.
Imad al Din al Isfahani, French translation: *Conquête de la Syrie* by H. Massé, Paris, 1972 in *Documents relatifs à l'histoire des croisades*; German translation: *Der Sturz des Königreichs Jerusalem (583/1187) in der Darstellung des 'Imad ad-Dîn al-Kâtib al-Isfâhani* by J. Kraemer, Wiesbaden, 1952.
Usama ibn Munqidh, *Autobiographie d'Ousâma*, translated by H. Derembourg, Paris, 1895, extract from *Revue de l'Orient latin*, ii–iii. Translated into English by P.K. Mitti with the title *An Arab-Syrian gentleman and warrior in the period of the crusades. Memoirs of Usâmah ibn-Munqidh*, New York, 1929 and (from the French version of Derembourg) by G.R. Potter with the title *The autobiography of Ousâma*, London, 1929.
Of other Eastern historians, we need only mention:
Michael the Syrian, *Chronique*, translated J.B. Chabot, 4 vols. in 5 parts, Paris, 1899–1904.

B) *Legislative sources*

The works of the jurists, essential for an understanding of the institutions of the Latin kingdom, still survive, thanks to the preservation of the law of Jerusalem in the kingdom of Cyprus. The texts drawn up in the two kingdoms are published together in *RHC, Lois*, 2 vols., by Beugnot. They include especially: the *Livre en forme de plait* by Philip of Novara, the *Livre des Assises de la haute cour* by John of Ibelin, the *Livre de Geoffroy le Tort*, the *Documents* concerning the succession to the throne, the regency and military service, and the *Lignages d'outre mer*. For the *Livre au roi*, however, and the *Livre des Assises de la cour des bourgeois*, we have used another edition based on a better manuscript: *Les livres des Assises et des usages dou réaume de Jerusalem*, ed. H. von Kausler, vol. i only, Stuttgart, 1839.

The Rules of the religious orders originating in the Holy Land have been published: by M. Perlbach, *Die Statuten des deutschen Ordens*, Halle, 1890; by J. Delaville le Roulx in the *Cartulaire général de l'ordre des Hospitaliers*; and by H. de Curzon, *La règle du Temple*, Paris, 1886, in *Société de l'histoire de France*. The French version of the Rule of the Templars is published in *Règle et statuts secrets des Templiers*, ed. C.H. Maillard de Chambure, Paris, 1840.

C) Documentary sources

Although relatively plentiful, documentary sources from the Latin East consist only of documents brought to the West before 1291. These are the cartularies belonging to religious foundations which possessed domains in Europe as well as in the Holy Land. A full collection was published at the end of the nineteenth century:
Röhricht, Reinhold, *Regesta regni Hierosolymitani. 1097–1291*, Innsbruck, 1893; completed by an *Additamentum*, Innsbruck, 1904; these are abbreviated as *RR* and *RR Add.* This collection has recently been reprinted in New York. Its use must be supplemented by reference to later discoveries and publications.

Albon, marquis of, *Cartulaire général de l'ordre du Temple. 1119–1150*, Paris, 1913–1922. See also Leonard, E.G., *Introduction au cartulaire manuscrit du Temple. 1159–1377*, Paris, 1930.

Blancard, L., *Documents inédits sur le commerce de Marseille au Moyen-Age*, 2 vols., Marseilles, 1885.

Delaborde, H.F., *Chartes de Terre-Sainte provenant de l'abbaye Notre-Dame de Josaphat*, Paris, 1880, in *Bibliothèque des Ecoles françaises d'Athènes et de Rome*, 19.

Delaville le Roulx, J., *Cartulaire général de l'ordre des Hospitaliers de Saint-Jean de Jérusalem*, 4 vols., Paris, 1894–1906.

Filangieri, Riccardo and Mazzoleni, Iole, *I registri della cancellaria angioina recostruiti (1265–1279)*, 20 vols., Naples, 1949–1966.

Filangieri, R., *Gli atti perduti della cancellaria angioina transuntati da Carlo de Lellis*, i 2 vols., Rome, 1939–1943 in *Regesta Chartarum Italiae*.

Huillard-Bréeholles, J.L.A. de, *Historia diplomatica Friderici secundi*, 7 vols., Paris, 1852–1861.

Kohler, C., *Chartes de l'abbaye . . . de Josaphat*, Paris, 1900, extract from *ROL* 7.

Liber jurium reipublicae genuensis, in *Historiae patriae monumenta* 2 vols., Turin, 1854–1857.

Marsy, count A. de, *Fragment d'un cartulaire de l'ordre de Saint-Lazare en Terre-Sainte. 1130–1220*, extract from *AOL* 2.

Michelet, Jules, *Le procès des Templiers*, 2 vols., Paris, 1841–1851, in *Documents inédits sur l'histoire de France*. See also Lizerand, G., *Le dossier de l'affaire des Templiers*, Paris, 1923.

Morozzo della Rocca, R. and Lombardo, A., *Documenti del commercio veneziano nei secoli XI–XIII*, 2 vols., Rome, 1940.

Muller, Giuseppe, *Documenti sulle relazioni delle città toscane coll'Oriente cristiano*, Florence, 1879.

Registres des papes edited by members of the Ecole Française de Rome, except for those of Innocent III (published by Baluze and then in *Patrologia Latina*) and of Honorius III (ed. Pressuti, *Regesta Honorii papae tertii*).

Rodenberg, C., *Epistolae saeculi XIII e regestis pontificum romanorum selectae*, 3 vols., Berlin, 1883–1894 in *MGH*.

Roziere, Eugène de, *Cartulaire de l'Eglise du Saint-Sépulcre de Jérusalem*, Paris, 1849.

Rymer, T., *Foedera, conventiones et acta publica*, i, 2nd edn, Hague, 1739.

Strehlke, E., *Tabulae ordinis Theutonici*, Berlin, 1869, reprinted with a foreword by H.E. Mayer, Jerusalem, 1975.

D) Other sources

Sandoli, Sabino de, *Corpus inscriptionum crucesignatorum Terrae Sanctae*, Jerusalem, 1974 in *Pubblicazioni dello Studium biblicum franciscanum*, 21.

Schlumberger, G., *Numismatique de l'Orient latin* and *Supplément à la numismatique de l'Orient latin*, 2 vols., Paris, 1872–1882.

Schlumberger, G., Chalandon, F. and Blanchet, A., *Sigillographie de l'Orient latin*, Paris, 1943, in *Bibliothèque archéologique et historique*, 37.

The chief literary source is the fictionalized history of the kingdom known as the *Estoires d'outremer*. This contains elements from the chansons de geste inspired by the First Crusade (see S. Duparc-Quioc, *Le cycle de la croisade*, Paris, 1955, as well as others taken from the kingdom's history. See R.F. Cook and Larry S. Crist, *Le deuxième cycle de la croisade. Deux études sur son développement*, Paris, 1972.

For archaeological evidence, see below, II F.

II Modern works

In view of the works by H.E. Mayer referred to above, there is no need to print a full bibliography here; the studies we have used on particular points will be found mentioned in our notes. But we cannot omit to mention the works which provided this book with its basis of fact, nor those studies which, carried out in parallel with our own, afford fresh viewpoints or enable readers to go more deeply into questions which we have had to treat briefly.

A) The geographical and chronological setting

Two maps are especially useful:

Johns, C.N., *Palestine of the crusades*, 3rd edn, Jerusalem, 1946.

Prawer, J. and Benvenisti, M., in the *Atlas of Israel*, part 9, sheet 12, Tel Aviv, 1961.

Abel, Father P., *Géographie de la Palestine*, 2 vols., Paris, 1936–1938.

Dussaud, R., *Topographique historique de la Syrie antique et médiévale*, Paris, 1927 in *Bibliothèque archéologique et historique*, 4.

Guide bleu: Syrie-Palestine. Iraq. Transjordanie, Paris, 1932 in *Les Guides bleus*; English edition: *The Blue Guides*.

Le Strange, G., *Palestine under the Moslems*, newly edited by Walid Khalidy, Beirut, 1965.

Rey, E.G., Etude sur la topographie de la ville d'Acre au XIIIᵉ siècle, in *Mémoires de la Société des Antiquaires de France*, 29, 1878, and 39, 1888.

For chronology and the genealogy of the principal families, see:

Du Cange, Charles du Fresne, seigneur, *Les familles d'Outre-mer*, ed. E.G. Rey, Paris, 1869, in *Documents inédits* (abbreviated Du-Cange-Rey).

Hagenmeyer, H., Chronologie de la Première Croisade in *ROL* 6–8, 1898–1901.

Hagenmeyer, H., Chronologie du royaume de Jérusalem, in *ROL* 9–12, 1902–1905.

Hiestand, R., Chronologisches zur Geschichte des Königreichs Jerusalem um 1130,
Deutsches Archiv, 26, 1970.
La Monte, John L., Chronologie de l'Orient latin, *Bulletin of the International com-
mittee of historical sciences*, 12, 1943.
Rey, E.G., *Sommaire du supplément aux Familles d'Outremer de Du Cange*, Chartres,
1881.
Röhricht, R., *Zusätze und Verbesserungen zu Du Cange. Les familles d'Outremer*,
Berlin, 1886.

B)   General works on the crusades

The fullest study is *A history of the crusades*, general editor K.M. Setton. Three
volumes have appeared, dealing with the history of events: i, *The first hundred years*,
ed. M.W. Baldwin; ii, *The later crusades. 1189–1311*, eds. R.L. Wolff and H.W. Hazard,
2nd edn, Madison, 1969; iii, *The fourteenth and fifteenth centuries*, ed. H.W. Hazard,
Madison, 1975. Three further volumes have still to appear.

Alphandéry, P. and Dupront, P., *La chrétienté et l'idée de croisade*. 2 vols., Paris,
1954.
Atiya, A.S., *Crusade, commerce and culture*, Bloomington, 1962.
Brundage, J.A., *The crusades. A documentary survey*, Milwaukee, 1962.
Chalandon, F., *Histoire de la Première Croisade*, Paris, 1925.
Cognasso, F., *Storia delle crociate*, Florence, 1967.
Grousset, R., *L'empire du Levant. Histoire de la question d'Orient*, Paris, 1946.
Grousset, R., *L'épopée des croisades*, Paris, 1939.
Grousset, R., *Histoire des croisades et du royaume franc de Jérusalem*, 3 vols., Paris,
1934–1936.
Mayer, Hans-Eberhard, *The crusades*, translated J. Gillingham, Oxford, 1972.
Morisson, Cécile, *Les croisades*, Paris, 1969.
Oldenbourg, Zoe, *Les croisades*, Paris, 1965, translated by A. Carter as *The crusades*,
London, 1966.
Rousset, P., *Les croisades*, Paris, 1957.
Runciman, S., *A history of the crusades*, 3 vols., Oxford, 1952–1954.
Saunders, J.J., *Aspects of the crusades*, Christchurch, 1962.
Waas, A., *Geschichte der Kreuzzüge*, 2 vols., Freiburg, 1956.
   For the crusades as an institution, an ideological concept and an organization, see:
Brundage, J., *Medieval canon law and the crusader*, Madison, 1969.
Erdmann, C., *Die Entstehung der Kreuzzugsgedanken*, Stuttgart, 1935.
Purcell, Maureen, *Papal crusading policy. 1244–1291*, Leyden, 1975.
Richard, J., *L'esprit de la croisade*, Paris, 1969.
Villey, M., *La croisade. Essai sur la formation d'une théorie juridique*, Paris, 1942.
For military history, see:
Smail, R.C., *Crusading warfare. 1097–1193*, Cambridge, 1956.

C) *The Latin kingdom's neighbours*

A brief account of the history of the Eastern countries is given in *The History of the crusades* along with that of the Latin states themselves. For Moslem and Mongol countries, see also:
Elisseef, N., *Nur ad-Din. Un grand prince musulman de Syrie au temps des croisades,* 3 vols., Damascus, 1967.
Gottschalk, H.L., *Al-Malik al-Kâmil von Egypten und sein Zeit,* Wiesbaden, 1958.
Grousset, R., *L'empire des steppes,* Paris, 1939.
Sadeque, Syedah Fatimah, *Baybars I of Egypt,* Oxford University Press, Pakistan, 1956.
Sivan, Emmanuel, *L'Islam et la croisade. Idéologie et propagande dans les réactions musulmanes aux croisades,* Paris, 1968.
Spuler, B., *Die Mongolen in Iran,* 3rd edn, Berlin, 1968.
    The other Latin states of the East, not including those founded after the Fourth Crusade, are studied in:
Cahen, Claude, *La Syrie du Nord à l'époque des croisades et la principauté franque d'Antioche,* Paris, 1940.
Hill, George, *A history of Cyprus,* ii and iii, Cambridge, 1948.
Longnon, Jean, *Les Français d'Outremer au Moyen-Age,* 2nd edn, Paris, 1929.
Mas-Latrie, L. de, *Histoire de l'île de Chypre,* 3 vols. with map, Paris, 1852–1861.
Richard, J., *Le comté de Tripoli sous la dynastie toulousaine,* Paris, 1945, in *Bibliothèque archéologique et historique,* 39.
Richard, J., Le comté de Tripoli dans les chartes du fonds des Porcellet, in *BEC* 130, 1972.

D) *Political history of the Latin kingdom*

The three fundamental works now are:
Grousset, R., *Histoire des croisades et du royaume latin de Jérusalem,* listed above; abbreviated: Grousset.
Röhricht, R., *Geschichte des Königreichs Jerusalem. 1100–1291,* Innsbruck, 1898 abbreviated *GKJ.*
Prawer, J., *Histoire du royaume latin de Jérusalem,* translated G. Nahon, 2 vols., Paris, 1969, 2^d edn, 1977; English translation, 1972.
Certain books superseded by the above were excellent in their day and are still worth reading:
Archer, T.A. and Kingsford, C.L., *The crusades. The story of the Latin kingdom of Jerusalem,* London, c. 1894.
Conder, C.R., *The Latin kingdom of Jerusalem. 1099–1291 A.D.,* London, 1897.
Munro, D.C., *The kingdom of the crusaders,* New York, 1936.
Stevenson, W.B., *The crusaders in the East,* Cambridge, 1907.
For particular events and periods, see:
Baldwin, M.W., *Raymond III of Tripolis and the fall of Jerusalem,* Princeton, 1936.
Clermont-Ganneau, C., *Recueil d'archéologie orientale,* 6 vols., 1888–1906.
Kohler, C., *Mélanges pour servir à l'histoire de l'Orient latin,* 2 vols., Paris, 1906.

Mayer, H.E., Studies in the history of Queen Melisende of Jerusalem, *Dumbarton Oaks Papers*, 26, 1972.
Nicholson, R.L., *Joscelyn III and the fall of the crusader states. 1134–1199*, Leyden, 1973.
Röhricht, R., Etudes sur les derniers temps du royaume de Jérusalem, *AOL* i and ii.
Schlumberger, G., *La fin de la domination franque en Syrie*, Paris, 1914.
   Numerous monographs have been written about individual towns and lordships; more than can be listed here. Exceptional in the depth of its treatment and in the number of texts it includes is:
Chehab, M., *Tyr à l'époque des croisades. i. Histoire militaire et diplomatique*, Paris, 1975; two volumes to come.
See also:
Mas-Latrie, L. de, Les comtes de Jaffa et d'Ascalon, *Archivio Veneto*, 18, 1879.

E)   *Institutions*

We have contributed a chapter to a forthcoming volume of the *History of the crusades* which will deal with the civil and ecclesiastical institutions of the crusader states.
Dodu, G., *Histoire des institutions monarchiques dans le royaume latin de Jérusalem*, Paris, 1894.
Grandclaude, M., *Essai critique sur les livres des Assises de Jérusalem*, Paris, 1923.
Hayek, D., *Le droit franc en Syrie pendant les croisades. Institutions judiciaires*, Paris, 1925.
La Monte, J.L., *Feudal monarchy in the Latin kingdom of Jerusalem. 1100–1291*, Cambridge, Mass., 1932; abbreviated, La Monte.
Prawer, J., Estates, communities and the constitution of the Kingdom, the *Israel Academy of Sciences and Humanities Proceedings*, 6, 1966.
Richard, J., Pairie d'Orient latin. Les quatre baronnies des royaumes de Jérusalem et de Chypre, *Revue historique de droit français et étranger*, 1950.
Riley-Smith, J., *The feudal nobility and the kingdoms of Jerusalem. 1174–1277*, London, 1973.
For ecclesiastical institutions, see:
Delaville le Roulx, *Les Hospitaliers en Terre Sainte et à Chypre*, Paris, 1904.
Fedalto, G., *La chiesa latina in Oriente*, i, Verona, 1973.
Hotzelt, W., Kirchliche Organisation und religiöses Leben in Palästina während der Kreuzzugszeit, in *Palästina-Hefte des deutschen Vereins vom Heiligen Lande*, 24–27, 1940.
Riant, P., Eglise de Bethléem-Ascalon, in *ROL* i and ii, 1893–1894.
Riley-Smith, J., *The knights of Saint John in Jerusalem and Cyprus. c. 1050–1310*, London, 1967 in *A history of the Order of the Hospital of Saint John of Jerusalem*, ed. L. Butler, i.

F) Life of the Frankish colonies in the kingdom

Ben Ami, Aharon, *Social changes in a hostile environment: the crusaders' kingdom of Jerusalem*, Princeton, 1969.
Benvenisti, Meron, *The crusaders in the Holy Land*, Jerusalem, 1970.
Boase, T.S.R., *Castles and churches of the crusading kingdom*, Oxford, 1967.
Boase, T.S.R., *Kingdoms and strongholds of the crusaders*, London, 1971.
Buchtal, Hugo, *Miniature painting in the Latin kingdom of Jerusalem*, Oxford, 1957.
Cahen, Claude, Notes sur l'histoire des croisades et de l'Orient latin, in *Bulletin de la Faculté des Lettres de Strasbourg*, 1950–1951.
Deschamps, Paul, *Les châteaux des croisés en Terre Sainte, i, Le Crac des Chevaliers; ii, La défense du royaume de Jérusalem*, 2 vols. and 2 albums, Paris, 1934–1936 in *Bibliothèque archéologique et historique*. The recently published third volume deals with the *Défense du comté de Tripoli.*
Deschamps, P., *Terre Sainte romane*, Paris, 1972.
Enlart, C., *Les monuments des croisés dans le royaume de Jérusalem*, 2 vols. and 2 albums, Paris, 1925–1927, in *Bibliothèque archéologique et historique*, 5.
Folda, J., *Crusader manuscript illumination at Saint Jean d'Acre. 1275–1291*, Princeton, 1976.
Prawer, J., Colonization activities in the Latin kingdom of Jerusalem, in *Revue belge de philologie et d'histoire*, 29, 1951.
Prawer, J., *The Latin kingdom of Jerusalem. European colonialism in the Middle Ages*, London, 1972.
Prawer, J., *The world of the crusaders*, London and Jerusalem, 1972.
Preston, Helen G., *Rural conditions in the kingdom of Jerusalem*, Philadelphia, 1903. Our chapter on Agricultural conditions in the Crusaders states will appear in a forthcoming volume of the *History of the crusades.*
Prutz, H., *Kulturgeschichte der Kreuzzüge*, Berlin, 1883.
Rey, E.G., *Les colonies franques en Syrie aux XIIe et XIIIe siècles*, Paris, 1883; abbreviated, Rey.
Smail, R.C., *The crusaders in Syria and in the Holy Land*, London, 1973.

G) Economic relationships and trade

Heyd, W., *Histoire du commerce du Levant*, translated Furcy Raynaud, 2 vols., Leipzig, 1885–1886.
Lopez, R.S. and Raymond, I.W., *Medieval trade in the Mediterranean world*, New York, 1955.
Mayer, H.E., *Marseilles Levantehandel und ein akkonensisches Fälscheratelier des 13. Jhdts*, Tübingen, 1972.
Schaube, A., *Handelsgeschichte der romanischen Völker des Mittelmeergebiets bis zum Ende der Kreuzzüge*, Munich and Berlin, 1906.

Further studies dealing in particular with the merchant colonies of the Italian cities are cited in our notes.

Lastly we should add that our own articles up till 1976 have been reissued in two volumes of the *Variorum Reprints* collection:

Orient et Occident au Moyen-Age. Contacts et relations, London, 1976, and *Les relations entre l'Orient et l'Occident au Moyen-Age: études et documents*, London, 1977.

Index

Abagha, mongol khan, 399
Abaq, emir of Damascus, 40
Abbasa, battle of, 345
Abraghinus, money-changer, 358
Abraham, xix, xx
Absalon, bishop of Ascalon, 156 n.
Abu Ali Tahir, vizier of Damascus, 34
Abu Imran Fadl, 29
Abu Tayi tribe, 29
Abyssinia, king of, 225
Acerra, count of, see Thomas of Aquino
Achaea, see Morea
Acre, bishop of, 262, 276, 368, 373–4;
    and see Florent, James of Vitry,
    Theobald
Acre, convent of Our Lady of, 438 n.
Acre, plain of; see Esdraelon
Acre, viscount of; see Gerard Le
    Raschas, Girard of Valence; viscoun-
    tess, see Peronelle
Adam of Adelon, 294 n.
Adam of Béthune, lord of Beisan, 86,
    91, 169
Adam of Cafran, castellan of Tyre, 429–
    30
Adalard of Ramleh, citizen of Gibelin,
    123
Adelaide, countess of Sicily, second
    wife of Baldwin I, 4, 100

Adelon, 85, 213, 256, 294 n.; and see
    Agnes
Adesia, casal, 137–8
Adhémar of Monteil, bishop of Le Puy,
    7, 8, 13, 16, 59, 287
al-Adil, king of Transjordania and of
    Egypt, 179, 194, 202, 204–5, 207, 208,
    209–10, 214–7, 219, 220, 221, 223,
    294 nn., 295 n.
al-Adil II, 323, 324
Adon of Cerisy, 86
Adriatic Sea, 9, 218
Aelia, 97
al-Afdal, vizier of Cairo, 22
al-Afdal, king of Damascus, 202
Afghanistan, 350, 434
Africa, 425
Ager sanguinis, battle of, 33
Agnes, abbess of St Mary Magdalen,
    Jerusalem, 105
Agnes of Adelon, wife of Thierry of
    Termonde, 257, 294 n.
Agnes of Courtenay, countess of
    Edessa, wife of Amalric, 3, 65, 78, 79,
    101, 167–9, 171, 289 n.
Agnes of Edessa, daughter of Joscelin
    III, 251, 256
Agnes of Franleu, wife of Daniel of
    Adelon, 294 n.

Simon of Montfort, earl of Leicester, 327–8, 398
Sinai, ix, xx, 49, 52, 161 n., 226, 350, 354
Sinjar, Mesopotamia, 202
Sinn al-Nabra, battle, xxii, 31, 32, 33, 57, 133
Sivard, goldsmith, 121
slaves, slavery, 40, 131–2, 179, 205, 217, 260, 264, 290 n., 351, 353, 388, 393, 430, 444 n., 456–7
Soissons, counts of, 331; *and see* Yves of Nesle
Solomon, 62
sorcery, 175
Spain, xvii, xix, 7, 111, 145 n., 211, 285, 458; *and see* Aragon, Castile, Catalonia
Spalato, 218
Spinola, *see* Thomas
Spring of Emmaus, *see* Emmaus
Stamford, 352
Stephanie of Armenia, queen of Jerusalem, 224, 248
Stephanie of Beisan, wife of Philip Le Roux, 293 n.
Stephanie of Milly, lady of Kerak and Montreal, 88, 91, 191
Stephen Boutier, viscount of Acre, 319
Stephen, count of Blois, 8, 9, 12, 16, 22
Stephen Lombard, citizen of Gibelin, 123
Stephen of Chartres, patriarch of Jerusalem, 21, 62, 100, 107, 158 n.
Stephen of Saisy, marshal of the Temple, 448 n.
Stephen of Sauvegny, 'syndic' of Jerusalem, 406
Stephen of Thornham, 196
Styria, 386
Subeibah, castle at Banyas, 85, 345–6
Sudan, 352
Suète, Terre de (Sawad, Gaulanitis, Yarmuk valley), ix, xv, 30, 31, 34, 54, 85, 86, 219
Suez, 149 n., 350
Sufi, 180
sugar, xv, 73, 125–6, 169, 176, 351, 369
Sully, Hugh Le Roux of, *see* Hugh

Sumatra, 351
Sunnite religion, 30, 50, 176
Swabia, duke of, *see* Frederick

Tabitha, xix
Table of Our Lord, church of the, xx, 393, 461
Tabriz, 399
Tafila, 149 n.
Tagliacozzo, 361
Taima, Arabia, 54
Tancred of Hauteville, 13
Tancred of Lecce, king of Sicily, 185, 203, 294 n.
Tancred, prince of Antioch, 9, 10, 11, 13, 14, 15, 19, 21, 23, 30, 32, 34, 60–1, 73, 85, 86, 94, 99, 101, 107, 153 n., 219
Tancred's Well, castle, 151 n.
Tanis, Egypt, 49, 295 n., 339
Taranto, 203; Bohemond of, *see* Bohemond
Tarsus, 219
Tartar, *see* Mongol
Taticius, Byzantine commander, 10, 11
Taurus mountains, 16
Teck, Walter of, *see* Walter
Tel-Danith, battle, 33, 109
Tel el-Saqhab, 34
Templars, order of, viii, xxi, 43, 44, 53, 80, 111–120, 123, 140, 142, 149 n., 156 n., 161 n., 168, 170–1, 172, 174–5–6, 179, 180, 183, 192, 198, 207, 215, 218, 219, 220, 223, 227, 232–3, 234, 235, 236, 243, 257, 264–7, 282–3, 290 n., 298 n., 308, 315, 318, 321, 325, 326–7, 329, 333, 336, 340, 342, 346, 355, 358, 362, 364, 365, 367, 370, 374, 375, 376–7, 380, 389, 392–4, 396, 403, 406, 409, 413–5, 417–8, 423, 425–6, 429–34, 435 n., 436 n., 437 n., 440 n., 458, 461
Temple, commanders/grand commanders, of the, *see* Giles, Matthew Sauvage, Theobald; grand masters of the, 57, 80, 215, 313, 324, 325, 335, 366, 380, 432, *and see* Girard of Ridefort, Robert of Sablé, William of